SAUDI, INC.

SAUDI, INC.

THE ARABIAN KINGDOM'S
PURSUIT OF PROFIT AND POWER

ELLEN R. WALD

PEGASUS BOOKS
NEW YORK LONDON

SAUDI, INC.

Pegasus Books Ltd.
148 W 37th Street, 13th Floor
New York, NY 10018

First Pegasus Books edition April 2018

Interior design by Maria Fernandez

Library of Congress Cataloging-in-Publication Data is available.

ISBN: 978-1-68177-660-6

10 9 8 7 6 5 4 3 2 1

Printed in the United States of America
Distributed by W. W. Norton & Company

For Sam

CONTENTS

THE REFUGEE BECOMES KING

Abdul Aziz woke quickly in the darkness. Around him, men and camels slept in clusters on the cool desert sand. Then just twenty-six years old, Abdul Aziz stretched his long limbs and sat up noiselessly. His hand automatically moved to grasp the musket by his side. Abdul Aziz began this particular day identically to the one that had preceded it.

Together, he and his men ate a light meal before dawn and then prostrated themselves in prayer. The group moved as one, answering the leader's benedictions in perfect unison. They rested in the shade of crudely erected tents, cleaned and polished their weapons, and competed to see who could recite more of the Koran from memory. Abdul Aziz judged their attempts harshly.

For twenty days in the month of Ramadan, Abdul Aziz ibn Saud and two hundred of his cousins, fellow tribesmen, and sympathetic Bedouins camped outdoors in a remote location in the Arabian Desert. The men were waiting for Abdul Aziz to decide when they would attack the city of Riyadh. After nearly three weeks, the Bedouins in his camp were growing restless. They had begun goading each other into increasingly vicious mock sword-fights after the *iftar* meal that broke the fast at nightfall. Abdul Aziz feared he would not be able to contain their fiery tempers much longer.

Riyadh, in 1902, was not an impressive city. Located in the center of the Nejd region of Arabia, its geographic isolation made it an unlikely seat of power. Riyadh sat atop a high plateau, three thousand feet above sea level. From the desolate center of the Arabian Peninsula, the journey just to Mecca took over a week by camel. In 1902, the city had few water resources and no important trading routes to sustain it commercially. In 1902, Mecca was the center of the Islamic world and Istanbul was the political center of the Middle East, but Riyadh was home to Abdul Aziz.

The tribe of *al Rashid* had captured it from Abdul Aziz's father and his tribe, *al Saud*, a generation earlier. Abdul Aziz's father had tried, again and again, to retake the city, but he had failed each time. Finally, in the winter of 1901 and 1902, young Abdul Aziz saw an opportunity. The local Bedouin tribes had become disgruntled with *al Rashid* rule and rallied eagerly to Abdul Aziz. Impatient, they wanted to march on Riyadh immediately, but Abdul Aziz knew from prior attempts that *al Rashid*'s governor guarded the city diligently. Cautious planning would help win the day, so he gathered supplies and took his restless allies into the desert to observe Ramadan away from the eyes of *al Rashid* sympathizers who might alert the governor to his intentions. Abdul Aziz dispatched a cousin to spy on the conditions within the city and awaited his return patiently.

On the twentieth day of the month, Abdul Aziz's spy returned with intelligence on the city, its fortifications, and the governor's schedule. As the sun fell behind the dunes, Abdul Aziz and his men performed their usual ritual of prayer and broke their fast. He ordered the men to gather their weapons and mount their camels. It was time.

Abdul Aziz rode at the head of the group, with a Jezail musket slung across his shoulders. A white *thobe* billowed out behind him and a *shomagh* shielded his eyes from blowing sand. A train of similarly clad and armed men followed him across the desert. They traveled quickly through small encampments and oases, stopping briefly only to refresh themselves and their camels. When the band reached the date palm groves that ringed the outskirts of Riyadh, Abdul Aziz had his men dismount and leave their camels by the oasis with a token force guarding them. The rest hurried on foot toward the mud wall protecting the city. At the gardens next to the walls, he instructed six men to quietly cut down a tall date palm and lean it against the wall to use as a ladder. Abdul Aziz and a preselected group of forty men prepared to scale the wall and enter the city. He left the rest of the men under the command of his brother, Mohammad.

"If," he said, "by tomorrow noon no message has come from me, hurry back to the others and flee together to Kuwait. Tell my father I am dead or prisoner of the Rashidis." He ended with a prayer, "There is no power nor strength but from Allah the Exalted." Under the cover of the cold, dark, moonless night, Abdul Aziz and his band climbed up the tree trunk and dropped silently down the wall on the other side. They hurried toward the Rashidi governor's house but stopped next door at the house of a shepherd and former *al Saud* servant named Juwaisir. When Abdul Aziz knocked on the door, he was recognized immediately and invited in with his men. Juwaisir allowed Abdul Aziz and his men to climb to the top of his house and gather on its flat roof, where they jumped onto the roof of the governor's house. From there, they climbed through the windows and quickly overpowered the governor's wife and her sister and locked them inside a room. As Abdul Aziz's spy had reported, the governor feared so much for his own safety that he spent his nights with his bodyguards inside the walled fortress nearby. He returned to his home every morning after dawn.

Abdul Aziz and his men hunkered down to wait until morning. They recited passages from the Koran and sipped strong coffee throughout the rest of the night. Meanwhile, Abdul Aziz sent a scout to bring Mohammad and the other men who had remained outside the walls. He posted guards to watch through the windows for the governor's approach. Just before dawn, Abdul Aziz led his men in prayer. According to his intelligence, the Rashidi governor, Ajlan, would soon return to his residence.

Indeed, just after dawn, the Saudis and their men heard the sounds of approaching horses. The governor and his bodyguards! The men tensed with excitement and apprehension at the coming ambush. They heard the wrought-iron lock open with a clank and the great wooden doors swing slowly open. The men waited for Abdul Aziz's signal and watched Ajlan step into the dimly lit courtyard. Suddenly, Abdul Aziz himself jumped out from behind a window and ran across the courtyard. Dust flew up in clouds behind him, making it difficult for his men to see exactly what was happening.

Ajlan was so shocked at the sudden attack that he did not draw his sword until Abdul Aziz closed in on him. He was able to recognize the son of his Saudi foe. The men saw the flash of Ajlan's sword and heard it meet the barrel of Abdul Aziz's rifle. Soon both men were tussling on the ground. Abdul Aziz's men fired on the governor's bodyguards to keep them from interceding, but the noise woke the garrisoned forces, who quickly joined the battle.

Ajlan managed to break free during the mêlée, and he raced toward the wooden gate to escape. Aiming carefully, Abdul Aziz fired a shot into the governor's arm. Ajlan's sword clattered to the ground, and Abdul Aziz caught up to him. Abdul Aziz grabbed the governor's legs, but Ajlan kicked the Saudi warrior hard in the groin. Momentarily free, the governor darted through the open gates, but when his soldiers tried to shut the gates behind him, Abdul Aziz's men threw themselves against the massive doors and kept them open long enough for Abdul Aziz to recover and rush through.

Ajlan fled past the walls and through open space toward a mosque. Abdul Aziz and his cousin, Abdullah ibn Jalawi, drew their swords and swiftly pursued him. The governor was no match for two young men in prime physical condition. Ibn Jalawi reached him first, and on the steps of the mosque cut him down with his sword. The governor collapsed, dead. Abdul Aziz and his cousin sprinted back to the battle that was still underway. Together with their men, they subdued the remaining Rashidi troops.

Later that morning, the city's denizens learned the news that their governor was dead and his forces had surrendered to young Abdul Aziz ibn Saud. The townspeople rejoiced in the victorious return of *al Saud* and assisted the Saudi forces in capturing any remaining *al Rashid* inside the city. As the day ended, Abdul Aziz stood on the walls of Riyadh and gave thanks to Allah for his victory. He was no longer a homeless refugee, living in Kuwait as the emir's guest. He was now the ruler of this small, mud-walled city. He watched the sun set over the vast desert before him and looked toward Mecca, many miles to the west, and many victories away.[1]

◆

In the early days of the 20th century, Abdul Aziz's victory in Riyadh meant little to that era's Western power. When the British sought to cultivate an Arab ally in the Arabian Peninsula in 1917 to help foment an Islamic revolt against the Ottomans during World War I, Abdul Aziz ibn Saud was still just a regional warlord. He had capitalized on his victory at Riyadh by expanding his control to the Arabian Peninsula's entire Nejd region. In fifteen years, Abdul Aziz had risen from a landless young man to a respected tribal leader, albeit in a desolate and remote region. The British briefly considered him as a contender for the job of rallying the Arab world to Britain's cause, but despite the formidable fighting force and tribal loyalties he commanded, the British chose the better-known Sharif Hussein of Mecca instead.[2]

Mecca was the religious center of the Islamic world, plus it was located along the more accessible and influential Red Sea coast. Riyadh's physical isolation from the rest of the Arab world was enough to discount any influence or military might that its warlord might bring to the British cause. Therefore, it made sense to the British, led in the region by T. E. Lawrence, to ally with Sharif Hussein of Mecca. The British promised Sharif Hussein power and land at the conclusion of the war in return for military assistance. His sons helped the British conquer the Levant from the Ottomans in 1917, and were rewarded with thrones in what became Jordan and Iraq. However, Abdul Aziz saw in that lost chance an even greater opportunity to exploit on his own.

Abdul Aziz ibn Saud struck while Sharif Hussein's sons and their fighting men were off with the British. He took his forces out of Riyadh and his Nejd region and began attacking the areas of the Arabian Peninsula under Sharif Hussein's control. By 1925, Abdul Aziz ibn Saud had conquered Mecca. By 1928, he controlled most of the Arabian Peninsula. In 1932, the refugee from Kuwait proclaimed himself king of the country he named for his family—Saudi Arabia. From that first battle for Riyadh's fortress, it took Abdul Aziz thirty years of nearly constant warfare to consolidate his control.

Even though he ruled an area just larger than Alaska, in 1932, Abdul Aziz's capital city of Riyadh still looked much as it had for one hundred years. The city had neither the religious consequence of Mecca and Medina, nor the commercial value of the port city of Jeddah. It was simply the ancestral home of *al Saud* and the place where Abdul Aziz had brought the family back to prominence after its long exile at the hands of its rivals. In 1932, Riyadh's main thoroughfare was a dusty road highlighted by the hangman's noose. By the start of the 21st century, Deera Square was still the site of the *shura* court's brutal justice, but instead it was framed by rows of carefully tended palm trees. The ground was paved and decorated with an intricate pattern of white, red, and gray stone. Benches were numerous and arranged so pedestrians could rest in the shade.

When Abdul Aziz captured Riyadh in 1902, the city consisted of only one square kilometer; a century later, Riyadh had grown to 1,300 square kilometers. When Abdul Aziz consolidated his kingdom in 1932, Riyadh had a population of fewer than forty thousand. By the beginning of the 21st century, its population approached six million. Riyadh became a bustling, modern city with terrible traffic, upscale malls, and neighborhoods stratified by class and wealth. In 1932, the man who ruled Saudi Arabia from Riyadh had barely a riyal to his name, but Abdul Aziz's sons, the succeeding rulers of Arabia, would enjoy immense wealth and come to own the most profitable company in the world—Saudi Aramco.

◆

In 1933, the year after Abdul Aziz consolidated power, American oilmen, suspecting that the newly formed Saudi Arabia might have oil beneath its sands, came to negotiate a partnership with the king. After discovering oil in the nearby island of Bahrain, the Americans were anxious to explore the Saudi desert for signs of petroleum. After several months of discussions, the king signed a concession agreement with an American company that later became Aramco. The oilmen were successful and discovered oil five years later. Almost two decades later, Saudi Arabia negotiated even greater profits. Then, after another two decades, Saudi Arabia maneuvered to take the upper hand in controlling its own oil assets. Abdul Aziz's son ultimately bought the company from its American owners, and Saudi Arabia transformed it into a diversified global energy powerhouse.

Along the way, Saudi Arabia also transformed. Its largely illiterate and pastoral population became urbanized and educated. Where there had once been fierce musket-wielding warriors on camelback, the Saudis purchased F-15 fighter jets and built a strong regional military. Radio, television, mobile phones, and the Internet became commonplace even in Saudi Arabia's more remote desert regions. The Saudi government and Saudi society grappled with the impact of these transformations on its patriarchal, monarchical, and conservative culture.

Throughout, the royal family ran the Kingdom of Saudi Arabia and managed its relationship with Aramco like a family business and with the twin objectives of long-term profit and power. The government and the company cultivated classes of business-savvy men and women with extensive training and education in their fields who managed the energy company's multifaceted global operations. The Saudi government, and the technocrats who have run Aramco, developed and adhered to a strategic vision designed to advance the long-term health and stability of the business and, therefore, the kingdom itself.

Aramco began as an American corporation established simply to drill for crude oil in Saudi Arabia, but within a single generation the Americans and the Saudis transformed it into a global energy conglomerate. The corporation purchased stakes in refineries around the world, developed cutting-edge technology research centers, built giant petrochemical plants, and managed shipping and pipeline operations. Saudi Arabia became the leader of the world's most entrenched cartel. The journey began when a tall, strong man and his cousins conquered a mud fortress from their family rival. One generation later Saudi Arabia became an international force in the energy market.

In spite of Saudi Arabia and Aramco's successes, misperceptions about the kingdom and its energy business persisted. In 1924, as Abdul Aziz was fighting in the desert, Saudi Arabia was an enigma to the outside world. The *Boston Daily Globe*, in describing his battle with Sharif Hussein, called it "a mystery war."[3] Similar language was used to describe Saudi Arabia's culture and society in Western publications throughout the 20th century. Even in 2015, Western publications wondered about "the mysterious Saudi prince leading the war in Yemen."[4] As a result, there has been an abundance of misperceptions about Saudi Arabia, its energy business, and its goals and intentions. A prominent pundit on global affairs wrote in 2015, that "Saudi Arabia can dig holes in the ground and pump out oil but little else."[5] He was wrong. He was ignorant of Saudi expertise in, for example, gas and solar power, desalinization technology, plastics and lubricant development, environmental disaster cleanup, and oil marketing. In 2016, the *Economist* called

Saudi Aramco "one of the world's most secretive oil companies."[6] Of course, as a private company, Aramco kept proprietary information secret. But that does not mean Aramco has been a mystery; much can be understood about its motivations, intentions, and goals from its story.

In the early 1950s, when Aramco was still owned by four American oil companies, the relationship between Saudi Arabia and Aramco—in fact between Saudi Arabia and its oil—was expressed in no clearer language than in the parting words of one of the rotating American ambassadors to Saudi Arabia. Shortly before he departed to take a new post in another country, he spoke with Saudi Arabia's finance minister, with whom he had developed a relationship of mutual trust. "A strong Aramco," this ambassador told his Arab friend, "means a strong Saudi Arabia."[7] The real accomplishment of Saudi Arabia, since the days when Abdul Aziz ruled Riyadh's dusty streets, was embracing this idea as an investment for future generations. After all, as Abdullah Jumah, Saudi Aramco's CEO, explained in 2008, "Oil is a gift from God." He paused for a moment before continuing. "The recovery of oil is really the work of men."[8]

◆

A note to the reader: This is a history of Saudi Arabia and Aramco together. As such the story ends at a specific point—in this case, the beginning of the reign of King Salman in January 2015—and does not directly address later plans of Saudi Arabia and Aramco, such as social liberalizations, Vision2030, or an Aramco initial public offering. Though this is a history, the plans, strategies, motivations, and goals of the past inform opportunities in the present and the future. The plans and the stories of the next generation of Saudis are yet to be told.

PART I

ONE

"A DEVIL OF A TIME"

S heikh Abdullah Sulaiman, commonly referred to as Sheikh Abdullah, was an anomaly in the Saudi court. He was neither a member of *al Saud* nor one of the Levantine or Iraqi-born Arabs who had come to Arabia to offer their administrative services to King Abdul Aziz in exchange for power, wealth, and opportunity.[1] Born sometime in the late 1880s, Sulaiman hailed from an old Nejd merchant family and grew up in Unaizah, a town in the middle of Saudi Arabia, just northwest of Riyadh. His family was poor, and in his youth, Sulaiman left Arabia to seek his fortune, beginning in Bombay. After a failed business venture in Bahrain, he returned to his home in the eastern desert region of Arabia richer only in his knowledge of bookkeeping and foreign trade. In 1919, he began his tenure in the king's court as an assistant to his uncle, a financial clerk. Sulaiman considered himself lucky to have been given this opportunity, considering his past failures. When his uncle died some years later, Abdullah Sulaiman took over his duties. It soon became clear to King Abdul Aziz that Sulaiman possessed a financial acumen above that of anyone in the king's immediate family, and he elevated Sulaiman to finance minister.

A British writer once described Sulaiman as "a frail little man of 'uncertain' age but with something of the inspiration of the prophets in his soul."[2] When the Americans from Standard Oil of California first arrived in Saudi Arabia in 1932, Sulaiman was still "lithe and skinny." One of the early geologists who came in the 1930s to survey the terrain described the finance minister as a "bright, intelligent, enthusiastic man" who was "full of energy and ideas."[3] The first American ambassador noted that "the Minister of Finance had four [wives], established in a like number of identical adjoining homes where he passed his nights in strict rotation."[4] As the Americans would discover, however, Sulaiman had a darker side that most often emerged when he drank. Though Islamic law proscribed the whiskey he loved, Abdullah Sulaiman could not seem to put away the bottle. Contemporaries said he would go through periods of sobriety that usually coincided with the month of Ramadan. When abstaining, the Americans observed, he was much more agreeable and even-tempered. Despite this vice, or perhaps because of it, Sulaiman often presented an image of religious devotion in front of foreigners. When meetings with oil company executives would run into one of the five set times for prayer, Sulaiman would always stop the discussion, go to the corner of the room where he would face Mecca and prostrate himself on his prayer rug.[5]

His title of "Sheikh" meant nothing more than a general honorific Arabs had used for centuries to indicate a man of power. As finance minister, Sulaiman exercised complete control over the king's entire treasury. It was said that "he had his own accounting system that nobody knew how it worked."[6] Of course, given the state of Arabia in the first decades of the 20th century, the king's wealth—kept in gold coins, cash, and other precious metals—fit into chests that Sulaiman reportedly stored in his family home. During those lean years, Abdullah Sulaiman's duties as finance minister mostly involved shaking down Abdul Aziz's subjects for tax money and collecting tolls from pilgrims on *hajj*. Once the money came in, Sulaiman's task was to figure out how to make the money last. In addition to supplying the royal family's needs, the funds needed to be distributed among the king's subjects in politically expedient ways to ensure continued loyalty from nomadic and settled tribesmen. The degree of loyalty an Arabian king commanded from his subjects depended on his ability to meet their financial needs.[7]

Sulaiman became a transcendent figure who bridged Saudi Arabia's lean early years and the period of newfound oil wealth. Among some of the Americans in Saudi Arabia, Sulaiman's early adventures, whether accurate or exaggerated, became part of the founding lore of the country. Tim Barger is the son of Tom Barger, who was a pioneer geologist in Saudi Arabia and the fifth CEO of Aramco. He relayed this story from his father, who first met Sulaiman while scouting the Arabian Desert for signs of oil in the 1930s. Before Abdul Aziz consolidated his kingdom, Tim Barger said, Arabians were "out there raiding people and engaging in all forms of warfare. . . . Raiding was sort of like a hobby."

In the midst of all this, Sulaiman "carried the trunk around with him with all the money." But, Tim Barger recalled, "the tide could turn really quickly. He'd have to pick the trunk up and leave real quickly. And the trunk was all the money they had." Sulaiman's trunk, at that time, "was filled with Maria Theresa thalers and gold rupees, and sovereigns and God knows what kind of currency." Tim Barger explained, "The king would give chitties [or vouchers] to people, and they would come to Abdullah Sulaiman. He would redeem the chitty with a handful of rupees or something, and then put the chitties in the trunk. That was the basic deal." This basic exchange remained at the heart of the Saudi compact between ruler and subject even after the Saudi government grew into a modern, bureaucratic state. A subject could appear at the king's open *majlis* (public audience) and make requests ranging from money for a new truck to a scholarship for his son to study abroad. The king would likely grant the request and send the man to see the finance minister. The finance minister, depending on the state of the government's treasury, might fulfill his request or send the supplicant through a bureaucratic maze long enough that he would likely give up and return home.

In the 1920s and early 1930s, while Abdul Aziz was still conquering Arabia, "when [Abdullah Sulaiman] didn't have any more cash, he would get lost. He would make himself scarce, and he and the trunk would just disappear. The King would still be giving you chitties, but you just wouldn't find the trunk to get the money." Observers often wondered "why the King was so loyal" to his quirky finance minister. "Those two were a pair," Tim Barger explained. "And [Sulaiman] had a lot of vision. He was more than just an accountant. He actually was, well he was the highest nonroyal person in the country."[8]

Later, Sulaiman became responsible for most of the financial interactions with foreigners in Saudi Arabia, and he played a particularly vital role in negotiating the initial concession agreement with American oilmen in the 1930s. He was undoubtedly a shrewd financial manager who grew to wield immense power within the kingdom despite his slight stature and soft voice. Sheikh Abdullah was a master at detailed negotiations. He personally handled all of the negotiations for that first oil concession and even signed the documents while King Abdul Aziz looked on. Several decades later, in 1950, he then renegotiated that same concession to achieve what no other Middle Eastern country had—an equal share of profits. But the tightfistedness that he was forced to employ over the lean early years of Abdul Aziz's reign left their mark on the finance minister. To the American oilmen and diplomats who worked closely with him, Sheikh Abdullah seemed to have a razor-sharp focus on the here and now. The Americans incorrectly believed his sole concern was cash flow and not strategic vision. Even after King Abdul Aziz died and his son dismissed Sulaiman from his position as finance minister, the astute negotiating tactics and attention to detail that Sulaiman brought to the Finance Ministry remained the foundation of the fledgling Saudi state.

◆

In 1933, the *New York Times* devoted just a few paragraphs of front-page space to news of an oil concession granted "in the Arabian Saudian Kingdom to the Standard Oil Company of California by King ibn Saud." The headline of the article read, AMERICANS GET OIL CONCESSION IN ARABIA; TRANSFORMATION OF DESERT LIFE MAY RESULT. "Another corner of the world has been opened to American commercial interests. . . . Exploration work is expected to begin soon. It is believed that if oil is found it will revolutionize all Arabia, transforming the desert into an industrialized country."[9]

As Standard Oil of California (abbreviated as Socal, and later renamed Chevron) told the story, the company made a huge gamble with Saudi Arabia.[10] Prior geological surveys looking for signs of petroleum deposits in the Arabian Peninsula proved disappointing but not conclusively negative. Despite the economic hardships of the Great Depression, Socal decided to take the risk and acquire a stake in Middle Eastern oil.

Standard Oil of California was a bit of a maverick when it came to the Middle East. The British had established themselves as the major player in the region when they became the first to discover oil in Iran in the early 1900s. The oil supplied by the Anglo-Iranian Oil Company (AIOC and later named BP) to the British Empire was deemed so vital that the British government had acquired a majority of the company's shares. After World War I, Anglo-Iranian, Royal Dutch Shell (a jointly owned British and Dutch Company), CFP (a French oil company), and several American companies negotiated a concession for Iraq's oil resources. Socal was not one of those American companies. In 1928, however, Socal purchased a concession for unproven oil reserves from Gulf Oil on Bahrain, a tiny island off Saudi Arabia's eastern coast.

In 1930, Socal dispatched geologist Fred Davies to survey the island. Davies hailed from Minnesota, where he had studied mining engineering at the University of Minnesota before serving in the chemical warfare unit of the US Army during World War I. He had worked on several smaller oil operations before joining Socal in 1922.[11] After Davies surveyed the Rocky Mountains for signs of petroleum, Socal sent him to the Middle East. In Bahrain, Davies made the discovery that would define his career. He chose to drill on the highest point on the island nation of Bahrain, an oval-shaped hill the Arabs called Jabal al Dukhan, or the "Hill of Smoke." On his first try he struck oil.[12] Socal was officially in the Middle Eastern oil business.

Bahrain turned out to be a small-time producer, but Socal's early success made the company eager for more. While in the Middle East, Davies had made a point of traveling to other oil sights in Iraq and Iran to study their geology. He was a "hunch and slog" oil prospector, looking for any sign that might prove commercially fruitful. In 1932, he was back in Bahrain, standing on the very same hill that had sealed his value to the company two years prior. Davies was a tall, slim man back then, and he climbed the 440-foot hill whenever he returned to Socal's base of operations in Bahrain.

As the company's story goes, Davies looked out across the deeply blue-green waters of the Persian Gulf and stared at the mottled desert landscape of the Arabian Peninsula rising before him. On that day he saw what he had seen every other time—a similarly shaped domelike hill—in the country that had recently been declared "Saudi Arabia." But that day Davies became convinced that the dome-shaped rocks thirty miles across the water also contained petroleum beneath. He tried unsuccessfully to obtain a permit to enter Arabia and inspect the domelike formations himself. Instead, he returned to the United States and took a position with a Socal subsidiary in Texas.[13]

However, Davies's initial reports on what he observed from across the water in Bahrain piqued Socal's interest in Saudi Arabia. The British, who then occupied the preeminent position in Middle

East oil with their massive operations in Iran, were unimpressed when they heard that Socal was interested in Saudi Arabia. Others had searched Arabia for oil before. Major Frank Holmes, a New Zealander, had searched and mapped the same region that would eventually interest Socal. Some historians have argued that Socal was inspired by Holmes's surveys and findings in the area, but Holmes's work, largely on behalf of the AIOC, never progressed.[14] Another American geologist, Karl Twitchell, was sent by a wealthy American industrialist to search for minerals and other natural resources at the request of Abdul Aziz, but his work never produced an oil concession either.

Once the Saudis knew Socal was interested, Abdul Aziz's British advisor and friend invited the Iraq Petroleum Company, a consortium that included British producer AIOC, to create a bidding war with the Americans. However, it seems that the extent of Iraq Petroleum's interest in Saudi Arabia was limited to preventing the Americans from getting a foothold in the region.[15] Socal never faced significant competition for assets in Saudi Arabia. The Socal executives in San Francisco quickly dispatched their own representatives to engage with the enigmatic Saudis. With British expat Harry St. John Bridger Philby serving as go-between and translator, King Abdul Aziz and Sheikh Abdullah Sulaiman found themselves sitting down with Socal representatives to talk specifics.

The Saudi kingdom desperately needed cash. Truthfully, Abdul Aziz never believed the Americans would find any oil underneath his kingdom's soil, but he was happy to let them try—for a price. King Abdul Aziz knew nothing about America, and the Americans knew nothing about Arabia. At that time the State Department did not even have a diplomatic representative in Jeddah, the only city in Saudi Arabia where foreigners were permitted to live. It took several months of back-and-forth negotiations between Abdullah Sulaiman and Socal's team to hammer out the details of a concession. Finally, on May 9, 1933, the finance minister presented the king with the final contract for his approval.

The Saudis would receive £35,000 immediately and another £20,000 after eighteen months. Socal would also pay Saudi Arabia £5,000 per year in rent, another £50,000 if the company discovered oil, and another £50,000 a year later, plus royalties from any oil sales.[16] From the perspectives of the king and the finance minister, this was £55,000 Saudi Arabia could get for nothing. The king was so skeptical that Socal would find oil that when he met with the engineers and geologists who would be surveying the concession area, he asked if they might let him know if they found any underground water cisterns that could be useful to his people.

In those days, in a premodern region that was largely devoid of population, water, electricity, and any amenities, drilling each oil well took a significant amount of time, manpower, and equipment. The process was further complicated because every piece of equipment and every man who operated or fixed the equipment had to be brought to Saudi Arabia's eastern coast from the United States. The contrast was stark between the Arabs and the American oilmen pouring into the desert with the newest technology. Philby, the British expat, observed at the time that to the Arabs, the American geologists and engineers just "descended from the skies on their flying carpets with strange devices for probing the bowels of the earth in search of liquid muck for which the world clamors to keep its insatiable machines alive."[17]

Details about Abdul Aziz's first encounters with the American oilmen from the Saudi perspective were all filtered through Philby's eyes, as he was one of the only people attached to the *al Saud* court who chronicled these events. Harry St. John Bridger Philby, born in 1885, was a British Foreign Service officer. He studied Oriental languages at Cambridge University and learned fluent Urdu, Persian, and Arabic while posted to the city of Lahore, in modern-day Pakistan. At age thirty-two he became a finance officer in Baghdad. Shortly thereafter, in 1917, the British dispatched him to central Arabia to gather intelligence on a powerful tribal leader—Abdul Aziz ibn Saud. The British were embroiled in the Great War and searching for a way to strike at their Middle Eastern enemy, the

Ottoman Empire. Philby's job was to determine whether Abdul Aziz could lead an Arab rebellion against the Ottomans.

At least that was what Philby thought he was doing in Riyadh. In reality, the British had already made up their minds to support Abdul Aziz's main rival in the Arabian Peninsula, Sharif Hussein of Mecca. T. E. Lawrence (later popularly known as Lawrence of Arabia) had already convinced the British government that Sharif Hussein was the man to back. In some ways, Philby and Lawrence lived parallel lives on opposite sides of the Arabian Peninsula. Both were tall, imposing figures, though Philby was thick whereas Lawrence was lean. Both wrote extensively about their time and experiences with the Arabs, but whereas Lawrence took liberties to craft a tale of love, war, and deceit, Philby wrote painstakingly accurate books detailing his explorations and interactions. Whereas Lawrence's book became an award-winning film, Philby's volumes were described by one reviewer as "a series of the dullest books that have ever been written about Arabia."

While in Riyadh, Philby became so enamored of Abdul Aziz that, despite Britain's decision to side with *al Saud*'s enemy, he decided not to return to England. Instead he embarked on a journey across the entire Arabian Peninsula by camel. Ostensibly, his purpose was to prove to his superiors that Abdul Aziz, not Hussein, controlled the territory, but his feat proved unremarkable to all except the Royal Geographical Society, which later awarded him their Gold Medal for this accomplishment.[18] As it turned out, Philby was correct, and the British were mistaken to support Hussein. Shortly after the conclusion of World War I (during which the British succeeded in capturing Iraq and the Levant from the Ottomans), Abdul Aziz attacked Hussein in Mecca and soundly defeated him. Philby's assessment of Abdul Aziz's strength and power had proven correct, but this did not help Philby's future advancement within the Foreign Office.

In the 1920s, Philby held positions in British mandate Iraq and Palestine, but in 1924 he resigned from the Foreign Service, ostensibly over his objection to British policies toward Jewish immigration to Palestine. In reality, he was forced out of the Foreign Service because it was discovered that he had maintained a correspondence with Abdul Aziz over the years that included conveying confidential information to the Saudis—technically espionage. He moved to Jeddah and worked for a trading company while continuing to explore the Arabian Peninsula and write books about his travels. His relationship with Abdul Aziz flourished after the Saudi ruler successfully defeated Hussein and declared himself king of Saudi Arabia. At some point, Philby converted to Islam and took the Arabic name Abdullah, though he was never religious. Philby realized that unless he converted he would never really be considered a member of the king's inner circle. Simply adopting the dress and customs of the Arabs, as he had done years ago, was not enough. Philby remained one of the king's closest advisors until Abdul Aziz's death.

Although Philby's loyalties seemed to lay squarely with his adopted tribe, the British expat remained devoted to his British wife. He returned to Britain regularly for business opportunities that rarely proved fruitful and for speaking engagements, where he earned a reputation for scandalous and scathing critiques of British foreign policy. His sentiments, however, did not seem to tarnish the reputation of his only son, Kim Philby, who rose through the ranks of British intelligence. Kim Philby tarnished his reputation on his own when he became a double agent for the Soviet Union. The younger Philby had been a Communist and Soviet sympathizer since the early 1930s and was, at one point, one of Stalin's most highly placed spies. In the mid-1950s he defected to Moscow after MI-6 became suspicious.

After Abdul Aziz died in 1953, Philby the elder openly criticized the king's successor, his son Saud, for not living up to his father's principles. In response, Saud exiled Philby to Lebanon, where he reconnected with his son in 1955. Kim Philby was living and working as a journalist there after his dismissal from MI-6. In 1960, a few years before Kim moved to the Soviet Union, Philby the father died in Beirut. His last words were reportedly, "God, I'm bored."[19]

◆

With a Saudi oil concession in hand and the king's blessing, Philby's American oil "magicians" chose the Dammam Dome, a rock formation right at the center of the hills that Davies identified from Bahrain. It took Socal eighteen months to prepare the first rig for drilling, but when it was finally ready, in 1935, breaking up the rock proved exceptionally difficult.[20] Engineers resorted to old-fashioned techniques such as heating the rock with fire and then cooling it quickly by pouring cold water on top.[21] The first well did yield some oil, but only about one hundred barrels per day. This was not sufficient incentive for Socal to run an oil operation eight thousand miles away from its headquarters. The company committed to drilling a second well. This one yielded a little over three thousand barrels, but then started gushing water instead of oil. Normally, two busts would not have been cause for concern, but with the expense of drilling halfway around the world, Socal needed to drill smarter.

The solution was to call on Fred Davies, whose initial scouting reports had set the Arabian concession in motion. When Fred Davies arrived back in the Middle East, he immediately assumed control of the Socal base camps in Arabia. Described by one of his colleagues in Saudi Arabia as "not a terribly warm and chummy guy," Davies brought a no-nonsense professionalism to the operation. The local Saudi officials respected him, though Davies himself was just as paternalistic toward the Saudis as any oil company executive of his time. He referred to Saudi culture as "tribal, patriarchal, Islamic, and ancient" and said that it "could not have changed much since the days of the Prophet."[22] Despite his attitude of cultural superiority, Davies's colleagues respected him. The geologist-turned-manager worked extremely hard. His colleagues respected his intelligence and imagination and were able to overlook his frequent mood swings and quick temper. Under his direction, Socal engineers went on to drill four more wells, two of which were completely dry. They wondered if it was just bad luck, or if Saudi Arabia was really dry. The Socal higher-ups began to question their commitment to the Saudi enterprise but decided not to give up just yet. They chose to continue searching, because, after all, the first two wells had produced some oil and nearby Bahrain was a small success.[23]

The company decided to expand the search area and sent more engineers, surveyors, and construction crews to Saudi Arabia. With packs of camels and local guides, these scientists took to the desert for weeks at a time, mapping the area and searching for signs of oil. One of these men was a newly minted geologist from Montana, Tom Barger. Barger had spent the majority of his working life in North Dakota, Montana, and the Arctic in a variety of mining jobs. Just as he started a position in Montana as an engineer with Anaconda Copper, the Depression hit and his job disappeared. No longer a salaried man, Barger found himself chipping away for copper far beneath Montana's surface. Though relieved to have any job at a time when unemployment hit 14 percent in the United States, Barger desperately wanted to get out of the mine and into a more respectable position. He was madly in love with Kathleen Ray, a North Dakota rancher's daughter, and he needed a steady salary to even consider proposing marriage.

In a Hail Mary pass, he wrote a letter to the assistant chief geologist at Socal, whom he had briefly worked with when surveying North Dakota for petroleum deposits. Barger's pluck was exactly what Socal was looking for at the time, because the company had just decided to send another team of geologists to traipse through the Arabian Desert in search of oil. After a quick interview in San Francisco, Barger signed on as a salaried geologist and left for Arabia less than a month later. In the interim, he married his North Dakota sweetheart in secret, because his parents objected to the union.

In Arabia, in 1938, Barger worked under the direction of Max Steineke, the Arabian operation's chief geologist, but he spent the majority of his time "out in the blue," or in the desert, with two other geologists, Walt Hoag and Jerry Harris. They were accompanied by an assortment of Arabs including two guides, two soldiers, a cook, and a mechanic to repair the jeeps that constantly broke down in the sandy hills.[24] The conditions were extreme, particularly compared to the cooler temperatures Barger must have been used to in the northern United States. The heat was so intense that the geologists were forced to use a specialized film for their cameras created by Kodak to withstand temperatures of 115 degrees Fahrenheit.[25]

In letters to his wife, Barger described how his team of geologists frequently ran into groups of Bedouins as they explored. The Bedouins were clearly puzzled by the sight of Americans crawling around caves and carrying armfuls of fossils. The geologists were actually examining fossils of ancient sea life to try to gauge the age of the rocks below, Barger explained. When news of the Americans' fascination with seashells reached Abdul Aziz, however, the king was amused. Unconvinced that the Americans would find petroleum, Abdul Aziz invited Tom Barger and his fellow geologists to Riyadh to ask him for a favor. There, after a traditional feast complete with platters of spit-grilled lamb and many tiny cups of cardamom-flavored coffee (etiquette dictated the guest consume at least three to be considered polite, according to Barger), the king asked the geologists to drill several water wells and test them for quality. At the very least, Abdul Aziz hoped he could get some water out of this crazy venture.

As they traversed the Arabian terrain, Barger and the other American geologists diligently mapped areas that even the king knew nothing about.[26] Separated from his young bride, Barger felt her absence acutely when traveling for weeks (and sometimes months) in the open desert. "The first night we camped at Ain al-Amrah, on the Qatar peninsula," he wrote to her. "It is a well that consists of some shallow holes amongst the dunes, which are completely innocent of any vegetation whatsoever. It's the most barren place I've ever seen."[27]

The sandstorms were especially intense, "but there's no dirt to blow, only sand. They are not as dirty as dust storms in North Dakota," he explained to Kathleen. "The current sandstorm has been blowing for the last three days." It was January, and even though "the thermometer [did not] go any lower at night, the wind whistling through our tin-roofed warehouse [sounded] like a blizzard and [made] it feel colder."[28] A few days later, after he returned to Socal's basecamp and picked up his mail, Barger learned that Kathleen might be pregnant. He was elated at the prospect of becoming a father but clearly scared of his parents' reaction, since they did not know he had married before departing for Saudi Arabia. Although Barger had "prayed that somehow they may [have] come to know and love" Kathleen, he wanted to be at his wife's side to deliver the news. As Barger found out several weeks later, Kathleen was not pregnant, though the two went on to have six children during their long marriage.

By the time Barger arrived in Saudi Arabia, Socal's management was already quite nervous about prospects in the area. Back at Socal's headquarters in San Francisco, they were questioning the value of the entire Arabian endeavor.[29] Several years and $10 million had yielded nothing of commercial value. Even if the geologists and construction engineers discovered oil in commercial quantities, Socal feared it would have nowhere to sell that oil. Saudi oil, like the crude oil Socal was already producing in Bahrain, generally had a high sulfur content. Most of the refining outlets that Socal had access to in Europe were not fitted to process that oil. The company was already having difficulty unloading its oil from Bahrain and chose to cut production there significantly. If Socal was going to invest more resources, time, and manpower into its Arabian venture, at the very least the company needed to know it could sell any oil it did find.

As it turned out, another American company, Texaco (later merged into Chevron) was facing the exact opposite situation. Texaco owned refineries and marketing outlets in Africa and Asia, designed to process the heavy-grade, high-sulfur crude the Middle East was already known for. Yet Texaco lacked sources of crude in that part of the world to supply them. Texaco feared that without a consistent supply of crude oil it would lose those outlets and the significant profits it saw developing in those regions. Forming a partnership for oil operations in the Eastern Hemisphere seemed the obvious course of action. The two companies joined forces, and Texaco received a stake in Socal's Arabian exploration venture, then called the California-Arabian Standard Oil Company, or Casoc.

The Americans had started to drill their seventh oil well in Arabia in 1936. Delays plagued the drilling process from the start when the sides caved in and blocked the shaft. Next, a delayed shipment of drill pipes stymied further progress on the well. By January 1938, the well had reached a depth of 4,500 feet, yet not a drop of oil had appeared. The company was having, as Barger put it, "a devil of a time" with that well.[30] While Barger, Steineke, and the other geologists scoured the company's concession area for signs of other oil deposits, Casoc's management reached a final decision. The company would curtail its spending in Saudi Arabia. San Francisco sent a cable to its teams in Arabia with firm instructions not to drill any new wells.[31] After nearly five years of unsuccessful drilling, the Americans were finally ready to concede what the British had told themselves all along—there was no commercially viable oil in Saudi Arabia.

In March 1938, the team in Arabia decided to deepen Well Number 7. Lo and behold, another two hundred feet beneath the surface, they found oil. Suddenly, Well Number 7 started producing 1,585 barrels of oil per day. Three days later, that number increased to nearly 4,000 barrels.[32] By mid-March, the oil was still flowing and all eyes in San Francisco turned back toward Dammam. Well Number 7 led to the discovery of an expansive oil field that spread out into the Persian Gulf. After the company expanded its concession an additional 440,000 square miles, another large oil field was discovered in the southwestern corner of the Arabian Desert.

A year later, King Abdul Aziz and his entire court assembled in Dhahran, a sleepy little town of animal herders near the Dammam Dome, where Casoc had decided to build its Arabian headquarters. On May 1, 1939, in front of his family, advisors, and Casoc's management, Abdul Aziz opened the spigot on Saudi Arabia's oil industry.[33] With a ceremonial twist of the tap, crude oil began to flow through the pipeline that Casoc construction crews had quickly built between Well Number 7 and Ras Tanura, a port on the Persian Gulf, where a tanker waited to bring Saudi oil to the world market.[34]

By 1940, Casoc was producing about 20,000 barrels of oil per day and the company had begun building housing and offices in Dhahran. Thanks to World War II, demand for petroleum had recovered from the Depression era lows, so the company's revenue was up. The war might have increased global oil demand, but it also made transporting that oil more difficult and dangerous as both the Allies and the Axis targeted each other's tankers and refineries. The Persian Gulf was over one thousand miles from the front lines in North Africa, and the Americans did not think their facilities in Saudi Arabia were in any danger.

However, a daring attempt by Italian bombers in October 1940 shattered the illusion of safety. The United States had yet to join the war, so Italy's real target was the tiny island of Bahrain, then under British protection. Mussolini, looking for a high-profile victory, approved a plan to send bombers from Greece, across the Middle East, to the Persian Gulf to bomb the oil refinery in Bahrain. He hoped to cut off a source of oil for the Royal Navy. The plan was incredibly risky. The squadron would have to overload its planes with fuel just to make the three-thousand-mile trip, fly through unmapped deserts in Syria, and avoid British reconnaissance planes in Iraq. Then, after bombing the refinery, the planes would have to fly across the Arabian Desert and the Red Sea to land in current-day Eritrea (then called Abyssinia, part of the territory Mussolini had seized during Italy's war with Ethiopian king Haile Selassie).

The planes shook with the strain of the extra weight as they took off in the Mediterranean dusk. A year and a half before the Doolittle Raid proved the United States could reach Tokyo by plane, this mission, if successful, would set a record for the longest-range bombing. If not, then the best-case scenario would find the pilots stranded in the Arabian Desert, forced to land as their fuel ran down. The

Italians had a cargo plane filled with fuel standing by on the Red Sea coast, but the likelihood of locating downed planes in Arabia's interior and successfully landing and taking off in the desert was a long shot. Everyone involved knew that a rescue would be unlikely. With a bit of luck and a favorable tailwind, the bombers made it over Iraq and saw Kuwait appear before them. Only nine hours had passed and only one plane had become separated from the squadron over Damascus. The planes dropped from nine thousand to three thousand feet and let loose a string of bombs aimed at the refinery in Bahrain.

The early morning sky lit up brilliantly as nearly two hundred bombs exploded. Thirty miles west of Bahrain, the Saudi Arabian city of Dhahran, which housed Casoc's headquarters, was also bombed. The squadron's lost plane had managed to catch up, but it mistakenly dropped its bombs over Dhahran instead of Bahrain. The four planes regrouped and immediately headed toward Eritrea. Now they were racing against their quickly diminishing fuel supplies. They managed to reach the Red Sea and land safely two hundred miles inland in Africa, but just in the nick of time. After flying for fifteen hours and thirty minutes that night, each plane had less than forty gallons of gasoline left in its tank.

The success they felt, however, was short-lived. Despite the signs of major explosions, the bombs had barely touched Bahrain's refinery or any important installations in neighboring Dhahran. One bomb hit a pile of coal on the island, creating an impressive explosion but doing little damage to the actual target. Another managed to hit an oil pipeline, but the remainder fell in the sand. The mission was botched because the pilots had been instructed to focus their bombsights on the orange-colored natural gas flares, which, it was assumed, indicated the location of the refinery and oil installations. These tall structures with gas flares at their top point were used by petroleum refineries to burn off flammable gasses released by pressure relief valves during the refining process and at oil extraction sites to reduce the raw natural gas that accompanied the release of oil from the ground. Later, petroleum engineers began regularly capturing the natural gas to use as energy, but in the 1940s, flaring the gas was extremely common.

Fortunately for the Americans, right before the bombing the refinery had moved its gas flares to a location farther away from the refinery, so in focusing on the gas flares, the Italians actually missed the refinery and the oil wells entirely. Damage in Bahrain and Dhahran was minimal, and the flow of oil continued almost uninterrupted. The only feat achieved by the Italian bombers was in completing the round-trip flight without refueling, although, at the time, *Time* magazine incorrectly reported that the planes had refueled from submarine tankers, so even recognition remained elusive.[35] In fact, two years later, the United States developed the B-29 Superfortress, which was able to carry much heavier loads and quickly surpassed the Italians' record for longest flight without refueling.

Even though the raid had resulted in only minimal damage, Socal and Texaco decided to evacuate almost all of the American personnel from Saudi Arabia, and they shuttered oil production almost entirely for the duration of the war. In any case, hostile powers patrolled the seas and would target any Allies they found. The Americans suspended all plans in Saudi Arabia indefinitely and left only a skeleton crew in Dhahran to maintain the oil installations and feed the refinery on Bahrain with as much crude oil as their tiny operation could manage during the war.[36]

As soon as the war ended, however, Casoc's parent companies, Socal and Texaco, were eager to restart production and pick up Arabian development where they had left off. Demand for petroleum remained high and was expected to grow as Western Europe started to rebuild its devastated cities. However, many American petroleum companies emerged from World War II short on capital. The war had required them to mobilize rapidly to provide most of the gasoline, petrochemicals, and high-octane fuels for the entire Allied war operation, but when the war ended, so did the steady flow of government cash.

Casoc, in particular, needed more resources than its parent companies had available in order to restart its operations in Saudi Arabia. First, Socal and Texaco tried to sell the entire Arabian company to a US government enterprise called the Petroleum Reserve Corporation. When that failed, they reached out to two other major American companies, Standard Oil of New Jersey (now ExxonMobil) and Standard Oil of New York (Socony, now part of ExxonMobil, as well), who decided to buy into the Arabian operations. The four companies renamed it the Arabian American Oil Company, or Aramco.

Demand for petroleum quickly soared as Western Europe's economic recovery took off and the American military presence around the world necessitated consistently available petroleum products. Aramco quickly ramped up oil production in Saudi Arabia to over 200,000 barrels per day in 1947. American carpenters, machinists, riggers, technicians, drillers, and managers poured into the Persian Gulf as Aramco began building extensive pipelines and deep-water ports to accommodate the rapidly increasing flow of oil. Soon, Saudi petroleum was filling new cars in Europe and fueling American military planes flying to Korea.

In late 1947, just as Aramco's business was taking off and Saudi oil was becoming vital for American policies in Western Europe and Asia, geopolitical upheaval in the Middle East appeared to threaten Aramco's operations. The United States had become heavily involved in the partition of Palestine that would, in 1948, lead to the establishment of the State of Israel. The State Department feared that American support for a Jewish state would compromise Aramco's oil business in Saudi Arabia, because King Abdul Aziz supported the Arabs. To the surprise of some in the State Department, King Abdul Aziz assured the Americans that he would not allow this conflict to interfere with Aramco and the production of oil. The king told the Americans that he was facing pressure from Arab neighbors to cut ties with American interests amid the regional tensions. King Abdul Aziz even feared a possible invasion because he did not intend to cut ties. He asked the State Department for assistance in securing his borders against possible incursions. King Abdul Aziz, who by then was seeing approximately $15 million per year in revenue from his Aramco contract, was not willing to compromise his growing and promising business relationship for regional politics.[37] In fact, at the time, Abdul Aziz was seeking "closer military and economic ties with the United States."[38]

King Abdul Aziz had given the State Department little reason to be concerned about US support for the Jews in Palestine. In 1946, King Abdul Aziz sent a letter to President Truman expressing concern about America's support for the immigration of 100,000 Jews to Palestine because he thought that Jewish immigration would expand beyond the borders of Palestine and into other parts of the Middle East. According to the American ambassador, the king said, "The Arabs would not object to the establishment on the Mediterranean coast of Palestine of a Jewish enclave. What the Arabs feared above all was that once a Jewish state was created extending over most of Palestine there would be no holding back Jewish pressure for further [living space]."[39] Abdul Aziz did not object to the establishment of a Jewish entity in Palestine. Rather, his concern was that if a Jewish state encompassed most of Palestine, Jews would eventually expand beyond the border of the British mandate into other parts of the Middle East.

Bringing Saudi oil to the global market had been no small feat. The Middle Eastern oil experts of the time had already written off Saudi Arabia as a lost cause by the time the Americans opened negotiations with King Abdul Aziz. Only a last-ditch effort by the American team in Saudi Arabia had saved the entire project from being shelved by management in San Francisco. World War II practically derailed the entire operation. It took a certain tenacity and foresight on the part of the American companies to continue to invest in a venture halfway across the world in a premodern country with harsh terrain and grueling weather conditions. Yet the Americans shipped steel, machinery, and products for development across the globe, consistently brought in new talent and technology to overcome these obstacles, formed and re-formed their corporate entities to provide capital, and worked within the confines of the Saudis' strict, fundamentalist culture.

As the Americans complained, cajoled, and generally fixated on trying to change the premodern elements of the Saudi economy, Sulaiman and others in the royal family's administration went about building a strong oil business and a strong Saudi Arabia. Perhaps the Saudis did not do enough to disabuse the Americans of their flawed notions that the Saudis were passive players. Or perhaps the Saudis considered this an advantage.

◆

While the Americans pumped God's gift to Abdul Aziz out of the ground, Abdul Aziz's appetite grew for gifts he could bestow upon his people. Sulaiman could no longer fit the king's entire treasury under his bed, nor was this arrangement practical for the kinds of changes Abdul Aziz had in mind. He had seen what the Americans built in Dhahran just for their company—massive housing structures for the oil field workers, office buildings and homes for company executives and geologists, an airport, a hospital, and a power plant to bring electricity to it all. Now that he had the money, he wanted those things—and more—for his wives and sons and grandsons. He wanted a palace with thick walls, indoor plumbing, and electric lights. He wanted a hospital and a school and a grand mosque in his city.

He had fought, conquered, and united Arabia with nothing more technologically advanced than guns. And yet, crossing Arabia was almost impossible by car in the 1940s, because the country lacked paved roads. He knew this was a problem. With money flowing into Abdul Aziz's treasury, he would spend it. He wanted the luxuries of modernity for himself, his sons, and his country. Conveniently, there was an American company right at his doorstep, eager for the opportunity to build what the king wanted in Saudi Arabia.

TWO

THE AMERICANS IN KING IBN SAUD'S COURT

When he arrived in the ancient port city of Jeddah, on Saudi Arabia's western coast, the humidity surprised Ambassador J. Rives Childs, and, in his words, "heat of an intensity unknown to me beat down in waves as if from an open furnace."[1] Socal had first sent Americans to Saudi Arabia in 1932, but the United States did not dispatch an official ambassador to the kingdom until the end of June 1946. Childs arrived at a critical juncture in the relationship between *al Saud* and the American businessmen. Aramco's operations expanded rapidly immediately after World War II to meet growing demand in Western Europe and America's global military operations. Money was pouring into the company and the

Saudi treasury, but this only fueled conflicts between American business operations and Saudi ambitions.

Ambassador Childs's diplomatic skills would be tested soon after he stepped onto Jeddah's "primitive airstrip" surrounded by a "limitless expanse of sand and rock." He arrived in Arabia just in time to patch the wounds in the relationships between the American businessmen and the Saudis, represented mostly by Abdullah Sulaiman and sometimes by members of *al Saud* themselves.[2] Through success and strife, over the following thirty years, American diplomats—eccentric characters and staid professionals—strove continuously to help each side. These men from the State Department kept a persistent focus on their one true aim in Saudi Arabia: keeping the oil flowing to the industrialized world and the machines of the Cold War.

By the time the winter months came around, Childs had hoped for cool ocean breezes, but instead the city's proximity to the Red Sea made it cling to moisture until it seemed the air was practically solid. Every day, Childs looked out over the azure waters that beckoned him from the embassy balcony. Swimming was out of the question, not because the Americans could not subvert the modesty laws that dictated men and women cover their bodies regardless of the heat but because sharks and barracudas lined the coast. These vicious animals swam back and forth, waiting for an unsuspecting human, overcome with the sweat and heat of the day, to jump in.

The ambassador wiped the sweat from his balding forehead and washed down another salt tablet with the tepid glass of water on his desk. The air-conditioning the embassy installed in 1948 (two years after his arrival in Jeddah) could do only so much against the oppressive heat and humidity. To avoid chronic dehydration, the entire embassy staff tried to consume at least a dozen salt tablets a day.[3]

Dealing with the Saudis, especially the higher-ups in the royal family, was as challenging as the weather. The Saudis ran on a different timetable than those from the West. Nothing happened when it was supposed to. Scheduled meetings could be put off for days or weeks, even audiences requested by the king himself. Every promise was really "*inshallah*"—God willing. As Childs saw it, this was not just a religious supplication but, in practice, an all-purpose excuse. It was nearly impossible to understand the rings and layers of power in the Saudi court, but Childs was realizing that no matter which prince or advisor he spoke to, unless word went directly from the king to his finance minister, everything was up for negotiation.

A career foreign service man, Childs had received tricky assignments before—as a young man he had delivered aid to starving Russians during a revolutionary purge in the early 1920s—but this position was especially challenging because Childs was the first US ambassador to the country. He would set the tone for America's relationship with Saudi Arabia.[4]

Childs's quirky personality and dogged insistence on "acquainting [himself] with less conventional circles" in the countries in which he served did not always endear him to the State Department. He had remained in the lower ranks of the Foreign Service until economic reports he had prepared while working in the American embassy in Bucharest somehow had caught the eye of Wallace Murray, the division chief of the Department of Near Eastern Affairs.[5] In 1930, he was finally promoted to second secretary and sent to the "American consulate" in Cairo.

In the Middle East, Childs's unorthodox approach to diplomacy was finally recognized as an asset, and he became "well known in Cairo as the first foreign diplomat who has made an effort to make friends with Egyptians." After stints in Iran and Morocco during World War II, he was finally offered an appointment as ambassador to Saudi Arabia in 1946. "Jeddah," where the new American embassy would be located, Childs wrote in his memoirs, "was subject to almost intolerable heat."

"A pressing appeal was made for my acceptance," Childs explained, as the American embassy in Jeddah was "known to be lacking in the most ordinary amenities." Childs accepted and became the first American ambassador to Saudi Arabia.

Each of his dealings with the royal family and government employees proved to Childs the value of "making friends" in the Middle East. The best way to get anything done in Saudi Arabia was a strategy of deference first and pressure later. His first audience with King Abdul Aziz introduced the ambassador to a set of customs he never had experienced before—even with years of service in Egypt, Iran, and Palestine behind him. When Childs arrived at the king's palace in Riyadh, after a tortuous flight from Jeddah's primitive airstrip, his first stop was the royal tailor. The tailor took his measurements. A day later Childs was presented with the appropriate white *thobe* robe, a *shomagh* to drape over his head, and an *igaal* to secure the red-checkered headdress with. The attire was a gift from King Abdul Aziz, which Childs learned he should wear to the palace on subsequent visits. None of his previous assignments had included a costume. However, Childs firmly believed that he should mix with the Saudi people, and dressing the part would help him penetrate this unknown society. Ambassador James B. Smith, who followed Childs's legacy sixty years later, and also donned native attire to celebrate with Saudi hosts, retold Childs's story with new details. "They did dress [Childs] up," Ambassador Smith said. "He was told that you should never turn your back to the king. So he went in and presented his credentials, and then, as he was backing up, he stepped on his *thobe* and tumbled over backwards."[6] Childs's willingness to adapt to the Saudi court's traditions was more indelible than his clumsiness; the king and Childs became close.

In subsequent visits, he came to think little of changing out of his stuffy Western attire and into the flowing robes before even landing in Riyadh. Of course, not everyone at the State Department was so inclined. The first time Childs brought George McGhee, an assistant secretary of state from Washington, D.C., to Riyadh, Childs began to don this outfit on the plane before landing. McGhee was outraged that an American diplomat would take on the dress of a foreign country.

Well, Childs explained, "as long as I am Ambassador I intend to respect the King's wishes the better to serve my country's interests. If Washington has other ideas, I am prepared to offer my resignation."

McGhee continued to "fume" at the perceived humiliation of putting on a robe and head covering, but ultimately warmed to the idea when he and Childs arrived at the palace and the tailor took his measurements. On McGhee's reaction to seeing his Arabian-clad reflection, Childs wrote, "When it was delivered, I observed, with an amusement which I was at pains to conceal, the admiring look with which he regarded himself."

Two days later, McGhee came around and apologized for his earlier rant. As the two were about to depart, McGhee put a friendly arm around Childs and said, "You were right and I was wrong." Showing deference to the king by conforming to Saudi customs yielded far greater benefits than making a point of not conforming.[7]

Childs himself cultivated what he described as an "unusually close" relationship with the king during his nearly four years of service. "On one of my visits to his capital," Childs explained, "[the king] went so far as to propose through one of his ministers that I accept a slave girl in my quarters during my stay. So significant a compliment was almost unprecedented, since the Moslem generally regards with abhorrence physical possession of a Moslem woman by an infidel."

Of course, Childs refused, but it was clear that other foreign dignitaries would have relished the opportunity. When Childs once recounted the story and his polite refusal to a French colleague, that man's response was "Only an American would."[8]

◆

As Saudi oil began to transform the global oil market, this newfound source of revenue began to transform Saudi Arabia. The oil concession, first signed in 1933, provided Saudi Arabia with a lump sum along with provisions for the country to receive royalties on Aramco's sales of Saudi oil. Before production skyrocketed after World War II, the Saudi government's primary source of income came from taxes and income generated by the annual Muslim pilgrimage to Mecca and Medina known as *hajj*. Suddenly, in 1946,

Aramco was providing the Saudi royal family with more money in a year than it had ever collected from *hajj*. Saudi Arabia could expect to make approximately $15 million per year from its concession with Aramco, although $7.6 million of that amount would be in oil royalties and thus susceptible to market fluctuations.[9]

Aramco put some of its own profits into building infrastructure in Saudi Arabia needed for its own operations. The king gave Aramco free reign to develop the sparsely populated area around Dhahran as it saw fit. As long as the Americans did not interfere with the traditional lives his people lived in the rest of the country, Abdul Aziz allowed the Americans to operate as they wished. The company built roads, ports, airfields, headquarters, houses, and amenities for American workers, and dormitories for Arab workers. Most of these projects were contracted to a San Francisco–based construction company called Bechtel. Almost overnight it transformed the tiny village of Dhahran into a modern Western enclave. Company videos from the early 1950s show a freshwater swimming pool, a golf course, suburban housing for American employees, and tennis courts. Modern elements such as better airports and faster airplanes in Saudi Arabia made work like that of Aramco executive James Terry Duce easier.

Duce joined Aramco as a vice president in 1939, but before 1948, he spent most of his time in Washington, D.C. As head of Aramco's government relations and public relations, "there was precious little that he did not concern himself with at one time or another."[10] Born in England, Duce immigrated to the United States as a child and grew up in Colorado. He studied geology at the University of Colorado before serving in the Chemical Warfare Service during World War I. Later, he joined the Texas Petroleum Company and served as president of one of its subsidiaries in South America. Like many oil company executives, during World War II he took a leave of absence from his company (in this case, Aramco) to serve in the Petroleum Administration for War. There, he acquired valuable contacts in Washington that served him well when he returned to full-time work with Aramco in the late 1940s.

Duce described himself as "just a country boy," though both the Saudis and American diplomats he worked with knew him to be a strategist who was always "planning for the future." Looking back, he found the challenges that faced Aramco in those early days "intellectually stimulating," though his communications at the time reveal great frustration with both Saudi and State Department representatives. Duce was one of the many eccentric Americans who ventured into Saudi Arabia in Aramco's early years and became a constant presence in the relationship developing between the Saudis and the Americans.

Upon his death, colleague William Mulligan described him as "discreet and unostentatious." His physical appearance, however, was anything but innocuous. He "had the face and figure of a Kewpie doll with thinning hair" and a "merry twinkle in his squinty little eyes [that] reminded one of Santa Claus." His wife was perhaps more outlandish than he. Ivy Duce met James in South America, but with her husband's frequent travels to the Middle East she became obsessed with Sufism, a mystical sect of Islam. She not only practiced the religion herself but also became a *murshidah* (spiritual teacher) and had as many as four hundred students during her lifetime.[11]

As Aramco grew in the 1940s, Saudi Arabia produced more oil, and oil meant money. The king and his government knew this. They also knew that although Saudi Arabia was blessed with a valuable natural resource, the country was not industrialized and lacked modern infrastructure. Its population was largely uneducated and premodern. Saudi Arabia's advantage was that it recognized its strengths and weaknesses in comparison to others. In the 1940s, Saudi Arabia lacked the domestic enterprise to build railroads, power plants, and ports. But it could entice foreign vendors with the promise of business funded by its oil fortune. Over time, the kingdom would come to leverage its assets to obtain the best bids from around the world and even incubate domestic enterprise in certain fields. But in the 1940s and 1950s, the Saudis looked to the most convenient vendor to bring their country into the modern era: Bechtel. Soon enough, Bechtel was building infrastructure for Aramco's growth and modernizing Arabia for its new client, *al Saud*.

The Saudi royal family put its newfound wealth into development—personal and public. The royal family appropriated funds for its own palaces and residences, and the government also embarked on an ambitious public works campaign. All of this construction brought more Americans to Saudi Arabia, particularly construction engineers and managers. The Saudis commissioned hospitals, roads, schools, and municipal buildings in Riyadh and Jeddah. They even ordered a quarantine area for pilgrims in Mecca. The Saudis wanted a modern airport, hotels, and restaurants to turn the mud-hut-dotted capital of Riyadh into a modern city.

Even the desert could not escape the changes the oil industry brought to Saudi Arabia. Construction crews from Bechtel plowed through large dunes, leveling the ground in preparation for roads and railroads that would connect the eastern and western parts of the peninsula. The company completed plans for the Trans-Arabian Pipeline (Tapline). This huge, new, 1,068-mile pipeline would carry Saudi oil directly through Iraq to ports on the Mediterranean Sea. But the desert posed its own set of challenges—never before had Bechtel had to take camel crossings into account when building its pipelines. Nor had Bechtel ever contended with roaming bands of Bedouins, who sometimes attacked the pipeline with swords and lit campfires dangerously close, a potential threat to ignite the oil.[12]

King Abdul Aziz desperately wanted a railroad built between the capital, Riyadh, and the eastern port city of Dammam, a nearly four-hundred-mile venture. In 1946, Sulaiman's treasury held about $10 million in oil royalties, and the king was eager to spend. When Sulaiman first showed the plans to Bechtel, vice president Van Rosendahl was immediately skeptical of the project. Engineers would have to cut through miles of isolated rocky terrain, level sand dunes as high as small mountains, and avoid lava fields. However, when Steve Bechtel, company CEO, made the trip from the company's San Francisco headquarters to personally negotiate the contract, he spoke directly with King Abdul Aziz. Steve Bechtel understood the significance of the railroad project.

Before Abdul Aziz had taken control of Arabia, the region had a single Ottoman-era railroad that linked the Arabian Peninsula to Baghdad. During World War I, however, the Sharif of Mecca and his British allies had destroyed the railroad in an attack later dramatized in the film *Lawrence of Arabia*. After World War I, the Sharif of Mecca had been the final adversary that Abdul Aziz and his forces had faced in their westward march across Arabia. A new railroad, though impractical, would cement the king's rule and his ability to care for his people in an important and symbolic way. Despite the problematic technical elements, Steve Bechtel left Saudi Arabia excited about his company's prospects there.

Tapline was Bechtel's biggest project "since the Boulder Dam" (later renamed the Hoover Dam) and "the mightiest ever laid."

"In the Middle East program," Steve Bechtel remarked, "I cannot help but foresee tremendous possibilities pointing toward the biggest development of natural resources ever undertaken by American interests."[13] After Aramco, Bechtel was the second company the king and his ministers invited into the kingdom. Its expertise in engineering, project management, and infrastructure development were vital in a country that lacked even the most basic modern amenities.

Bechtel's Saudi Arabian venture was really like a second career for its CEO. Steve Bechtel's father, Warren, had been a man who—at least in his own mind—forged his own destiny, much like Abdul Aziz. He started a construction company in San Francisco right after the 1906 earthquake and fire leveled the city. After working on the railroad for years, Warren simply purchased an old steam shovel, slapped W. A. BECHTEL CO. on the side, and set out to build what would become one of the most successful private American corporations.[14] California flourished over the next two decades, and Warren Bechtel's construction company built highways, railroads, dams, and irrigation projects. Steve Bechtel grew up as his father's business thrived, and enjoyed the physical comforts of that labor. When he was a sophomore at

Berkeley, Steve Bechtel killed two pedestrians and injured a third in an automobile accident. All of the charges against him were inexplicably dropped, but Steve Bechtel left school anyway and joined his father's business.

In his early years at the company, Steve Bechtel concentrated mostly on oil pipelines, but when Bechtel (along with five other construction companies) won a bid to participate in building what would become the Hoover Dam, he joined the project as chief of administration. The project's scale dwarfed everything Bechtel had built previously. The sheer scope only fueled Steve Bechtel's growing ambition to go after bigger projects. After his father's death (from insulin shock while on a trip to Russia), Steve Bechtel took over the company and quickly won contracts from major oil companies like Socal to build pipelines, refineries, and chemical plants. By the time World War II was over, Bechtel had grossed $100 million and was starting to look at foreign markets.

Steve Bechtel thought Saudi Arabia was the right customer for his company. He wanted Bechtel Corporation to shed the heavy infrastructure that he had seen become a liability for other construction companies coming out of the war. Instead of making large capital outlays, the company would accept the jobs it wanted to do. It looked for select, "sweetheart" clients who could pay up front for massive projects. "We," he told his senior staff, "are not in the construction and engineering business. We are in the business of making money."[15]

Throughout the 1940s, Steve Bechtel had been keeping track of Socal's activities in Saudi Arabia. In fact, in 1943, Bechtel had built a pipeline for Socal to connect its refinery in Bahrain to the port of Ras Tanura in Saudi Arabia. In 1946, Socal (now operating as part of Aramco in Saudi Arabia) was number one on Steve Bechtel's list of potential "sweetheart" clients. He and Rosendahl created a special division, International Bechtel, Inc. (IBI), just to focus on the Middle East.

IBI executives had not even received their business cards before Steve Bechtel took off for Saudi Arabia to meet with Aramco executives about building Tapline. There he learned that the Saudi government had made $10 million in royalties from Aramco in 1946 alone. Saudi Arabia's oil industry was beginning to take off. It was obvious to Steve Bechtel that the Saudi treasury would be able to pay and that the Saudis' appetite for modern building would continue for quite some time. To Steve Bechtel, the match could not have been more perfect. IBI would build its largest pipeline ever for Aramco while simultaneously picking up the basic building projects from the Saudi government, a client whose needs were endless and whose funds came directly from a reliable source.

Saudi Arabia hired IBI for its first public works campaign with the unwritten understanding that more projects from the royal family and the government would be forthcoming. Saudi Arabia spent lavishly and quickly on its building program, often burning through its monthly oil royalties and then borrowing against future months' royalties to pay off the growing expenses. The Americans, from the newly installed diplomatic entourage to managers from IBI and Aramco, grew increasingly concerned about *al Saud*'s sharp increase in spending. At this early point in Saudi history, the royal family's treasury and the government's treasury were one. As soon as the royalty money rolled into Abdullah Sulaiman's coffers, he quickly dispensed it to a variety of building projects the royal family had commissioned. On the side some members of the royal family also tapped IBI to build grandiose new palaces to replace the mud-walled palace the family had occupied since taking control of Riyadh several decades before.

The railroad that had first created the opportunity for IBI with *al Saud* took four years to build and generated $50 million in bills. By the time it opened, IBI was deeply intertwined in Saudi development. At the end of 1949, IBI had built an impressive resume of ongoing and future projects for the Saudis: railroads, highways, power plants, hospitals, sanitation facilities, and hotels. IBI saw the Saudi public works campaign as a sure source of profit, given the company's near monopoly in the kingdom. However, when the time came to settle the bill, *al Saud* proved to be less of a "sweetheart" client than Steve Bechtel had thought.

Looking back at the relationship between Bechtel and the Saudi government, its contentious end seems a foregone conclusion. Unlike Aramco, which invested heavily in programs to build rapport between Saudis and Americans—and especially in worker training programs—Bechtel never seemed to hit its stride with the Saudis. The ink on the first $17 million contract was barely dry when the problems began, giving IBI president Van Rosendahl and CEO Steve Bechtel headaches from their San Francisco headquarters. The first whispers of discontent came from Tom Borman, IBI's project manager based in Jeddah.

"We have a situation over here," he wrote directly to the CEO in October 1949, "which I consider quite serious [and] has developed into an untenable position. Relations between myself and Mr. Fahoum (Borman's Saudi contact and one of Sulaiman's deputies) have retrograded steadily during the past five months even though we have bent over backwards in an effort to cooperate with him."[16]

According to most accounts, Tom Borman was a decent guy but a poor fit for IBI's operations in this vastly different culture. Borman was straightforward and honest—qualities that earned him the respect of US ambassador J. Rives Childs—but this did not serve him well in maneuvering among Saudis, who were accustomed to more subtlety. At the end of 1948, Borman discovered that Saudi Arabia owed IBI over $1 million. He immediately visited the finance minister and asked him where the missing money was. Sulaiman leaned back in his chair and smiled. The treasury, he explained, had simply kept the money as IBI's Saudi "income tax" payment.[17]

Borman knew Sulaiman had the king's absolute trust and saw no benefit in taking the matter further up the Saudi hierarchy. Instead, he complained to his IBI superiors. Though Borman thought he was making a pragmatic decision to ignore intransigent Saudis, the Saudis saw this as a character deficiency. To them, it seemed that Borman lacked cunning, wit, and spirit—qualities valued and respected by the Saudis with whom he had to operate. Once

Sulaiman and his deputies saw Borman's weakness, they walked all over him.

At first, Steve Bechtel and the executives in San Francisco hesitated to blame the Saudis for problems with the construction projects and the withheld payments. Because IBI was the first engineering and construction company to land lucrative contracts in Saudi Arabia, the last thing Steve Bechtel wanted was to upset the Saudis and lose his near monopoly. He and Rosendahl showed Borman's letter to John Rogers, a rising executive in the CEO's inner circle who had accompanied them on their first trip to Saudi Arabia.

Borman himself was the problem, Rogers told Rosendahl and Steve Bechtel. After making a visit to Borman's jobsites in Saudi Arabia, Rogers reported that "the situation in Jeddah continues to deteriorate because Tom is spiritless and has lost his punch, but more because his wife is talking too much about many subjects."[18]

When Steve Bechtel pushed Rogers for more concrete evidence, he explained that "Tom Borman, as project manager, has tried to control every move on his project without consideration to his associates or to Government officials and has been unduly influenced by his wife."[19]

Apparently, Borman's wife frequently drank to excess and became indiscriminate with her words when intoxicated. Borman, according to Rogers, listened to his wife's meddling far too much. Rogers faulted Borman for failing to control his wife's alcohol consumption and for listening to her advice. If the Saudis discovered the alcohol, Rogers cautioned, Borman could find himself expelled from the country, not to mention that the company would have to justify breaking this cultural and religious taboo. In fact, whether Rogers was aware or not, alcohol consumption by non-Muslim foreigners was accepted in cities like Jeddah and Dhahran in 1949. It was not until 1952 that it became a problem for foreigners to have alcohol in the kingdom. This crackdown was a reaction to an incident in 1951. King Abdul Aziz's nineteen-year-old son, Mishaari, had been at a party at the home of British consul Cyril Ousman in Jeddah. Foreigners like Ousman regularly served alcohol at such functions. Prince Mishaari became agitated and left the party. When he returned, drunk and carrying a gun, he opened fire and killed Ousman. Mishaari was imprisoned but allowed to live. The following year, Abdul Aziz forbade foreigners from importing alcohol.[20]

The accusations against Borman and his wife proved to be the last straw for senior management. Borman did push back, protesting that Rogers was "after his scalp," but a visit from Rosendahl sealed Borman's fate.[21]

"In general," Rosendahl explained to Steve Bechtel as he was on his way back from the Middle East, "it has been a one-man show, managed with almost complete disregard for organization principles and proper procedures in the handling of other people's money. A change in management is imperative and, as you know, we are taking steps in that direction."[22]

Borman and his wife were removed from Saudi Arabia and reassigned. Once Borman was out of the picture, senior management dispatched another high-level executive and personal friend of CEO Steve Bechtel to oversee all of Bechtel's projects in Saudi Arabia. His name was C. Stribling Snodgrass. The C stood for Cornelius, but everyone called him "Stribs."

Stribs was a former navy officer who had studied petroleum-processing engineering at the US submarine school in 1922. His real expertise, however, was working with the men who ran the petroleum companies. After four years of active duty in the navy, he moved to London and sold his services as a consultant to major oil companies—including Socal—which is how he met and befriended Steve Bechtel.

When World War II broke out, Stribs returned to work for the navy, this time in the safety of a Washington intelligence office. In 1942, he left the navy to become the head of the foreign petroleum supply division of the Petroleum Administration for War, a government agency tasked with coordinating the petroleum supplies that American forces and civilians would require for the duration of World War II. Not coincidentally, James Terry Duce, an Aramco vice president, served as director of the Petroleum Administration for War's Foreign Division and knew Stribs well from their time in Washington. During his government service, Harold Ickes, President Roosevelt's interior secretary and "oil czar," dispatched Stribs on a top-secret mission to survey the world's oil reserves. As part of this mission, he found himself trudging through Saudi Arabia with geophysicist Everette DeGolyer, trying to estimate how much oil might be buried under all that sand, and how the United States might use it in the war effort.[23]

The three weeks he spent in the Saudi desert convinced Stribs that Saudi Arabian oil would become an integral part of American national security in the future. In his report, Stribs recommended that the United States make every effort to develop Saudi Arabia's oil resources. His good friend Steve Bechtel hired Stribs as a vice president for IBI and sent him off to Saudi Arabia to become the primary liaison between IBI and the Saudis. His letter of introduction to Abdullah Sulaiman described him as "Executive Representative in charge of all affairs and relations between the Saudi Arab Government and International Bechtel, Inc. pertaining to operations in the Kingdom of Saudi Arabia and elsewhere."[24]

It was rumored that Stribs was, in fact, a CIA spy, but it is more likely that he was at most a CIA asset who provided information to the intelligence agency while conducting his traditional business. It is unclear who may have recruited him, but it is likely that Stribs had connections to the Office of Strategic Services (OSS), the CIA's predecessor during World War II, through his work overseas during and immediately after the war. William Eddy, a former OSS agent and later CIA agent, also worked for Aramco in Saudi Arabia during this time, and it was not uncommon for CIA agents to have positions with companies that had extensive contact with the State Department. Stribs's papers include cryptic accounts of events and contacts he had with Saudi government officials in which the names of major players, some of whom may have been important Saudi officials, were replaced with biblical pseudonyms such as "Matthew," "Mark," and "Peter."[25]

In response to a Freedom of Information Act request, the CIA would not confirm or deny whether it officially employed Stribs. The CIA did release a December 1951 memorandum of understanding (MOU) signed by Cornelius S. Snodgrass and a representative of the US government whose name was redacted. The MOU may not relate to Stribs's work in Saudi Arabia at all, but it may, instead, relate to later employment with the government in D.C. It may even relate to still later work as an independent petroleum consultant, which he began shortly after signing the document. However, even during his government stint in the 1950s, Stribs continued assisting IBI and its parent company in Saudi Arabia, so the rumors persisted. As part of this memorandum of understanding, Stribs acknowledged that "because of the particular relationship between myself and the U.S. Government," he would be receiving sensitive information that would "adversely affect the interests, and possibly the security, of the United States."

As part of this MOU he pledged that he would "never divulge, publish, nor reveal either by word, conduct, or by any other means such information or knowledge."[26] Indicating that Stribs may, in fact, have collected intelligence for the CIA, the MOU stated that he recognized "the paramount interest of the US Government in information which I or my organization may possess, compile or acquire as a result of requests placed upon me by Government representatives." Regardless of his possible affiliation with the CIA, Stribs demonstrated zeal on behalf of his true employer, IBI. His real value to IBI came from the connections he brought with him.

Stribs was photographed frequently for the corporate magazine, *Bechtel Briefs*, but never without sunglasses, a bow tie, and a goofy grin. Even standing next to a considerably shorter and more rotund Ambassador Childs, Stribs looked small in his baggy pants and oversized suit jacket. Regardless of how awkward and uptight Stribs appeared, his attention to detail served him well in the field.

When he arrived in Saudi Arabia, Stribs found that IBI's problems ran much deeper than organizational malaise, and he was quick to blame the Saudis. The company's contract with Saudi Arabia specified that Saudi Arabia would advance money into Bechtel's account "so that at all times there will be sufficient money available to meet therefrom all expenditures."[27] After all, Steve Bechtel's business plan was based on those "sweetheart" clients who could pay up front. In fact, the financial discrepancies were so great that IBI suspended a number of projects and compelled Deputy Finance Minister Najib Bey Salha to promise an immediate payment of $100,000 and 100,000 Saudi riyals.[28]

Stribs had little hope that Salha and the Finance Ministry would follow through. IBI knew that Saudi Arabia had the funds: after all, IBI also worked for Aramco and saw firsthand just how much oil was being pumped from the ground and sold to Western Europe and the US military. To Stribs and others at IBI, the Saudis were too incompetent to manage this wealth appropriately, or too indolent to pay up. Stribs, however, had a plan to overcome this roadblock. When Steve Bechtel wondered whether his company should even be working for the Saudis anymore, Stribs defended the program.

"In spite of the immediate financial mess," Stribs explained, "which is due to extravagances, wastefulness and lack of method— I still feel that Saudi Arabia is the best credit risk in the Middle East."[29]

This assessment confirmed Steve Bechtel's initial instinct about Saudi Arabia. The Saudi government had a secure source of income that was likely to grow. What then, Steve Bechtel wanted to know, did Stribs propose to do about the current situation and the immediate lack of cash? "The gap in finances," Stribs said, "can be bridged only by an advance from Aramco or by an external loan."[30] In other words, IBI needed to bypass the Saudi government altogether.

Essentially, Stribs's plan was to get the US government or Aramco to front Saudi Arabia the cash to pay IBI immediately. Then the Saudis would be indebted to Aramco and the US government— two entities with the most leverage to force the Saudis to repay, or enough funds to simply write off the loan if repayment proved too difficult. Conveniently, the US government was in the business of offering such loans—though not without some fairly significant strings. When apprised of IBI's cash-flow problem, Ambassador Childs himself suggested that Saudi Arabia apply for a loan from the Export-Import Bank to cover the costs of some of IBI's major infrastructure projects.[31]

President Franklin Roosevelt created the Export-Import Bank of United States in 1934 under the National Industrial Recovery Act. At that time, its purpose was to finance the export of American goods and services to other countries. Essentially, the Ex-Im Bank functioned as a way to help US companies secure foreign contracts that would stimulate jobs in America. In providing loans to other countries for the purpose of purchasing American products, the bank was designed to accept "credit and country risks that the private sector is unable or unwilling to accept."[32]

Stribs pretended that the idea had never occurred to him and prevailed on Ambassador Childs to present the idea to King Abdul Aziz, who promptly appointed Deputy Finance Minister Najib Bey Salha to prepare the application. Upon review, however, the Americans told Salha that his application was "badly presented" and recommended, in January 1950, that Stribs take over the loan application process to ensure its effective completion.[33]

Steps still had to be taken to conceal the truth that IBI was actually preparing the loan application to the Export-Import Bank, because, as an IBI employee, Stribs "could be judged as having an axe to grind in this particular matter." Which, in reality, he did. The money from the loan would go directly to pay IBI for ongoing projects. Stribs justified this by portraying Saudi Arabia in the application as "devoid of administrative controls and procedures" and generally not competent to manage its own affairs—not a stretch in his mind.[34] Eventually, the Ex-Im Bank loaned Saudi Arabia $15 million to finance specific IBI development projects.

Despite the loan from the US government, Saudi Arabia's debt to IBI continued to build. The construction work in Saudi Arabia continued unabated, and the company even used some of its own capital to meet operating costs because IBI was confident that

Saudi Arabia did, in fact, have plenty of money to pay IBI's costs. The Saudis, in the minds of IBI's managers, were just refusing to part with it. So, even though the Saudi government had only paid half of its outstanding balance to IBI, the company signed on for another year.[35]

Stribs, however, did not see the projects through. He had been offered a position in the US government's newly formed Petroleum Administration for Defense and departed for Washington, D.C., later that year.[36] Stribs was to become the head of the foreign petroleum division and, in this position, maintained many of his contacts in the Middle East.[37]

Before he left, Stribs wanted one last try at stabilizing IBI's financial situation. He arranged a meeting between himself, Steve Bechtel, and several members of the State Department to discuss the situation in Saudi Arabia. During the meeting, Steve Bechtel made his dissatisfaction known with the "business conduct of the Saudi Arabia Government." He was frustrated to the point that he asked George McGhee—the same diplomat who had resisted Childs's adoption of Saudi attire—if he thought it advisable that IBI continue its work in Saudi Arabia altogether. Steve Bechtel was hoping to get some help from the US government in directly dealing with the Saudis and obtaining payment.

"We consider the work of [your] firm in Saudi Arabia an important contribution to the development of that country and in the promotion of American influence and goodwill" was McGhee's diplomatic answer. Immediately, Steve Bechtel knew he was being rebuffed. McGhee and the State Department would help Aramco, because the oil it pumped was vital to national security. However, it would not help Steve Bechtel's company past a certain point. IBI's services in Saudi Arabia were not vital. They could, and would, be replaced by the work of any number of other construction companies. Aramco's services, however, were unique and vital to America's strategic goals.

Steve Bechtel had not even arrived at the point in the conversation where he had planned to request that the State Department pressure the Saudis to pay their bill. The only assistance McGhee was willing to offer was to request that the Ex-Im Bank relax the conditions placed on its loan to Saudi Arabia "so that the proceeds can be utilized in non-dollar markets." This meant nothing to Steve Bechtel, and he left the meeting annoyed at having wasted his time.[38]

With Stribs now working for the government, Steve Bechtel put another Bechtel Corporation vice president in charge of the Saudi public works campaign. Earl English's primary function in Saudi Arabia was to squeeze the Saudis and get every possible penny IBI was owed. He also oversaw IBI's new contracts. Finally, in late 1951, Steve Bechtel decided it was time for the Saudis to really start paying. He got on a plane himself and traveled to Saudi Arabia for a sit-down with Abdullah Sulaiman himself. According to Steve Bechtel's account, the Saudis had yet to pay for Crown Prince Saud's palace, Saud's opulent trailer, electrical material for Prince Feisal's palace, and other road, water drilling, and transportation equipment that the Saudis had ordered from IBI.

During the meeting, Sulaiman dismissed these as minor costs. The trailer, at least, was no minor matter. It cost $60,000 in 1951, and was, by IBI's account, "a very special piece of equipment . . . something which has never been built before and [could not] be bought off a floor similar to an automobile. . . . There was never a trailer like this built and we do not believe a better one could be built." Some of the specialized elements included a full-size bathtub and shower combination and china bidet in the bathroom, wall-to-wall carpet in the bedroom and living areas, two-way radio, 30 KW generator, telephone, bell system to call servants, and an eight-cubic-foot electric refrigerator.

As Steve Bechtel recalled these details, Sulaiman sat silently and listened to the CEO's complaints. When Steve Bechtel had exhausted his litany, the finance minister explained, in his careful and measured tone, that he would "take care of" these expenses. Meanwhile, as if there was no tension between the two parties, Sulaiman said he wished to order several new items for Riyadh.

Steve Bechtel and the managers who accompanied him were flabbergasted. How could the Saudis, with what the company considered an extreme amount of debt with no way to repay it on the horizon, consider commissioning more projects? When Rudy Grammater, a company vice president, tried to remind Sulaiman that he still owed them for its recent purchase of company construction equipment, Sulaiman just smiled.

Steve Bechtel was furious and ready to issue an ultimatum. He said, "Unless the government [meets] its financial obligations [which at that point totaled $1.5 million] promptly, Bechtel will terminate its contract with Saudi Arabia." Even in the face of this ultimatum the finance minister remained, at least to American eyes, unflappable.

As it turned out, this ultimatum was not something IBI was ready to follow through on—yet. It was simply a ploy Steve Bechtel had designed to get the State Department and Aramco to pressure the Saudis to pay.[39] What IBI really wanted came out in a meeting that the new US ambassador to Saudi Arabia, Raymond Hare, arranged. The ambassador gathered Earl English, an Aramco representative named Garry Owen, Sulaiman, and Salha in his office in Jeddah to try to resolve the issue between IBI and Saudi Arabia face-to-face.

English wasted no time delving into what IBI considered the major problem. Saudi Arabia's income, he explained to Hare, had been steadily increasing as its oil production rose. According to English, IBI needed a direct line to those funds in order to finally clear up Saudi Arabia's debts. As English explained to Hare, only an agreement whereby Aramco would withhold royalty payments from the Saudis and pay IBI directly would satisfy them.[40] Upon hearing this, Garry Owen, Aramco's representative, looked askance at English. There was absolutely no way Aramco would ever consent to this arrangement, he explained, barely containing himself at the IBI executive's suggestion. In Owen's mind, and in reality, IBI was asking Aramco to circumvent its vital partner, Saudi Arabia. It seemed that English assumed the Saudis would not notice or care, even though the Saudi finance minister and his deputy were sitting in the same meeting. Unlike English, Owen had come to realize that the Saudis were more sophisticated than that, and Aramco was not about to ruin its good deal with its hosts.

Sulaiman, sitting calmly beside Hare, also rejected English's proposal outright. He knew what IBI was asking. English was perturbed and tried to argue his point by reminding the Saudis and Aramco that they, in fact, already had such an arrangement in which Aramco simply withheld royalty payments in return for a railroad that Aramco had built for the Saudis.

The words were barely out of English's mouth when the cordial tone of the meeting that the US diplomats had carefully cultivated evaporated. Salha turned toward English and exploded in anger, shouting at him that "[We were] wrong! [We] should never have done it because if [we] had gotten bids for the railroad it would have cost [us] a great deal less."[41]

It was then that English realized the entire hair-splitting effort to cajole the Saudis into exercising some fiscal restraint or at least prompt payment had been a waste. The Saudis had no intention of continuing to employ IBI despite the unfinished projects. While IBI had been negotiating, entreating, and even threatening to up and leave Saudi Arabia unless the government paid its debts, the Saudis, as it turned out, were the ones who really wanted to cancel the contract.

Back in 1947, Saudi Arabia lacked basic modern infrastructure. At the time, IBI was already completing projects for Aramco, so the company had been the natural choice to contract for the public works campaign in 1947. By 1951, however, major cities were already electrified and transportation routes had been built. Sanitation services, hospitals, hotels, and even cafés had sprung up around Riyadh and Jeddah. The equipment, plans, and logistics for further expansions were in place. The easily accessible knowledge and personnel that, in the 1940s, made IBI such an advantageous choice now took a back seat to cost.

IBI had greatly underestimated the Saudis. Though the Saudi Finance Ministry might have been unsophisticated by Western standards, Sulaiman and Salha had kept their own records and knew exactly what IBI was charging them. They had compared the costs of construction in Saudi Arabia with their counterparts in other countries and knew that IBI was overcharging their government. This became abundantly clear when Ahmed Fakhri, the newly appointed director of the Bureau of Mines and Companies within the Finance Ministry, arranged for an introduction with Emile George. George, an American of Lebanese descent, was the son of Fakhri's "friend," and had recently become the Middle East representative for a firm from Pittsburgh, Pennsylvania, called Michael Baker Jr. Inc. George spoke Arabic fluently and had traveled to Saudi Arabia multiple times since 1949. Slowly, he had befriended Abdullah Sulaiman and had worked diligently to bring together the Saudi finance minister and the construction firm from Pittsburgh.[42]

Before Steve Bechtel ever threatened to cancel the Saudi public works campaign contract, Emile George had brought Baker representatives to Jeddah to meet with Sulaiman, Salha, and Fakhri. The two sides had quickly begun negotiations for Baker to assume responsibility for the unfinished IBI projects and some maintenance work. Baker, a smaller firm without a major foothold in the Middle East, was willing to do the work for less, particularly if the Saudis purchased IBI's equipment. The Saudis did acquire IBI's equipment, though Sulaiman made clear to Steve Bechtel after the fact that he did not intend to pay for it.[43]

By the time the State Department brought Earl English, Garry Owen, Sulaiman, and Salha together, the Saudis had already practically signed a new contract with Baker. Making good on their word to open the market to competition, the Finance Ministry hired Baker to design and oversee new projects, but it would hire other firms to undertake the actual construction. Some of these firms came from overseas, like the West German firm Govenco. Other firms, like the Binladin Group, came from within Saudi Arabia. The Binladin Group, started by Mohammad Binladin, the father of al Qaeda mastermind Osama bin Laden, grew rapidly through its royal contracts and had become the third-largest employer in Saudi Arabia by the late 1950s. In fact, *al Saud* was so pleased with Mohammad Binladin's work that he became known as "the King's builder."[44] Mohammad Binladin's construction company went on to receive lucrative contracts to expand and maintain the Grand Mosque in Mecca, and Mohammad was later appointed director of government construction by Abdul Aziz's son, Saud. The two families were so close that the Binladin children, including Osama, grew up alongside the children and grandchildren of Abdul Aziz. Mohammad Binladin died in a plane crash in 1967, but his construction company continued to grow under the leadership of his oldest sons (not Osama). Later renamed the Saudi Binladin Group, the company continued to be one of the most prominent construction firms across the Middle East.[45]

After discovering that Sulaiman had signed with Baker, IBI had no choice but to abandon the Saudi public works campaign. IBI continued to work for Aramco in Saudi Arabia. It completed Tapline, the pipeline that traversed Saudi Arabia, Iraq, and Syria to bring Saudi oil to ports on the Mediterranean. Tapline would be maintained and operated until the early 1990s. IBI tried for months to force the Saudis to pay their debts to the company in full, but for every charge English brought to the Finance Ministry, Sulaiman and Salha came back with their own accounting to dispute the charges. Eventually, the Saudis paid what they felt they owed, and no more. Without any leverage in a country where the king's word was law, English eventually gave up and returned home. Steve Bechtel did not know it at the time, but his adventure in Saudi Arabia was not over. The oil money would prove too enticing. He and his company would return a decade later to manage and build Jubail and Yanbu, the first major petrochemical complexes for Saudi Arabia and Aramco. For Saudi Arabia, the disputes of the early 1950s did not sour later opportunities for increased profit.

The Saudi experience with IBI, though brief, proved instrumental and became a model for how the Saudis went on to conduct business. Saudi Arabia understood that it lacked the resources of more developed nations. These included a large population, an educated populace, capital, credit, and native businesses. What Saudi Arabia realized it did have was an immense quantity of a very desirable resource: petroleum. Because it lacked so many resources, it could not drill for, extract, refine, transport, or sell that petroleum on its own. It needed outside firms to access the value of the petroleum, at least initially.

The Saudis considered the petroleum under their soil a gift from God, but accessing its value laid within man's capacity. Until the Saudis developed the capabilities themselves, they would simply import the human capital they needed to make that petroleum valuable. This meant importing Aramco to run the oil industry, IBI and, later, other companies to build modern cities and transportation, and even American financial advisors to create a modern banking system. The trick was to buy what they did not have from the outside, and then to make it their own. In the case of IBI, that meant buying the company's equipment and leasing it to other construction firms to build more palaces, roads, and power plants at cheaper prices. For the royal family, it meant sending princes abroad for education at the finest Western institutions like Princeton and Oxford. In the case of Aramco, it initially meant encouraging Saudi workers to accept training as welders, carpenters, machine repairmen, and roughnecks. Ten years later, it meant sending promising young Saudis abroad to school to learn geology, petroleum engineering, logistics, and law. These men, and later women as well, took positions in Aramco and worked their way up into management. Sometimes the Saudis assumed full control almost immediately after buying or importing what they lacked.

And sometimes the process took nearly fifty years.

THREE

ACTUAL ACCRUED BENEFIT

In the midst of the Bechtel fiasco, Aramco and the State Department were facing their own concerns caused by Saudi Arabia's finances. King Abdul Aziz's cavalier spending was beginning to alarm Aramco. The company worried that financial insolvency would destabilize the royal family and potentially threaten the company's concession agreement. Aramco worried that if the king was overthrown, Aramco's access to the country's oil could be cut off. This, in turn, concerned the State Department, as America's global interests at the time required easy access to foreign sources of oil. Saudi Arabia's vast reserves were providing just that. Both Aramco and the State Department thought Saudi Arabia's best interests—and their own—would be served by limiting spending and postponing massive development projects. The Saudis, however, had other ideas about how to finance their national development programs, personal luxuries, and social welfare.

This dissonance quickly began to spoil the friendly and successful relationship Aramco enjoyed with the king and his advisors. The Saudis saw great wealth streaming into Aramco from the sale of Saudi Arabian oil and could not justify tightening their belts and making due with the relatively small share of royalties Aramco provided them. Instead, the Saudis looked at this money and wanted a larger portion. Why go hungry when Aramco had everything *al Saud* needed to satiate its appetite? *Al Saud* would not be satisfied; *al Saud* had ambitions.

◆

By 1950, Ambassador J. Rives Childs suspected that Saudi Arabia was running out of money even before his friend, Garry Owen, stopped by his office in the US embassy in Jeddah. Childs and Owen had both lived in Jeddah for several years by then, and they knew each other socially as well as professionally. Garry Owen had joined Aramco in 1941, working in the San Francisco office during World War II before transferring to Jeddah, where he worked as Aramco's chief representative and liaison with the Saudis in Jeddah. Owen was a lawyer by training, and his job was to represent company interests to both the Saudis and the American diplomats. He was very good at what he did, and Childs respected him.

Owen's visit to the embassy that morning was not out of the ordinary, but the message he delivered alarmed Childs enough to warrant an immediate cable informing the State Department in Washington. In the "strictest confidence" Owen told Childs that Aramco had just approved an exceptionally large loan to the Saudi government—$6 million without interest, to be repaid in eight monthly installments starting in July.

"Why?" Childs asked.

Garry Owen showed Childs a copy of a letter to the Saudi government from Fred Davies (who had risen from chief geologist at Socal to executive vice president at Aramco at that point). Davies had written, "[The] company depends on a sympathetic understanding and cooperation with His Majesty's Government on company market and monetary problems."[1]

Aramco, Owen explained, wanted to avoid falling into the troubled relationship that other Western oil companies had in countries like Mexico and Iran. The "market and monetary problems" that Davies mentioned referred to the potential for decreased oil prices or demand, which would adversely affect the Saudis' royalty revenue. Essentially, he was asking the king to be patient with his coming wealth. The loan was less than ideal, he conceded, but worth it to the company to cement a positive relationship. Hopefully the loan would improve the king's patience despite Saudi Arabia's increasing desire for revenue. Childs, who boasted of his "relations with His Majesty," which had taken on "a friendly and almost familiar character," needed no convincing. He recognized why Aramco prioritized satisfying the Saudi government.[2]

The good-natured and friendly relationship that Childs had consciously cultivated with the royal family and Saudi bureaucrats might come in handy for Aramco now. Childs understood that Owen was telling him that the Saudis were beginning to tread on dangerous financial ground, even after the generous $6 million loan. Saudi financial insolvency would threaten American interests in the kingdom, which daily were becoming ever more mixed with oil. Something had to be done, and Aramco wanted a united American front to present to the Saudis when the time arrived to tell them, finally, no more handouts.

Working to keep friction between the Americans and the Saudis to a minimum was wise, Childs agreed. Along with Aramco's interest-free loan, the company also established and funded a program to treat trachoma, an eye disease that was prevalent among the people of Saudi Arabia. Trachoma is a bacterial infection of the eyes that, if untreated, can cause blindness. In its early stages, the disease is easily cured with a course of antibiotics. It is preventable with clean water and improved sanitation. Aramco also regularly sent American gifts to the royal family. These payments in kind (or in dollars) were not exactly bribes. The State Department and the company considered them all part of Aramco's method of maintaining and deepening the positive relationship the company needed to have in a country where the king's word was law.

However, Childs was still cautious about the strategy. He had his staff begin to track, as best they could, Saudi expenditures, loans, and royalty payments from Aramco. The numbers were distressing and convinced him that this overly conciliatory approach was not working. Armed with information that demonstrated an exponential growth in Saudi Arabia's budget deficits, he told Garry Owen that Aramco should resist giving the Saudis any more interest-free loans. Referencing the financial information his staff had managed to scrounge, Childs showed Owen how the financial problems had ballooned.

The $6 million, Childs said, "may have [had] the merit of keeping Company-Government friction to a minimum, [but] it renders impossible the institution of modern budgetary procedures so desperately needed by the country."[3] Faced with the actual figures, Owen had to agree with the ambassador. He would recommend to Aramco that the company withhold any future "gifts" to the Saudis unless the Finance Ministry took steps to improve their financial management.

While the Americans busied themselves looking for more examples of Saudi fiscal irresponsibility, the Saudis were preparing their own case against the Americans. As Davies, Owen, Barger, and other Aramco executives convinced themselves of the Saudis' immaturity and foolhardiness, the Saudis continued to manipulate the Americans into helping them secure loans from the US Export-Import Bank. When the two sides finally faced off against each other across the negotiating table, it would be the Saudis who held the upper hand and caught Aramco off guard with their shrewdness and depth of knowledge about Aramco's situation in the Middle East and the global oil industry. At the end of the day, the company found itself outmaneuvered and flummoxed. Luckily for them, the State Department would be there to pick up the pieces.

◆

Saudi Arabia did not necessarily see its budgetary shortfall as a problem. King Abdul Aziz took a risk back in the 1920s when he conquered the western parts of Saudi Arabia and united the country under his rule. He faced rebellions from tribes that chafed under his rule, and after putting an end to these upstarts, King Abdul Aziz cemented his dynasty's power over these tribes, which had been historically hostile to *al Saud*. Military superiority was only part of the battle—a tribal leader in Arabia needed to demonstrate his strength and control on a continuing basis by providing for the tribe financially. This meant responding to the needs and bequests of his people promptly, and with gifts, justice, and cash.

Abdul Aziz regularly heard the complaints of his subjects in open court, as custom dictated. His palace provided meals to anyone who knocked on the door. In a land where luck often determined survival, generosity served the king well. The Western, Protestant work ethic, popularized by the writings of scholars like Max Weber, famously disapproves of handouts, but Arabian culture and society embrace these gestures as a sign of prosperity and health. Before oil, King Abdul Aziz possessed only minimal funds to dispense to his subjects. That money was simply not enough to continue to prove his power and legitimacy to a population spread across a vast land. To maintain his rule, King Abdul Aziz had to show the people of Saudi Arabia, in material ways, that they were his subjects. Without the funds to do so, his rule would crumble.

Abdul Aziz took a risk when he invited the Americans into Saudi Arabia to look for oil. That risk paid off, and now the king had the opportunity to show his subjects a comfort they had never known before. *Al Saud* could thus provide hospitals, schools, sanitation facilities, medical care, transportation, and business opportunities to its subjects and, in so doing, secure the dynasty's rule. Cutting back at this point would have been tantamount to inviting rebellion and dissent into what had been only a little more than a decade of civil tranquility. While Aramco worried about every penny the Saudis spent, Abdullah Sulaiman, who had negotiated the original concession agreement, set about crafting a strategy to increase Saudi revenues.

The Saudis used the Americans' misperceptions of them as unintelligent, greedy, and unmotivated to their own advantage in this situation. Sulaiman and his deputies deliberately led the Americans on, telling them what they wanted to hear, and temporarily placating them until the time was right. Ambassador Childs was unintentionally complicit as well. He even brought in a US currency specialist from Egypt to study the Saudi situation, meet with Sulaiman's deputies, and prepare recommendations for financial reform. Sulaiman was courteous during the presentation, and sat calmly and listened to the recommendations. Then he told Ambassador Childs and the currency specialist exactly what they wanted to hear: Saudi Arabia welcomed the assistance of the American specialists and he would take these recommendations to the king for consideration and implementation, immediately.

The State Department expected the Saudis to accept their offer graciously and allow US government specialists to inspect their books and even tutor them in Western accounting practices. The Saudis had other ideas. Rather than continue to subsist on royalty payments that varied from month to month and loans from Aramco to tide them over, the Saudis wanted a more permanent solution. For that, the king handed Finance Minister Abdullah Sulaiman free reign. The king would step in when needed, but Sulaiman would take charge of Saudi Arabia's relationship with Aramco.

Several months later, Abdullah Sulaiman made his first move. At the end of May in 1950, Sulaiman failed to send Aramco the kingdom's regular monthly payment on the railroad loan.[4] Sulaiman placed a call to Aramco headquarters in Dhahran, inviting Aramco vice president James Terry Duce to the palace for an audience. Now that the Saudis had run out of dollars to pay the loan installment,

Duce entered the meeting expecting to finally discuss fiscal reforms and modern accounting practices.

Abdullah Sulaiman looked as gaunt and as gruff as ever. According to Duce, the minister immediately "made claim to a larger take from the Company enterprise." What could possibly justify this entitlement? "Large company profits," offered Sulaiman. Duce tried to explain that Aramco needed "to keep costs down to be competitive to create royalty producing sales" and that the current state of global oil supply and demand meant that Aramco could not afford to charge a higher price for Saudi oil.[5] (In truth, even when demand was low, Aramco's effective return on its capital investment rarely fell below 200 percent.)[6]

Sulaiman was not convinced. "The Company can well afford to pay more," he told Duce. "The Saudi Arabian government has a good idea of Company profits." In fact, Sulaiman continued, "In connection with a query . . . and from available statistics such as the 38% rate of taxes and amount paid to the U.S. Government, the Saudi government has working knowledge of Aramco's profits." Duce understood what Sulaiman was telling him. Sulaiman's point was that the Saudis had been able to discover Aramco's profit by examining Aramco's tax returns and other information.

Duce could not deny Sulaiman's claims. Instead, he tried to explain why Aramco could not part with any more of its revenue. "Everything the Company makes is plowed back into the venture. It is only because of this policy that the Company has been able to achieve such remarkable success."[7]

Abdullah Sulaiman was not easily swayed. He told Duce yes, he would "acknowledge that the Company has pursued an enlightened policy." The Saudi government and country "alike have benefitted," he said. "But," Sulaiman continued, "increased payments to the Saudi government would not detract from these contributions materially."

His purpose in calling Duce in for an audience was "only to impress upon [Aramco] the Saudi government's determination to get what it believes to be its rightful share out of the Company's undertaking." Aramco had known the king's views on this issue for "more than a year," Sulaiman continued. The king, he said, "has waited a long time for a favorable answer and now is getting impatient" and "cannot wait longer." According to Duce, Sulaiman kept his cool and with "no histrionics . . . threatened that drastic action would be taken to secure more revenue from the Company but did not reveal its nature."[8] There should be no more delays, Sulaiman said. A yes or no answer was expected in two weeks.[9]

It was clear to Duce that his audience with Sulaiman was over. As his car was leaving the palace, he noticed Prince Feisal arriving. Prince Feisal was the king's second son. Feisal was widely known as demanding and rigid. It was possible, Duce told the Aramco board in San Francisco and the State Department, that Sulaiman's sudden and swift demands were simply for Feisal's benefit. In that case, the finance minister would certainly be able to report truthfully to Prince Feisal that he had spoken to Duce and delivered the king's warning. If Duce ever considered that Sulaiman was manipulating him, he never mentioned it to either his superiors at the company or to his allies in the State Department.

Aramco executives in San Francisco read Duce's letter with care. In response, they dispatched Fred Davies to Saudi Arabia to handle this delicate situation. Before he departed for the Middle East, Davies called Ambassador Childs to fill him in on Aramco's intended course of action. First, the company would suspend collection of Saudi Arabia's payments on the Aramco-built railroad as a gesture of goodwill. Without the pressure of monthly payments of $600,000 hanging over his head, hopefully Sulaiman would be in a better mood.

Aramco's strategy, Davies explained, would be to "ease the increasing pressure on the company for a greater share of profits." But, he explained, "no actual increase in the [Saudi] government's share of Aramco's profits has yet been agreed upon."

Childs thought Davies should know that Sulaiman's office had been talking about Aramco's profits and corporate taxes with other

American officials. "Saudi officials referred to the fact that Aramco paid, in 1949, U.S. government taxes totaling 38% of its profits, an amount equal to some $40 million," he said.

Davies confirmed that the Saudi figures were indeed accurate. He had no idea how Sulaiman had figured this out and continued to pump Childs for more information.

Childs did not know Sulaiman's sources, but he did have some important intelligence for Davies. The finance minister would soon be taking an extended vacation. Before he departed, he was scheduled to meet with Crown Prince Saud, the king's oldest son. The rumor was that Sulaiman would present the Crown Prince with a letter "pointing out that he has done all he can to obtain concessions from Aramco."

It was believed that the Crown Prince or other high government officials "may then take up the question of revising the concession, or," Childs said, "registering the company in Saudi Arabia in order to enable the Saudi government to obtain taxes now paid to the U.S. government." Childs cautioned Davies that this was only rumor and that Sulaiman could be bluffing.

Childs's meaning was clear. If the Saudis thought Aramco would not negotiate anymore, they were prepared to take more drastic actions. "The Embassy does not believe the matter ended," Childs explained. "We fully expect continued Saudi government efforts to obtain a larger share of Aramco profits."[10]

Aramco was genuinely scared of Sulaiman's demands. Before ending the conversation, Davies revealed that Aramco president Fred Moore was also planning a visit to the kingdom later that month. The worst-case scenario, which Aramco saw playing out between Iran and the Anglo-Iranian Oil Company (later BP), would be popular unrest, strikes, and nationalization. Davies, Moore, Duce, and every other Aramco executive knew their directive was to avoid this—at all cost.[11]

By the time Moore made it to Saudi Arabia, however, the situation had deteriorated considerably. He was almost immediately "confronted by Sheikh Abdullah's demands for a reply from the company." Moore explained that the company had decided to grant the Saudis another year's respite from the $10 million railroad payments and that he was "unwilling to reopen discussion [on Sulaiman's demands] at this time."

Back at Childs's office, Moore relayed the experience to the ambassador. The ambassador knew the Saudi mind better than he did, but it seemed as though "new demands from the Saudis appear each time Aramco makes a financial concession."

"Aramco is unwilling to make further concessions now," Moore told Childs, "which would lay [the company] open to probable new and further demands." The board recognized that this could lead to a possible shutdown, but, Moore explained, the directors "believe [the Saudi] government in its present financial straits can afford a shutdown much less than can the company." At this point, the Americans thought that Sulaiman was trying to drive a hard bargain with Aramco and that the king and other royal family members would, in the end, lack the nerve to follow through.

Barring interference from the royal family itself, Childs counseled Moore to remain firm. "We believe . . . there is no indication that the King and Princes are as determined to force concessions from Aramco as are Finance Ministry officials." Childs did not explain why he thought the Finance Ministry's demands did not reflect those of *al Saud*. Perhaps he did not understand the loyalty of Sulaiman to his king, or perhaps Childs underestimated the fortitude of *al Saud*.

Childs would continue to impress upon the Finance Ministry the importance of putting the Saudi fiscal house in order instead of "supporting the policy of milking Aramco and all comers for sufficient funds to balance the budget." However, Childs was not sure he would have much of an impact. As he remarked to another embassy official after Moore left, "Perhaps the only way to correct the situation might be for it to be brought to a head by a really first-class crisis."[12]

Aramco's final reply to Sulaiman appeared in the form of a written statement:

> Aramco notes with concern and disappointment the Finance Minister's threat of unfriendly relations. The Company has found and developed oil in Saudi Arabia with speed without precedent in the oil industry. The Company has been generous with its assistance and has produced actual revenues to the government in amounts beyond all expectations. We are happy that this has been possible; but there is a limit to which the Company can provide support. In the final analysis the oil must pay its way.

Childs reported this dutifully to the State Department, adding that the "next move is apparently up to the Saudi Arabian government, but timing is uncertain."[13]

With that, communications between Aramco and the Saudi government broke down entirely. Sheikh Abdullah Sulaiman must have felt aggrieved that Aramco executives had taken such a hard line on paper and refused to sit down with him, as equals, and negotiate based on common problems. This, he had his deputies tell Ambassador Childs, was a great breach of the courtesy he expected of Aramco. After all, Aramco's lifeblood came at the grace of the Saudis.[14]

In truth, Aramco officials did not take Sulaiman as seriously as they might have a finance minister from a Western country. By their own admission, Aramco executives considered the Saudis less than capable, but they had never before behaved dismissively toward government officials. Moore, Duce, Davies, and others believed that Saudi Arabia would not actually threaten Aramco's position in the country, because royalties from Aramco funded the entire Saudi government operation. The problem with directly calling Sulaiman's bluff was that Saudi Arabia was an autocratic country. Abdullah Sulaiman might have been cantankerous and possibly even a bit corrupt, but he had King Abdul Aziz's complete confidence. He could make life in Saudi Arabia frustrating and miserable for Aramco—which is exactly what he did.[15]

After Moore refused to sit down with him, Sulaiman ordered Saudi customs inspectors to "open and examine thoroughly every package arriving for Aramco." A few days later the Saudi government mysteriously ordered Aramco "to terminate its radio communication facilities."[16]

◆

In 1950, the month of fasting and prayer known as Ramadan fell in July. During Ramadan, Muslims abstain from food and drink during daylight hours, so the particularly long, hot, sunny summer days of fasting added a layer of tension and frayed nerves to the already strained relationship between the Americans and the Saudis. Finally, though, Childs managed to get a meeting with Sulaiman to try to break the logjam.

When Childs called on Sulaiman in his Jeddah office, the finance minister had broken his fast only "a short time before." Childs observed that Sulaiman "reportedly imbibed nothing stronger than Coca Cola" at the traditional *iftar* meal.[17] Sulaiman's penchant for alcohol, despite Islam's strict prohibition against it, was well known among the Americans. Aramco had previously reported to Childs that the finance minister had once appeared drunk at a meeting and "signed a check drawn to the order of a Saudi Arabian merchant for one million dollars without reading what he was signing."[18]

Childs and the other Americans were surprised to find Sulaiman in such an agreeable mood, even after the sunrise-to-sunset Ramadan fast. According to Childs, Sulaiman "appeared more normal and reasonable than he had seen him in some time." Although, the ambassador added for good measure, "He has developed an annoying habit of unending repetitions of the same point which only serves to obscure the true facts at issue." Obscuring the issue and wearing down the Americans was likely a deliberate tactic the finance minister had chosen to adopt.

Sheikh Abdullah opened the meeting with what appeared to be an offer of congeniality, saying that he was perfectly willing to negotiate with the company. He did, however, "expect one thing from Aramco." Sulaiman explained this as he uncharacteristically struggled to "open the container of a long black cigar."

"Namely," Sulaiman remarked, "that [Aramco] have the courtesy to answer his communications." Finally, "he successfully lit the stogy and continued in the same vein"—that he had sent "several important communications to the oil company over the past few months," none of which had been answered.

Ambassador Childs explained that he "was not really in the position to counter [these] arguments" but that he would convey the message to Aramco when he met with Davies and Moore on Saturday. Childs took it all in stride, offering to play the role of an "honest broker," and bring the two parties together.[19]

Childs and the embassy staff tried furiously over the next several days to bring the Finance Ministry and Aramco together. Their efforts largely failed, because the Americans fundamentally misunderstood Saud Arabia's position. Childs, Duce, Davies, and the other diplomats and Aramco executives involved thought the Saudis were grasping for funds due to seemingly poor financial decisions. The Saudis, though, were confident in their financial situation because they knew the value of the oil beneath their land. *Al Saud*'s decision to build infrastructure was a cultural necessity—the people needed to see and experience the benefits of the oil industry, and they needed to see that those benefits came from the hands of their king. *Al Saud* did not consider running a deficit to build an irresponsible decision.

Childs found his efforts at diplomacy constantly stymied, because he did not understand Sulaiman's goal or his tactics. In 1950, Sulaiman wanted to force Aramco to renegotiate a concession agreement that, when he signed it in 1932, was supposed to last until 2012. Sulaiman chose to cause enough problems for Aramco that the company would be forced to come to the table long before the concession was due to expire. At the same time, Sulaiman laid the groundwork for a more favorable negotiating position for Saudi Arabia. He portrayed himself as a victim, complaining that Aramco disrespectfully refused to answer any of his letters even though Sulaiman was the one who had failed to pay the loan installment, had ordered Aramco shipments stopped and searched, and had shuttered Aramco's radio operations.

During a low-level conversation between Deputy Foreign Minister Yusuf Yassin and the American embassy's native Arab secretary, Mohammed Massoud, Yassin continued to pressure Aramco. "If Aramco is not prepared to help the Saudi Arabian Government, the Government will probably find it necessary to revise Aramco's Concession," he told Massoud. "This is not strange or unusual since Iraq is at the present time demanding a revision of the Iraq Petroleum Company concession in Iraq."

Massoud replied, pointing out "that Aramco is now paying higher royalties than any other oil company in this area, and, in addition, has made extremely large investments in Saudi Arabia."

Yassin disputed this assertion. "Iraq," he said, "obtains twenty-five percent from the mouth of the well while Saudi Arabia does not have the same privilege."[20]

Sulaiman knew that the Americans would never take him or *al Saud* seriously unless they feared for the existence of their oil business. Once they recognized that the seemingly backward Saudis, with their traditional dress and culture, commanded real power, the Americans would be motivated to sit down and negotiate a new agreement.

Despite Sulaiman's efforts to make business in Saudi Arabia difficult for Aramco, Moore and Davies remained resolute. They sent Childs back to Sulaiman with a letter explaining their position. Though the executives were willing to meet in Jeddah, Riyadh, or any other location to discuss important issues, "on the matter of further assistance, however, we have only one answer, and that is 'no.' This answer has been repeated over and over again both verbally and in writing. We are reluctant to initiate ourselves [*sic*] further discussions." Regarding Sulaiman's "general appeals for increased participation in the revenues of the industry," the Aramco executives were firm. "We," they wrote, "must in the mutual interest maintain our costs on a competitive basis."[21]

This told Sulaiman that Aramco did not yet understand the power Saudi Arabia held over the company. Sulaiman and *al Saud* were patient people. They would not confront Aramco violently. Instead, they would wait, and watch, and increase the pressure on Aramco incrementally, until Aramco would see it had no other choice but to renegotiate with the Saudis as equals. The Aramco executives would come to see profit sharing as a mutual interest. In the meantime, Sulaiman stepped up his pressure on the company with new customs duties. He added quarantine fees, aircraft landing fees, and pipeline security fees, all with the goal of showing Aramco who truly controlled the country and its oil.

Months went by without any resolution. In the interim, the State Department contacted Ambassador Childs to inquire about the possibility of extending his tour in Saudi Arabia for another year. By that time, Childs had spent four years in the desert kingdom, though the State Department initially promised him only a two-year stint. He had readily agreed to extend his stay in both 1948 and 1949 owing to delicate situations that required a knowledgeable and well-connected diplomat, but by August 1950, Childs could no longer stand the heat.

"My vitality had been so sapped by temperatures rising at times as high as 136 degrees that I was compelled to decline, particularly as there were no longer compelling political reasons for the prolongation of my stay," he wrote in retrospect.[22] King Abdul Aziz, however, was not pleased when he heard the news, and, in fact, "announced categorically that he had no intention of allowing [Childs] to leave."

The king's affinity for the beady-eyed American ambassador knew no bounds. As Childs explained in his memoirs, "In a tone which implied that I was as much a subject to his orders as to those of my government he added that he had sent a telegram to his ambassador in Washington to convey to the American Government his insistence that I stay."

Standing in front of the king in his ceremonial Saudi dress for the last time, Childs clearly was not immune to the nostalgia the meeting conjured. "I expressed deep gratification with these marks of his confidence but informed him that there was no possibility of obtaining any countermanding of my orders. . . . The perplexity on his face was almost pathetic; the idea that his orders would not be executed was one which he found difficult to grasp. It was only after I hastened to add that the state of my health was what stood in the way of my remaining that his countenance relaxed. He placed his hand on my arm and stated that under the circumstances he would not stand in my way."

Ambassador Childs's health was less an issue than his pride. He had hoped, after spending four years in the Arabian Desert, for a European post. Instead, he was appointed ambassador to Ethiopia. Though Ethiopia provided more physical comforts, he "had comparatively little of moment in the way of diplomatic activity with which to occupy [himself]."[23] After not quite two years in Ethiopia, Childs came to the realization that his career with the Foreign Service had reached a standstill. Six years before the mandatory retirement age, and after the State Department denied him permission to travel to Rome to confer with the ambassador there on an issue of relevance for Ethiopia, Childs quit.

"If my judgment carried so little weight," he wrote several years later, "it was more than clear that every day I spent in office was a waste of my time."[24] Perhaps those qualities that had made Childs such a good match for Saudi Arabia from the king's perspective—his willingness to wear traditional Saudi dress and adopt the customs of the court—were what made him such a poor match for the 1950s-era State Department.

In 1953, he retired from public service and moved to Nice, France, where he indulged in what had always been his true passion—the life and writings of the Italian adventurer, spy, and sometimes diplomat Giacomo Casanova. By the time he died in 1987, Childs had written fourteen books, including four on Casanova, traversed European archives in search of information about the elusive adventurer and his lovers, and served as the president of the International Casanova Society. His biography of Casanova was published posthumously.

In place of Childs, the State Department appointed Raymond Hare as ambassador. Like Childs, Hare was "a soft-spoken man." Unlike Childs, however, he did not seem to resent the fact that his approach to diplomacy often relegated him to the shadows. The staff at a prior post took to calling him the "Silent Ambassador," a nickname he "almost relished."[25]

Ambassador Hare was of a different ilk than Childs. He had not cut his diplomatic teeth in pre- or postwar Europe but came to the Foreign Service immersed in the language and culture of the Middle East. As a student at Grinnell College in Iowa in the 1920s, Raymond Hare aspired to be a journalist, but after graduation he found himself teaching history and English at a small college that had been established by Protestant missionaries in the mid-1800s in Istanbul, Turkey.

After several years in Istanbul, Hare sat for the Foreign Service exam. Hoping to capitalize on his present knowledge of the Middle East, the State Department sent him to study Arabic and Turkish at a language school in France. Although the instruction there did not include the practical application Hare and his American colleagues hoped for, Hare was an accomplished scholar and soon became capable in both languages. In the 1930s, this ability proved invaluable, as Hare was one of the few Foreign Service officers who spoke fluent Arabic. Intellectually, Hare occupied himself with the study of Islamic architecture, a pastime facilitated by multiple assignments in the Middle East and India.

Ambassador Hare and his wife, Jule, arrived in Jeddah in the fall of 1950. Previously posted to Cairo, Beirut, and London, Saudi Arabia was Hare's first ambassadorship. They found Jeddah largely unchanged from World War II, when Hare had first journeyed to Saudi Arabia as part of the US ambassador to Egypt's entourage to initiate diplomatic contact with King Abdul Aziz. He noted that the US embassy in Jeddah was simply one of many "old traditional buildings with overhanging balconies and intricately constructed wood shutters."[26] The phones worked only intermittently, and, Hare remarked, "when they did it was usually a call from the Foreign Office saying that the king wanted to see him right away in Riyadh."[27]

His residence held little of the finery the Saudi royal family was in the process of acquiring for its own palaces. The ambassador used orange crates turned into side tables. The dining table was so flimsily built that when his wife rested her elbows on its surface the entire table flipped over. Luckily, air conditioners had arrived prior to his posting, but they were old and hummed noisily in the bedroom windows all night. The Hare family made do with their shabby and decrepit furniture until finally the chief of foreign buildings, Fritz Larkin, came to visit Jeddah. Hare instructed his wife not to remark on the conditions of the furnishings for the duration of the visit, because Larkin was known for his stinginess in dispensing government money; she should simply allow the house to speak for itself. On the second day of the chief's visit, Hare recounted, "We were having cocktails before lunch. I'd not said a word to him about the state of furniture or residence. Finally, after his second martini, Fritz said, 'Oh hell Ray. Give me a pad of paper and I'll write the orders for you.'"[28]

Despite King Abdul Aziz's affinity for Ambassador Childs and his odd sense of humor, the king extended an equally warm welcome to his new American ambassador and his wife. Although the Saudi court typically did not host women, on some occasions the king would invite foreign women for a reception. Shortly after Hare and Jule arrived in Jeddah, the king sent a plane to bring the two newcomers to Riyadh. Just as Childs and Hare received traditional Saudi dress upon their arrival at the king's palace, so too did Jule. She was invited to the harem, the section of the palace where the king's wives, concubines, daughters, and female relatives lived, and treated to great feasts and hours of gossip, makeovers, and stories of Saudi royal intrigue. The Hares must have endeared themselves to King Abdul Aziz, because he jokingly asked her whether she would take offense if he offered the ambassador another wife. With an impressive display of wit and courage, she replied, "I am afraid, Your Majesty, my husband finds that one wife is already too expensive for his taste!" King Abdul Aziz responded with a rumble of laughter. Ambassador Hare was clearly not to be consulted on this matter.[29]

With regards to Abdullah Sulaiman and Aramco's apparent impasse, it seemed to the Americans as though the finance minister had either accepted Aramco's decision as final, or had turned his attention toward other issues. In truth, Sulaiman had not budged an inch from his real goal of renegotiating the concession along the principles of profit sharing. The Americans were simply experiencing the effects of the Arabians' patience. A few months were nothing in the grand scheme of *al Saud*'s dynastic future. The kingdom had always figured out a way to meet its immediate needs and would make due with its present financial situation—either by delaying payments on construction projects, taking loans, or cutting expenses—in order to secure much, much more in the future.

Finally, in October 1950, the Saudis renewed their pressure on Aramco, this time coming at Aramco from a different angle. Instead of confining their efforts to the small circle of Aramco executives and American diplomats in Saudi Arabia, the Saudis took the issue straight to Washington. The Saudi ambassador to the United States, Ambassador Asad al-Faqih (commonly referred to as Sheikh Asad), met with Aramco executives in the United States. Fred Davies, James Terry Duce, and the other Aramco executives arrived at the Saudi embassy in Washington, D.C., armed with what they thought were enough charts and graphs to overwhelm any remaining Saudi aspirations for more funds.

When they arrived and assembled their cadre of easels, however, they found that the ambassador "gave little regard to . . . the graphic support for their position." Instead, he "stressed that the ability to pay must be the criterion for settlement with the Saudi Arabian government and not equality of payments in the area." Ambassador al-Faqih was a short, rotund man who persisted in wearing a dark *thobe* and white Saudi headdress despite many years in Washington. The Aramco executives seemed to have bought into the image of congeniality that his doughy face and dimpled smile forecast.

"There is no doubt that Aramco can pay more," Sheikh Asad said firmly. "And they must, therefore, do so. Otherwise," he continued, the Saudi government "will make other arrangements for the exploitation of its oil."

Davies asked whether Sheikh Asad thought these negotiations should take place in the United States or in Saudi Arabia. Sheikh Asad replied that he would refer the matter to the Saudi government. With nothing else to discuss, the Aramco delegation gathered its charts and its easels and exited the Saudi embassy.

There was "no doubt" that the Saudis would want to move the talks to Saudi Arabia. Davies explained this afterward to Fred Wilkins in the Near East division at the State Department. He still hoped Aramco would be able to review the charts with Sheikh Asad at another meeting scheduled for a few days later, but otherwise Aramco had a board meeting the following week and would have a strategy in place by then.

Duce decided to appeal to the State Department's biggest fears. He talked about a "partnership," meaning any relationship that gave the Saudis more power. He told Wilkins that a partnership "might force Aramco to withdraw from Saudi Arabia, that Middle East oil stability would be upset, and that because total oil production would be reduced, rationing might result in the U.S." Wilkins saw through Duce's fearmongering and dismissed those concerns. He had already "discussed this point with Mr. McGhee previously, and . . . Mr. McGhee did not believe developments would take such a pessimistic turn."[30]

At the Aramco board meeting in early November 1950, Davies and Duce reported on their meeting with Sheikh Asad. Aramco president, Fred Moore, and the other members of the board of directors took the Saudis' threats more seriously than Aramco's Saudi Arabia–based employees. With the board "conclusively convinced that the Saudi Arabian government meant business," Aramco's strategy flipped.[31] The company would now seek a mutually amicable agreement. The next step was to structure this new relationship. For that, Aramco would rely on the company's best legal and financial strategists.

The Aramco board's decision was reinforced when Sheikh Asad called on the Near East division himself and stressed directly to the State Department that "his government was serious in its demands for a revision of the Aramco concession." Perhaps unwisely, the State Department conveyed to the Saudi ambassador the impact his "strong stand" had had with the Aramco board of directors.[32] Sheikh Asad filed this information away for future use and went on to confirm that negotiations with Aramco would take place in the kingdom, in Jeddah.

With a little patience and a strategic approach, Sulaiman had succeeded in bringing Aramco to new negotiations over the very nature of the oil concession he had settled not twenty years prior. Back then oil was just a gamble. In 1950, oil was the future of the monarchy. The question was how much control he could wrest away from the Americans.

On November 28, 1950, negotiations between Aramco and *al Saud* finally began. Sulaiman had successfully maneuvered the discussions from his original issue into a situation in which everything about the oil concession was on the table. The Americans were still not quite sure how they had gone from loan repayments on a railroad to discussing whether Saudi Arabia would levy an income tax on the company and come away with half of Aramco's profits. Unbeknownst to the Saudis, however, the Americans had done their homework, too.

As the weeks dragged on, Owen, Davies, and Duce knew Aramco was only postponing the inevitable. Aramco would have to fundamentally alter its concession agreement with Saudi Arabia. But before meeting with Sulaiman, Aramco had thoroughly investigated new contract options. The existing contract, or concession agreement, was based on a fixed percentage of royalties that Aramco paid the kingdom. It was based on the amount and price of oil

Aramco sold in return for the rights to exclusive oil development for sixty years.

A week before Aramco's first meeting with the Saudis, Duce and Davies met with McGhee from the State Department to discuss Aramco's options. During this contentious conversation, the Aramco men revealed the plan the company had been working on for months.[33] It would, they hoped, finally put an end to the Saudis' "policy of milking Aramco . . . for sufficient funds to balance their budget."[34] It might finally put an end to the months of increasingly difficult and contentious relations between Aramco and the Saudis.

Instead of a mere increase in royalty payments, the Aramco executives were prepared to offer something no other Middle Eastern oil-rich country had—a 50-50 profit-sharing contract in which Saudi profits would take the form of an "income tax." George McGhee did not like the idea of such a drastic change in the contractual relationship between Aramco and Saudi Arabia at all. However, after listening to the explanation offered by the oilmen, he did admit that this type of arrangement was not without precedent. In 1943, Venezuela had instituted a similar relationship with Jersey Standard and Royal Dutch Shell, the foreign oil companies responsible for that country's petroleum exploitation. McGhee explained that "the Department could not take a position on this matter" but wanted to know why Aramco favored this option.

Aramco's legal counsel, W. "Spike" Spurlock, explained that if the Saudis levied such a "tax" on Aramco, then the company could claim a foreign tax credit on its US tax returns and likely the entire situation would "involve no extra expense to the company." This was an inherently risky move, since the IRS would not rule on whether Aramco could use a foreign tax credit until after the "tax" was instituted and the company filed its tax returns. But, Duce said, the company "had spoken to Treasury officials who did not seem 'particularly concerned' with any difficulties." In addition, the IRS had recently ruled in favor of the foreign tax credit for the companies in Venezuela, so Aramco's legal and financial experts were confident.

Would the Saudis be satisfied with this relationship? the State Department wanted to know. At this point, the Americans could not predict what, if anything, would satisfy the Saudis. Spurlock offered that "Saudi Arabs in his experience has [sic] always basically favored some sort of 'partnership' relationship with Aramco and that any agreement would have to take this principle into consideration if it were to last." Aramco felt that increasing Saudi Arabia's financial benefits based on income rather than royalties would be fairer to the company and "give the Saudis a feeling of participation." Spurlock was careful to add that "partnership" with Aramco would not entail any "stock partnership or participation in management." This would be purely a "partnership in profits."

Duce and Davies were apprehensive because they had just received confirmation that Prince Feisal would lead the Saudi negotiating team himself. No one knew how the Saudis would react to Aramco's profit-sharing proposal. McGhee said that he would draft a memo that the new ambassador, Raymond Hare, could deliver to the Saudis before the negotiations began, reminding them that "Aramco had done an extraordinary job in developing Saudi Arabia oil resources." The Aramco officials thanked the State Department for its support and assistance before setting off for the negotiating table.[35]

◆

Ambassador Hare hosted the negotiations at the US embassy to provide a neutral backdrop. Prince Feisal, second in line for the crown, headed the Saudi delegation. Although he was King Abdul Aziz's second-oldest living son, he was widely known in both Saudi and American circles as more capable than his older brother, Saud. He had traveled extensively at the bidding of his father, and his experience representing the kingdom abroad "had given him a knowledge and interest in international affairs that was the frequent subject of comment by foreign ministers and envoys who met him."[36]

Feisal was not especially handsome, but his presence was unmistakable when he entered a room. Whereas his older brother, Saud, was easily identified by his jovial smile and rotund frame, Feisal appeared aloof and enigmatic. His most prominent features included a large, hooked nose, thick black eyebrows, and a protruding chin that his rangy facial hair only succeeded in emphasizing. Feisal kept himself lean and trim, owing to his rigidly devout and austere lifestyle. The austerity extended to his children, as well. Whereas Saud spoiled himself and his children with extravagant cars to chauffer them to and from school, Feisal sent his sons to a traditional mud-walled school, where they lived in simplicity with their schoolmates. He had high academic expectations, however, and later sent them to private high school at the Hun School in Princeton, New Jersey, and on to Ivy League colleges or prestigious military schools. He held his sons, and everyone else who worked with him, to the highest, exacting standards.

After a perfunctory opening, the Aramco delegation presented the plan they had scrambled to put together since the board decided to engage with the Saudis. The process proceeded amicably enough. Aramco began by proposing an "equal participation in net profits." In true Saudi fashion, Feisal expressed no "opinion for or against," instead allowing Abdullah Sulaiman to aggressively question the Aramco officials.

Sulaiman's primary concern, of course, was in the "actual benefit which would accrue" to the Saudis. He pressed the Aramco officials for a "specific guarantee in that regard." Davies and the other Aramco negotiators responded that it "was impossible to do so." All Aramco wanted to know at this point was "whether the plan was acceptable in principle" to the Saudis. "If so," the company "would bring tax and financial experts here to go into details." Sulaiman indicated that the Saudis would consider it, though Feisal was notably silent on the matter. With that, the negotiations adjourned for several days.[37]

Aramco wanted to avoid further discord with its Saudi host at all cost, because that, more than anything else, threatened its profits.

As would be made clear in congressional testimony two decades later, the Americans never truly feared that the Saudis would end the relationship, but animosity could hinder productivity. But for the Saudis, some friction with Aramco was not a bad thing. It drew attention to the royal family, made *al Saud* appear powerful in the eyes of its subjects, and, perhaps most importantly, sent a message of power about the Saudis to the rest of the Arab world. The Americans, in both Aramco and the State Department, seemed oblivious to this objective. They continued to perceive the Saudis as less shrewd, less intelligent, and less powerful than they actually were. Meanwhile, the Saudis used Aramco's fear of nationalization and political upheaval to manipulate the Americans into agreeing to the most progressive oil agreement between a producer country and an oil company in the Middle East—one that gave the Saudis significant control over the future of their own oil.

The disconnect between the Americans' perception of the Saudis and the reality of the situation is revealed in conflicting accounts of a "chance" incident between Ambassador Hare and Abdullah Sulaiman on December 12, 1950. Compellingly, Hare related this incident in two very different ways. The day after the event occurred, he described it in a memo to Washington that was intended to demonstrate his own upper hand with the Saudis. However, to his wife and son, he told a much more humble and, one can only assume, honest version of events. The difference in the accounts reveals just how much of an upper hand the Saudis actually had, while the Americans maintained a façade of superior sophistication.

The incident occurred during the most contentious period of the negotiations between Aramco and Saudi Arabia. Talks had broken down entirely, when Hare and Sulaiman found themselves both attending a ceremony marking the beginning of construction on a road in Medina.

According to the description he relayed to his wife and sons, Hare's car broke down on the way back to Jeddah, and Sulaiman happened to pass by the ambassador and his car. The finance minister stopped and invited the stranded Hare back to his palace for coffee. Hare went through with the preliminary courtesies demanded of the elaborate Saudi coffee ritual, until the ambassador finally turned the conversation to the oil contract negotiations, which had been stalled for over a week. Hare's son later recounted:

> Employing analogy, much favored by the Arabs, Hare said, "You know, Sheikh Abdullah, my daughter is very unhappy."
>
> "You have a daughter?" Sheikh Abdullah asked.
>
> "Yes," Hare replied, "I have a daughter. You know my daughter, her name is ARAMCO; she married you some time ago and wants to be a good wife and get along well, but sometimes she has difficulties, and this makes her unhappy."[38]

As Hare explained it to the State Department, however, he and Sulaiman just happened to run into each other at the ceremony in Medina. At the ceremony, Sulaiman invited Hare back to his residence in Jeddah "to have a cup of coffee."

According to this account, which is found in the State Department records, it was Sulaiman, not Hare, who "brought up the ARAMCO negotiations."

In the State Department's version, Sulaiman began by putting all of his cards on the table. This openness would have been uncharacteristic of Sulaiman. In the State Department memo, Sulaiman began, "I favor the profit-sharing principle but on the condition that we are guaranteed an increase in revenue." Sulaiman then told Hare that he would be happy if Aramco could assure the Saudis that their revenue would increase by 40 percent per barrel of oil. If so, "he would accept immediately and undertake to persuade Prince Feisal to accompany him to Riyadh to convince the King."[39]

In the story he told his family, Sulaiman was a rescuer (picking him up by the side of the road), Hare spoke first (giving up that advantage), and Hare portrayed Aramco as weak and eager to please—like a woman who "wants to be a good wife." In the story he sent to the State Department, Hare portrayed himself as stoic, while Sulaiman was eager to compromise. The story Hare told his superiors perpetuated the misconception that the Saudis were disadvantaged, when, in fact, most of the advantages lay with *al Saud*.

Armed with the true knowledge of Aramco's weakness, Sulaiman contacted Fred Davies the day after his encounter with Hare and had him repeat Aramco's profit-sharing proposal, but this time with actual figures detailing the estimated profits. Sulaiman told Davies he was "personally prepared [to] accept [the] proposal without reservation" and would "convince" Prince Feisal.[40] Feisal was still concerned about the outcome of Aramco's proposed "tax" scheme. His contention was that the Saudis should receive more than 50 percent of Aramco's profits and that the king should levy a "tax" that would, with Aramco's foreign tax credit, ensure that the company paid no taxes to the United States and everything to Saudi Arabia.[41]

Sulaiman then traveled with Prince Feisal to Riyadh, "where they remained about a week to discuss matters with the King."[42] None of the Americans had any idea what went on behind the palace walls, although the rumors abounded.

Talks resumed on December 29, 1950, at which point, Aramco was told that King Abdul Aziz had issued a new income tax decree. This was apparently in line with the settlement preferred by Aramco. Two days later Davies, Owen, and Duce concluded negotiations on what became known as the December 1950 Agreement. The full details of the agreement did not become public until many years later, when congressional hearings revealed that Aramco had basically traded its American tax bill for a Saudi one.[43] In effect, Aramco had done exactly what McGhee had the most reservations about: it had fundamentally changed the nature of its concession agreement with Saudi Arabia by entering into a 50-50 profit-sharing agreement with *al Saud* that the American treasury would pay for.

The December 1950 Agreement (actually taking effect as a fee, a tariff, and two "tax" decrees from the king) had four components designed to divide Aramco's profits in half through a complicated system of taxes, royalties, rents, and duties. Aramco would continue to pay royalties and rents to the king for use of the country's natural resources and land. Some of the proceeds for Saudi Arabia would come from this. Aramco would also continue paying duties on goods it imported and exported to and from Saudi Arabia. The rest of the proceeds would reach Saudi coffers through two new payment plans decreed by the king.

One of the two new payment plans, referred to as the October Tax, taxed Aramco's profit (revenue after expenses) before US taxes at the rate of 20 percent. The second payment plan, called the 50 percent December 27 Tax, was not really a tax according to the standard definitions and definitely not a tax at a 50 percent rate. It actually reflected additional charges on Aramco that would be calculated at a separate rate each quarter with the purpose of making the sum of all payments to Saudi Arabia—royalties, rents, duties, the 20 percent October Tax, the 50 percent December 27 Tax—equal to all Aramco profit. Aramco and the Saudis called it a "tax," and apparently so did the IRS after a lengthy review of Aramco's foreign tax credit application.[44] In reality, it was not an income tax at all. It was a variable rate payment plan intended to make both sides equal in terms of profit.[45]

Aramco was thrilled, because the new Saudi tax laws "virtually eliminated all U.S. taxes."[46] This did not mean that the United States would see no revenue from Aramco operations. Aramco's parent companies still paid the IRS an 8 percent tax on dividends, a 30 percent tax on stockholder dividends, and a duty on oil imports from Saudi Arabia, but the US Treasury did give up millions of dollars each year.[47]

Yet Aramco and the State Department continued to puzzle over what had transpired in King Abdul Aziz's palace during those days in late December. The story, as told by Hare, was that of a power struggle between the finance minister and Prince Feisal. In the end, Hare concluded that Abdullah Sulaiman must have sidelined Feisal by making his case directly to the king.[48] Despite Hare's assumptions about what went on in the king's court in December

1950, any royal intrigue was immaterial. In the end, the Saudis got exactly what they had sought from the beginning—a renegotiation of the concession, equal share of the profits, and a still satisfied partner. The Saudis made off with 50 percent of the oil profits at the US Treasury's expense, set a precedent in the Middle East for 50-50 profit-sharing oil concessions, and, most importantly, took the first step toward what would become their complete ownership of the American company.

FOUR

AN ARABIAN DAWN

n other Near Eastern countries," King Abdul Aziz told the Americans he had brought to his court in June 1951, "although the people are good Arabs, they are of many sects, political parties, and conflicting desires."

Neighboring countries had invited him to "extend his rule and domain" there, but he would always refuse. The king of Saudi Arabia preferred to rule a "heterogeneous nation," rather than deal with the conflicts that arose between peoples of different languages, ethnicities, traditions, and religions. His typical bravado might have been intended, as usual, to impress his foreign visitors, much as he often used the retelling and embellishment of his conquest of Riyadh. However, there is no evidence against his claim that fielded requests to extend his kingdom to the lands of other Middle

Eastern peoples. He was, after all, the protector of the Muslim holy places, Mecca and Medina, as well as an imposing figure who had brought peace to his country.

The king continued his musings, shifting to a new topic—the state of Saudi-American relations. He was satisfied "with the recent agreements concluded with the United States" and believed "in full cooperation with the United States." The king "praised the men in Aramco, their work, and its results," especially since the company had recently discovered new oil fields in his land.

His mind was clearly still preoccupied with the animosity and tension that had preceded the recently negotiated 50-50 profit-sharing deal with Aramco. "I don't want you to go," he said to the Americans, "either now nor later. The number of years of the Concession Agreement are not important; I want you," he said to the ambassador, "and Aramco to stay here forever to work with us in developing our wealth and our prosperity. You are our sons, and I don't want to hear any talk of your going away. Neither do I want any other oil company (speaking to Aramco officials) in here besides you."[1]

To Aramco officials, this was confirmation that their relationship with the Saudis was solid. The company believed its profit-sharing deal had concluded the discussion of Saudi Arabia's place in the oil business. However, they were misguided; Saudi Arabia's maneuverings for greater control had just begun. Regardless of any negotiated contract, Aramco still relied on the king's permission to access the oil, and Saudi Arabia recognized that this was its advantage. The company would have nothing but a bunch of pipes in the desert without access to that commodity. Over the next several years, the Saudis successfully played off this lurking fear to take more of Aramco's profits for the kingdom than Aramco had thought possible—not because Aramco needed Saudi Arabia more than Saudi Arabia needed Aramco but because the Americans were too scared to truly risk their investment.

◆

In a country where the king's word was law, Aramco was relieved by his reassurances. After months of threats (whether delivered obscurely over a cup of coffee or by ultimatum delivered directly to Dhahran), Aramco had returned to the king's favor. Of course, Abdul Aziz had never offered anything other than unquestionable hospitality to the Americans, but with almost two decades of experience in Saudi Arabia, some of the Aramco executives were becoming adept at picking up the subtle shifts in Arab behavior that signaled deeper turmoil.

Since the 50-50 profit-sharing agreement, everything about the Aramco-Saudi relationship had changed. No longer did Finance Minister Abdullah Sulaiman seem on the brink of losing his temper every time he met with James Terry Duce, Fred Davies, or Garry Owen. Prince Feisal's face retained its perpetual snarl, but the man now "seemed much more friendly with regard to the United States than a year ago."[2]

Aramco thought the Saudis' improved disposition was a result of the revenue now accruing in their treasury. Garry Owen conservatively estimated Aramco's payments to Saudi Arabia for the 1950 calendar year at approximately $110 million.[3] Prospects for 1951 appeared even better. In May, Aramco increased its production target by 100,000 barrels of oil per day to a maximum of 850,000 barrels.[4]

It had taken little effort from Abdul Aziz and Feisal to reduce Aramco's anxiety. The feasts, audiences, and acclaim worked wonders over the next several months. Garry Owen and Fred Davies believed the tax deal had finally resolved issues with Saudi Arabia for good, because the Saudis now had what no other Middle Eastern country did—an equal profit-sharing agreement. Thus, it came as a complete surprise to Garry Owen that less than a month after the reassuring meeting with the king, Sulaiman submitted a request for an advance on the next year's payments. Davies, Owen, and Moore went to Riyadh to discuss this request with the Saudis. When the Aramco executives arrived, they were received not by Sulaiman or one of his deputies but by Crown Prince Saud.

As Abdul Aziz grew weaker with age he finally began delegating some responsibilities to his oldest living son and presumed heir, the large and gregarious Saud. Aramco was anxious to get to know the man who would soon be king. From among the many princes, Aramco had dealt primarily with the king's second son, Feisal. They saw Feisal as "a hard nut to crack" but found Crown Prince Saud almost the exact opposite.

When Davies, Owen, and Moore met with Crown Prince Saud, they found a corpulent man with an easy and broad smile. His immense body dwarfed almost every chair he sat in. A double chin jutted out from beneath his robe, and his eyes recessed in his large face. The Aramco men explained that Abdullah Sulaiman had requested an advance of the next year's payments. Saud "expressed great surprise" and asked the Aramco officials how they would respond.

When Moore said the company would not grant such a request, Saud "agreed wholeheartedly," and even offered to write to the finance minister himself.

"This will probably not be necessary," Moore said. This was when the Aramco men overstepped the line of protocol between the king and the oil company. Curious about why the Saudis needed such a large advance, the Aramco officials inquired of the Crown Prince as to the state of Saudi finances. Davies expressed that the Crown Prince himself, now taking a larger role in the "responsibilities of government," must also be curious about how the funds were being used. Saud agreed with the Aramco men, whose audience concluded shortly thereafter. The American men left charmed by this Crown Prince. Here, they thought, was a man who finally understood what Aramco wanted.[5]

This hope, it turned out, was both premature and ill founded, as Saud turned out to be a weak leader. He wanted to please, and the person he most sought to please was himself, generally with extravagant luxuries, opulent palaces, and copious amounts of food and drink. Making others happy, placating them by telling them what they wanted or needed to hear, was simply another form of quieting his psyche. Saud had no stomach for conflict, with his brothers or with the Americans. As long as the oil flowed, Saud was happy. His job, or at least part of his job, was to keep Aramco happy. Sheikh Abdullah Sulaiman's job was to figure out how to make it all work.

◆

After the meeting with Saud, Owen spoke to Sulaiman in person and denied his request for a tax advance. The finance minister, as more than one American ambassador had observed, had the difficult job of managing the bills for the Saudi royal family's excessive spending along with the entire country's budget. Crown Prince Saud was a major spender. Sulaiman's tasks also included ensuring that Abdul Aziz had the ability to spend money freely to satisfy his subjects' needs, just as he had managed the trucks of treasure and disbursed coins for chitties in years past.

Abdul Aziz saw his kingdom as a giant tribal confederacy that he had painstakingly crafted and diligently bought, married, and fought into submission. Maintaining order throughout the vast territory was best accomplished by maintaining the traditions that had worked for generations. For example, anyone who came before the king's *majlis* (public audience) would receive a free meal and a fair hearing. If the man had no money for necessities, the king would provide. Public gestures of charity reinforced Abdul Aziz's power in times of peace, when there were no rebellions to make examples of. Sulaiman's responsibilities were many, and the king relied on Sulaiman. None of his tasks were quite as important, however, as negotiating with Aramco.

Aramco continued to refuse the requests for more money that came from Sulaiman and his deputy, Najib Bey Salha. Finally, Salha told Owen that Sulaiman was prepared to bring the issue to the king, and that "if the King would not support him, he must ask to be relieved of his responsibilities." As Owen showed Salha to his car, Salha "remarked half-jokingly that maybe it would not be long before they were talking about the 'Saudi Arabian national petroleum company'" instead of Aramco.[6] The undertone, as well as the threat it delivered, was clear. Owen understood that the Saudis were raising the possibility, for the first time, that Aramco could one day be a Saudi company. After all, nationalization of oil resources seemed contagious at that time.

Salha later informed Owen that the king and the finance minister would be arriving at the king's summer palace in Taif (a city in the mountains near Jeddah) on July 19 and that the king "desired to see Aramco president Moore and executive vice president Davies at that time." The company made arrangements to attend.[7] However, Moore and Davies were extremely late for their appointment with the king. "Various complications" kept them in Dhahran until July 20, so the two of them, along with Owen and Floyd Ohliger, another Aramco vice president, did not reach the king's palace in Taif until the morning of July 21. Then, they waited from 8:00 A.M. until 4:00 P.M. before being admitted to an audience with the king. Even though they were two days late, the Aramco men began to wonder, based on their wait, whether the king had even been consulted about this meeting or whether this was another ploy by Sulaiman.

When the oilmen were finally invited into the king's hall, Moore, Davies, Owen, and Ohliger found the session in full court. In addition to King Abdul Aziz, Sulaiman, Salha, Prince Feisal, the king's brother Amir Abdullah, and three other sons awaited the Americans in the room. Crown Prince Saud was noticeably absent. According to Owen's account, "Ibn Saud opened the discussion by inquiring whether Moore had any business to discuss. On being told 'no,' the King stated that he had several distasteful matters to raise and proceeded to castigate the company for allegedly demanding to know of the Finance Minister what the Saudi government does with its funds."[8] Saud must have shared details of his earlier meeting with Davies, Owen, and Moore.

Owen, after requesting permission to speak, tried to explain that this was a misunderstanding based on a comment he had made when he was responding to the Saudi government's request for an advance. Sulaiman then "presented the Saudi case." As he listened, Owen came to believe that "the King had been given the understanding that the company had refused to honor current obligations." Owen and Sulaiman argued, in front of the king, about the nature and deadlines of various payments.

The king finally turned away from Owen and Sulaiman to face Aramco's president, Moore, and two of the company's vice presidents, Davies and Ohliger. He told the executives that he wanted payment "when it was due to him." He did not want "money now, but only a letter to a bank that money would be paid to that bank when due." The king was telling them that he was looking for a letter that would vouch for future income he would receive, even though a specific sum could not be accurately predicted. This letter, according to the king's plans, would be presented by Sulaiman to a bank to obtain a loan.

Moore responded that yes, the "company would give the bank a letter and copy of the December 1950 agreement and that Aramco will pay money due under that agreement when it is due."

Ohliger pointed out that the "company could not now give a guarantee" on taxes for 1950–1951, since the taxes had to be "computed based on the entire 1950–1951 business" and there were still several months to go. The bank, he said, "might not accept the type of letter the company would write."

Owen also expressed concern that this point was not clear to the king. It is not known why Ohliger and Owen belabored this point and doubted the king's understanding of his own relationship with the banks. Perhaps it was just another display of the simplicity with which Aramco viewed the king and his aides. Both Sulaiman and Salha tried to break into the discussion, but the finance minister "was briskly cut off by the King." According to Aramco, the king "appeared satisfied" with Moore's promise and Aramco's willingness to write the letter. Owen suggested that Sulaiman draft the letter and present it to Davies for review. With that the king said, "I do not want a cent from the company one half hour before it is due." He made Owen and Sulaiman shake hands before the Aramco delegation departed.[9]

Afterward, the Aramco delegation discussed the situation with their friends at the embassy and expressed incredulity at what had transpired. The ambassador wrote to the State Department that, "while the King may feel he has induced a spirit of compromise," the company men believed that "any type of letter [Aramco] was in the position to furnish to a bank will almost certainly be not satisfactory to the bank." The ambassador believed Sulaiman had to be aware of this, even if the king thought it a satisfactory solution. The ambassador fully expected the issue to repeat itself, "probably in several months," when the Saudis discovered the inadequacy of the letter.[10] Months later it would become clear that the king had a better understanding than anyone else of the banks' desire to do business with him. Until then, the Americans would continue to underestimate.

The next month, Hare visited the king at Taif to present his deputy before going on leave, but he ended up staying for hours. Hare reported that the king was in his "usual frank and friendly mood" while the two discussed a situation in Jordan. Hare had been about to ask permission to leave, when the king mentioned that he would like to discuss a situation with Aramco.

According to Hare, "At that point his attitude changed completely. . . . The following hour and a half were [*sic*] very heavy going."

The king said that he "had long been unhappy with relations with Aramco," and that "Aramco officials had been discourteous to him and his people." Abdul Aziz explained that he "had been patient but the point was now reached where he could no longer cooperate." He had decided to request that the current group of Aramco officials be replaced.

Specifically, Aramco officials had questioned how he used his money—"this was none of their business," the king said, and he "would not tolerate such interference in his affairs." An Aramco official had been heard ridiculing his people, and "Aramco personnel would avert their faces in passing 'my people' in order to avoid greeting them."

The final offense, the king said, was that Aramco had gone back on its word. At the meeting in Taif with Moore, Davies, Owen, and Ohliger, Abdul Aziz had asked if Saudi Arabia "had money due to it by Aramco." The king then told Hare that the Aramco executives had said they did owe him money. According to the king, all he wanted was a letter for the bank explaining that his treasury had undetermined receivables coming due, but he had yet to receive that letter.

At that point, the king became truly irate and started to lecture Hare. He had "struggled for years to build up his kingdom and a King's honor could not," he repeated, "could not be violated." The Aramco officials had insulted him and "they must go."

"Necks," he said, and made a slashing gesture with his hand, "had been cut off in the past to maintain [my] honor. Honor," the king concluded, "could be maintained only with blood." The ambassador had not known Abdul Aziz during his years of struggle when the king united the warring peninsula. In fact, the ambassador rarely saw the king other than seated in his receiving room, but this glimpse of emotion must have impressed upon him what a powerful figure Abdul Aziz had been in his youth.

Hare tried in vain to interject several times throughout the king's speech, but Abdul Aziz was so "wrought up" that the interpreter could barely keep up. Finally, Hare began speaking and reminded Abdul Aziz that he personally had known the Aramco men for years, and "it was unthinkable that they could have intended any insult to His Majesty."

Clearly, Hare continued, "for one reason or another, there had been a misunderstanding. Darkness," he said, "had descended where formerly there had been light. It was necessary for frank discussion to let in the light again."

The king was not impressed by Hare's petition and "indulged in another outburst" in which he turned on the ambassador as well, saying, "If the United States would say that such an insult coming from an American company was justified—that would be another matter."

Hare realized that logic and diplomacy were not working. He needed to address the king anew. Hare later recalled, "I indulged in a little emotional histrionics myself and said that I was sure there was no question of any insult to His Majesty. . . . If what I said was not true let it be on the heads of my two sons who had visited His Majesty several months past."[11] And with that, he offered his own sons as collateral on the king's benevolence.

As Hare said, the king had met the ambassador's sons the previous spring. They had been flying home to Jeddah for vacation from their high school in Beirut. They had landed in Dhahran for a layover and were about to take off for Jeddah when Abdul Aziz learned of their presence and ordered the flight diverted to Riyadh. He wished to meet the children of the American representative in his kingdom. Abdul Aziz's fondness for children was widely known—he had thirty-seven sons who'd survived past childhood and many daughters as well, most of whom had children of their own at that point. Neither the pilot of the plane nor Hare's sons, Ray Jr. and Paul, knew why the plane was being diverted to Riyadh. There was cause for apprehension.

As they taxied down the runway, the two boys saw their father waiting on the tarmac. He ushered them into a luxurious Mercedes, which drove them to the king's palace. A young Saudi air force major greeted the boys and explained that they would be meeting the king. While the court tailor measured them for robes and headdresses, the young Saudi officer instructed the boys on court etiquette and what to expect during an audience with the Saudi king. They spent the evening with their father in Riyadh, and the next day, they were presented with the traditional Saudi dress to be worn at the king's court.

Ray Jr. and Paul accompanied their father to the palace. The boys later recalled the thrill of carrying the small gold daggers that accompanied their ensembles. The boys approached the king and bowed three times, as they had been instructed. Each in turn greeted the king in Arabic. Upon hearing the traditional greeting, the king smiled and motioned for them to come closer and stand at his right, a place of honor. Their father, the ambassador, stood beside his sons while Abdul Aziz addressed the boys directly. For an hour he talked to them, through an interpreter at his other side, about his country; particularly how beautiful the desert could be, especially in the spring when the colorful flowers briefly bloomed. The king loved hunting, though spasms from injuries received during long-ago conquests now plagued his back. He regaled the young men with the famous story of his daring capture of the city of Riyadh. Dressed as they were, listening to a tale of guile and deadly swordplay, in a room thick with carpets and heavy with incense, the boys were truly spellbound. Finally, the audience came to an end, and, as instructed, Ray Jr. and Paul backed out of the room, bowing three times.[12]

Ambassador Hare swore on his sons' heads, months after their visit, as a last attempt to save a faltering relationship. The king seemed to recall the visit fondly, and it "had the effect of easing pressure."

Of the Aramco officials' fate in Saudi Arabia, the king said he would "leave this matter in [Ambassador Hare's] hands." However, he repeated that Hare should know "it had otherwise been his intention to demand the recall of the Aramco officials."[13]

King Abdul Aziz threatened Hare with the removal of these Aramco executives, not the company. He was not threatening nationalization, and he surely knew that these executives could be replaced by the Aramco parent companies. Even though the king possessed absolute authority in his land, he did not want to cancel the concession and force Aramco to leave Saudi Arabia, because Aramco was virtually his only source of revenue. Any disruption in the flow of oil would have meant a loss of profit for the kingdom. Although Aramco employed many Saudis for basic jobs in the oil industry, Saudi Arabia lacked the engineering expertise, industry knowledge, and marketing outlets to take over the business with domestic talent.

Saudi Arabia was not eager to invite a different international oil company into the kingdom either. At the time, only a few oil companies not involved in Aramco were capable of operating in foreign countries as far afield as Saudi Arabia. These companies were all European and had other oil interests in the Middle East. Enticing them to take over for Aramco would have been extremely difficult, if not impossible, particularly if the Americans refused to purchase any oil from Saudi Arabia as a result of the breakup. Despite these negotiating advantages, the Americans often seemed to lose faith in their own positions when challenged by the Saudis.

After Hare's apology before the king, Aramco finally provided the letter.[14] The Saudis immediately obtained a loan and began drawing against future payments to accommodate their expenses. The Saudis' plan, despite the Americans' doubts, had worked.[15] Aramco depended on the king for access to oil; without Saudi oil there would be no Aramco. As the Saudis were then learning from their experience with Bechtel, contracts could be broken and competition invited in. The Saudis preferred the Americans to the British, Dutch, or French (the only other major oil producers with the capital and experience to develop Middle Eastern oil fields), but Sulaiman was not afraid to threaten a realignment to use as leverage against Aramco.

For Ambassador Hare and the State Department, Saudi oil was becoming an absolute necessity in the Cold War. It was 1951. Though Middle Eastern oil had not yet reached American cars, which were still being fueled largely by domestic and South American oil, Saudi oil was fueling Western Europe's economic recovery from World War II and providing for the security of the free-market bloc. Saudi oil, in particular, went to American and other allied planes in the Korean War and served as a critical source of fuel to American forces deployed across the world.

Sulaiman might have manufactured or, at the very least, embellished some of the grievances Abdul Aziz brought before the Americans. Sulaiman might have deliberately cultivated the financial misunderstandings that led to the confrontation, but there was one thing he had not lied about or exaggerated. Salha's seemingly offhand mention to Owen that soon the two might very well be discussing a "national Saudi oil company" was real—"soon," of course, being a relative term, and "national" taking an entirely different meaning in Saudi Arabia than it did in Iran. But the warning was real.

By the end of October 1951, Iran had successfully nationalized its entire oil industry. The Iranian government took control of the Abadan refinery by force, causing all British personnel to flee, and established the National Iranian Oil Company (NIOC). The British responded by sending warships to blockade the Persian Gulf near the refinery. They also used their navy to stop tankers carrying Iranian oil from leaving the area, effectively embargoing Iranian oil. Iran's economic situation devolved and the government could barely operate due to lack of funds. Public opinion began to turn against Iranian prime minister Mohammad Mossadeq, the firebrand politician who had championed the oil industry nationalization. Mossadeq could not negotiate with the British, because anti-British sentiment still ran deep among Iranians eager to take to the streets. Nor could he help Iran's floundering economy without the ability to export the country's oil.

Sulaiman probably could not have chosen a better time to bully Aramco with the Korean War and the beginning of the crisis between Iran and the Anglo-Iranian Oil Company. There is no evidence for or against the argument that these global crises were the impetus for Saudi Arabia's actions or whether Saudi Arabia intentionally took advantage. However, the 50-50 profit-sharing agreement was made at the New Year; the Iran oil crisis began in March 1951; the king reassured the Americans in early June 1951, saying he wanted Aramco in his country "forever"; and by July 1951, Sulaiman submitted the request for an advance that led to the dispute. The Americans watched events in Iran. Surely, the Saudis did too.

The Saudis also watched Aramco's corresponding increase in oil production as the American company filled the hole left by Anglo-Iranian's sudden drop in exports. King Abdul Aziz refused to let his relationship with the Americans go the way of the once strong British-Iranian partnership, but the situation did present an opportunity for the Saudis. This was precisely the time for Saudi Arabia to try to gain lasting influence on Aramco. The Americans' insecurity, combined with the king's absolute power, could mold Saudi Arabia's relationship with Aramco to benefit *al Saud*'s long-term needs.

Ever so subtly, the finance minister informed Aramco's directors that wealthy Saudi businessmen, along with the Crown Prince himself, were interested in purchasing shares of Aramco stock. At the time, only four powerful American oil producers owned stakes in Aramco: Jersey Standard (Exxon), Texaco, Standard Oil of New York (Mobil), and Standard Oil of California (Chevron). Aramco's directors staunchly opposed this proposal. George McGhee, from the State Department's Division of Near Eastern Affairs, called Ohliger and Duce to inquire about their concerns.

"The company suggested that [these wealthy Saudis] might invest in the [Aramco] parent companies," Ohliger explained to McGhee. Aramco's parent companies were not willing to cede any ownership over the private company, Aramco. However, the publicly traded parent companies would welcome Saudi shareholders among the thousands of others, according to Ohliger.

Ohliger continued, "But [investment in the public parent companies] was not acceptable to the Saudi Arabs, first because they had less interest in investing abroad than in putting their money in Saudi Arabia, and second because investment in the parent companies would subject them to payment of a 30 percent income tax in the United States."

McGhee pressed Ohliger and Duce. What was the "objection . . . to allowing Saudi Arabs to invest in Aramco itself?"

Ohliger responded, "The sale of stock would offer the possibility of some of it getting to the hands of Jewish investors, which would be objectionable to the Saudi Arabia Government." Ohliger was trying to argue that if Aramco stock was offered for sale, Saudis might find themselves as co-owners alongside Jews. This, Ohliger claimed, would be problematic for the Saudis. McGhee, however, did not accept or believe this excuse.

McGhee pressed him further until Ohliger admitted, "It would be possible to control the initial sales and to restrict the transfer of stock by purchasers in such a way as to avoid Jewish investment." So, the concern of mixing with Jews was just an excuse concocted by an Aramco executive.

McGhee quickly discovered that the real reason for Aramco's objection to selling stock was that Aramco's parent companies would have to sell shares they already held. Their initial investment in Aramco had been $11 million, but the value of the firm was, in 1951, much higher. The value of the firm was calculated "exclusive of the oil reserves," which the king owned.

"Consequently," Ohliger continued, "any change in Aramco's stock position might require revaluation and subject the company to a very heavy capital gains tax." McGhee finally accepted Ohliger's claim that the real reason for the Aramco parent companies' hesitancy to sell was a desire to avoid capital gains taxes. Further questioning led McGhee to establish that there was very little likelihood that any possible tax situation for Aramco would impact actual oil production. Oil production, after all, was what the State Department cared about. Oil production was a matter of national security. Aramco's tax liability was not.

Stock participation was not the only request coming from Abdullah Sulaiman. "There seems," Ohliger said, "to be developing in Saudi Arabia an urge to have a Saudi Arabian on the Aramco Board of Directors." This request appeared to come, he said, "more by considerations of prestige than by any expectation that such a member could make an important contribution to their deliberations."

"Why . . . would it not be a good idea to appoint someone because of the good will which will undoubtedly arise from it?" McGhee asked.

Ohliger disagreed. "It would only enhance the prestige of the individual and not of the country generally." He was grasping for an explanation.

From the State Department's perspective, this was exactly the kind of obstinate thinking that got the British into so much trouble with the Iranians. The situations were not identical, but the comparisons were there.

McGhee then asked if "the people of Saudi Arabia were generally satisfied with Aramco." He hoped to ascertain the likelihood of a similar nationalization catastrophe.

Ohliger explained that most people in Saudi Arabia were satisfied with Aramco, though "there was a considerable disappointment" with the king's illness and lax control over his court as a result. Of course, Ohliger added, this reflected the opinions of "about 25 percent of the population who [are] the more alert and substantial section of the population.

"If Saudi Arabia [wants] to nationalize," Ohliger said sarcastically, "[Aramco] would be glad to hand it over tomorrow and work out an arrangement with the [Saudi] Government for the operation of the company. The biggest ace in the hole for [Aramco]," he continued, "would be the necessity of the Government assuming the responsibility for operating costs . . . running at the rate of $150 million a year at present."[16] These claims, as recorded by McGhee in State Department memos, must have been either sarcasm or bravado, because Aramco did not want to lose the company.

Ohliger's claims betray an almost mocking arrogance that the Saudis could not possibly run the company like the Americans could. In 1951, that was true, but Ohliger's attitude also betrayed a lack of foresight. He was blind to the Saudis' true plan to become more involved in Aramco so that one day they would be prepared to acquire the company and, as Salha had said, own the "Saudi Arabian national petroleum company."

The call ended when McGhee excused himself for another meeting. The situation in Iran was the State Department's first priority in the Middle East at that time. McGhee believed that if Aramco could pacify the Saudis for a time, it would help US policy immensely. The last thing the State Department needed at the time was for Saudi Arabia to mimic Iran's national resources policy. Of course, Saudi Arabia did not have a firebrand, ultranationalist, rabble-rousing politician like Mohammad Mossadeq. Abdullah Sulaiman might have been conniving and ambitious, but his loyalty was always to his king, Abdul Aziz. There was not a nationalist bone in his body.

In the end, Sulaiman was willing to temporarily forgo the stock purchases and seats on the board of directors for other, more immediately significant compromises from Aramco—namely, increased revenue. Aramco, however, saw the writing on the wall. The company knew that even though it had staved off Sulaiman's demand for Saudi directorship (at one point the finance minister even demanded that Aramco elect an equal number of Saudis to the board as Americans) it would eventually have to concede this point. As a precaution, in 1952, the Aramco board decided to shift a number of key functions from its board to the company's stockholders—the four major American oil companies.[17] It was not until 1959 that Aramco would finally elect two Saudis to its board of directors: Abdullah Tariki, Saudi Arabia's first oil minister, and Hafiz Wabha, a former Saudi ambassador to the UK.[18]

◆

The absence of Iran-style nationalist fervor did not make Sulaiman any less of a thorn in Aramco's side. Just when Aramco thought the Saudis were satisfied with an essentially guaranteed $10 million in revenue a month from Aramco, Sulaiman stumbled upon a serious discrepancy in the price per barrel sold of Aramco-Saudi oil and the recorded price per barrel on which Aramco was basing its payments to Saudi Arabia. The finance minister believed the company was hiding a significant amount of money that the Saudis deserved.

Sulaiman discovered that Aramco sold its crude oil for more money than the per barrel price that the two sides were using to

determine payments to Saudi Arabia. Aramco had been calcu-
lating its payments to Saudi Arabia for the 50-50 profit-sharing
agreement based on a fictional $1.43 per barrel price of oil. In
fact, Aramco received more per barrel than that $1.43. At that
time Aramco sold all of its oil to its parent companies. The price
Aramco received for oil sold to its parent companies out of the
Persian Gulf port at Ras Tanura was $1.73 per barrel. The price
Aramco received for oil sold to its parent companies through
Tapline was $2.41 per barrel.

Aramco was underpaying Saudi Arabia by a significant amount.[19]
Sulaiman was going to get what was due to Saudi Arabia, but this
time he would do it the American way. The American way meant
hiring an American consulting firm. In June 1952, Sulaiman
selected the Texas firm DeGolyer and MacNaughton. According
to Duce, this firm was "known to be extremely competent on oil
pricing problems."[20] By the time Sulaiman brought the matter to
Aramco in November 1952, DeGolyer and MacNaughton had estimated that Aramco was pocketing an extra $20 million by selling
the oil at a higher price per barrel than the price at which it calculated its taxes to Saudi Arabia.[21]

When the Saudis and the American oilmen sat down for negotiations, the finance minister included Lewis MacNaughton on
the Saudi side of the table. MacNaughton proposed an entirely
new solution—instituting a clear pricing formula like that used to
determine the price of oil in the Western Hemisphere. He compared
Saudi crude grades to American crude grades, determined that it
was most similar to West Texas sour crude with a specific gravity
rated at 36.5 degrees APS, and then applied "a complex series of
mathematical adjustments" along with "added transport charged
from Saudi Arabia" to a variety of locations to determine the base
point price.

Garry Owen reported that Aramco was "disturbed over the
competitive disadvantage" these prices would cause, as well as the
"possible retroactive effect of this formula." Sulaiman had already
requested that MacNaughton "calculate how it would work out if

carried back to January 1950." Aramco later calculated that the company would owe the Saudis around $50 million in back payments.[22] After this initial meeting, serious negotiations did not continue until 1953, after Prince Feisal returned from a diplomatic visit to the United States.[23]

By that point, an atmosphere of acrimony seemed to have settled firmly into place. Ambassador Hare was facing pressure to intervene on the matter with the king, but his intuition told him an audience with the king would not accomplish much. Instead, he decided to focus on the finance minister. Several months prior, when he had been in the midst of particularly challenging negotiations for the US military to continue its lease of a key airfield in Dhahran, he had found Abdullah Sulaiman to be especially helpful. In that case, Hare had found it especially helpful to allow the Saudis to take credit for the compromise.[24]

Perhaps a similar accommodation could be reached with Aramco and Sulaiman. Aramco could get what it wanted, Hare hoped, "but the Saudis could claim it was on their terms."[25] He realized he would have to act quickly, as his posting in Saudi Arabia was rapidly approaching its end. President Eisenhower had nominated him as ambassador to Lebanon, and he would be leaving the Arabian Peninsula shortly.

Jeddah's population sweltered in the late June humidity, but Hare and Sulaiman sat in relative cool in Sulaiman's office. Hare called on the finance minister to discuss the Aramco situation and to remind Sulaiman that after Hare left Saudi Arabia, his duties would be assumed by an interim chargé d'affaires until his successor could be confirmed. He then asked the old Arab about the apparent lack of progress in reaching an agreement with Aramco over the price of oil. Sulaiman was uncharacteristically upfront and told the ambassador that he was "glad that [Hare] mentioned the matter."

He went on to explain how he "endeavored to facilitate a settlement by letting the Americans [i.e., Aramco] deal with Americans [i.e., MacNaughton]. But they had failed." Sulaiman was ready to give up and "turn the matter over to other authorities." Sulaiman did not offer any details as to who these "other authorities" might be, but Hare inferred that Sulaiman probably meant the Saudi foreign minister, who had the power to close ports, deny telecommunications use, and, with the king's permission, deny Aramco executives entrance into the kingdom.

Hare told Sulaiman that he appreciated his account. "There [are] certain . . . general comments which I [would like] to make regarding the relationship between Aramco and the Saudi Arabian Government," Hare began. "If one were frank," he continued, "one would have to admit that prior to the coming of Aramco and the exploitation of Saudi oil resources, Saudi Arabia had been little more than a geographic expression. Other countries of the area such as Egypt, Syria, Lebanon, Iraq, etc., had experienced long periods of development in various fields of activity. They had communications, schools, hospitals, industries, roads, and the various other attributes of a normally modern state, but Saudi Arabia had none of these. It had been an economic vacuum, and, being so, a mere skeleton without flesh.

"All that has been changed by oil and Saudi Arabia [is] now in the process of building itself up. . . . Flesh [is] being put on the bone. Saudi Arabia is becoming strong, but it has only become strong because of Aramco and Aramco, in its turn, has grown strong too. All this leads, as I see it, to the conclusion that, dependent as it is on a single source of income, a strong Aramco means a strong Saudi Arabia; a weak Aramco means a weak Saudi Arabia."[26]

"That was quite true," Sulaiman responded. He agreed with Hare "that a strong Aramco means a strong Saudi Arabia. The trouble," he explained, was "that Aramco was resorting to undue haggling when clear-cut action was required.

"A case in point," Sulaiman said, "the payment for services rendered by the Government on Tapline." The negotiations had gone on for some time without resolution.

Hare asked Sulaiman if the finance minister "had any recommendations as to how this problem might be put right?"

"Aramco should quit quibbling and settle the Tapline payment question," Sulaiman answered. On the issue of pricing, Sulaiman explained that if Aramco would include back payments from 1951 in the new pricing scheme, then he would try to persuade Prince Feisal to accept MacNaughton's proposed figures. He "thought that he would have quite good prospects of being able to do so."[27]

This was exactly what Hare needed. Sulaiman was telling him that as long as the Saudis won on the issue of back payments for higher-priced oil dating to 1951, along with some remuneration for oil that went through Tapline, the Saudis would agree to a negotiated price per barrel for upcoming payments. The reconciliation meant that no animosity would linger on the part of the Saudis for any deception, real or perceived. It would take some time to settle the details and Aramco would have to deal with another drop in profits, but when Hare relayed his conversation with Sulaiman to the Aramco officials, he found them agreeable to the compromise.

Floyd Ohliger in particular "was very appreciative." He told Hare that during a subsequent conversation with Sulaiman, the finance minister "admitted that he was personally responsible for certain restrictive measures being imposed on Aramco." In fact, he "frankly thought that the whole Aramco-Saudi relationship at the present time was rather absurd and that both sides were acting like children." The time had come, the finance minister concluded, "that they should settle their differences in their mutual interest."[28]

Ultimately, fourteen months later, Saudi Arabia and Aramco reached an agreement finalizing the financial arrangements between the two on a long-term basis. Fred Davies, who by that point had become president of Aramco, and Prince Feisal agreed that Aramco and Saudi Arabia would use the market price of oil less a 2 percent sales discount as the basis for their profit-sharing agreement.[29] Aramco paid the Saudis $70 million in back payments, but the Saudis agreed to relinquish all other claims on back payments. On the surface, this deal seemed to cut deeply into Aramco's profits.

To ameliorate this, Aramco and its parent companies decided that Aramco would keep all of the profit the company would make from the price increase to $1.79. The parent companies would absorb the loss instead of Aramco by agreeing to purchase the entire output from Aramco at the higher price. Ultimately, given their foreign tax credit, Aramco "under certain circumstances would realize a net financial gain by their action," though this was only an unexpected benefit.[30] It had not been planned or foreseen at any point during the disputes. Finally the financial friction between the company and the kingdom was put to rest.

PART II

FIVE

HE MET HIS DUTY

When King Abdul Aziz died, he was surrounded by his prodigious family. They had been preparing for this moment for some time. The king's health had been declining for several years. His eyesight had dimmed and his circulation had grown so poor he needed to wear thick socks to keep his feet warm. An injury to his back that he had suffered during his early years of conquest made walking difficult, and he was plagued by arthritis. He had become less and less involved in state business and preferred to sit in his palace, drinking hot coffee and reminiscing. Periodically, he would handle the seven-foot spear that still stood at his bedside. Abdul Aziz was clearly disheartened by the slow, but determined, deterioration of his body. The death of his sister, Nura, several years earlier, followed by the sudden passing of his son Mansour, who was only twenty years old, brought a sadness that the king had not been able to shake.[1]

In April 1953, an ill Abdul Aziz was transported from Riyadh across the country by plane to his summer palace in Taif. At that point, his health was so precarious that he spent the trip laid out on a pallet on the floor of the plane, which had been specially modified to accommodate the king's needs. The hope was that the mountains' "cool, clear air would revive him."[2] Most of the royal family made the trip as well. They were concerned the king's health would continue to disintegrate and wanted to be there with him especially in the event of a succession crisis. Even though Abdul Aziz had affirmed his eldest living son, Saud, as Crown Prince in 1933, the future of the kingdom's leadership seemed tenuous. There were powerful people who still had not indicated they would support Saud, including tribesmen who had submitted to Abdul Aziz but did not seem content to pledge loyalty to his untried son; the country's powerful and independent Islamic establishment, or *ulama*, who wanted to see what kind of Muslim Saud was; and some members of the royal family who were holding out for personal reasons.[3]

In his last years, Abdul Aziz was clearly concerned about potential friction and perhaps even sensed that Saud might not be up to the task of governing. Royal Councilor Sheikh Hafiz Wabha recalled witnessing a critical moment between the king and his two oldest sons. The story came from Parker T. Hart, who heard it directly from Sheikh Wabha. Hart was a longtime diplomat and spent many years at the US embassy in Saudi Arabia before he was named ambassador to Saudi Arabia in 1961. Hart was a frequent observer of Saudi politics, and because of his ease in the country, his notes and recollections provide valuable insights. Hart was equally comfortable with Americans and Arabs alike. Dr. J. Winston Porter, an American engineer who worked in Saudi Arabia, described how Hart would host large parties at the US embassy on the Fourth of July. "All the Saudis would come to the American embassy, and they would praise America," he said. Hart would stand in front of everyone and give a speech in English and then, "he would give the whole thing in Arabic . . . thirty minutes in English, thirty minutes in Arabic. He was very good in Arabic," Porter recalled.[4]

As Hart relayed Wabha's story, King Abdul Aziz "obliged [Wabha] to witness . . . a pledge repeated seven times by his sons . . . to respect and support each other to the death: Feisal to Saud as Crown Price and future ruler and Saud to Feisal as future Crown Prince and senior advisor."[5] The king sought to ensure family tranquility even if he had to will it past his own lifetime. In earlier times, he had dismissed the personal hostility and competitiveness between Saud and Feisal, but as he grew weaker, he feared the consequences of their rivalry for the kingdom's future. Bedridden at that point, he called both Saud and Feisal to his side.

He directed them to "join hands across [his] body." Then he said, "Swear that you will work together when I am gone. Swear too that, if you quarrel, you will argue in private. You must not let the world catch sight of your disagreements."

Saud and Feisal had no choice but to do as their father commanded. They leaned over his body and clasped hands while swearing to work together as stewards of the tremendous opportunity their father had engineered.[6]

That summer, however, King Abdul Aziz defied expectations. His health rallied, and he even resumed some of his state duties, occasionally receiving foreign dignitaries and oil executives. An Aramco executive (it is not clear who), after a trip to the United States to receive treatment for a life-threatening illness, spoke to King Abdul Aziz about his recovery and the new perspective on life he had gained as a result. Family relationships and connection to God were the most important aspects of life, he mused to the king. Wealth and professional success were enjoyable, but true meaning could be found in religion, he said. King Abdul Aziz, usually gracious and welcoming to Americans on social visits, was perhaps not in the mood to hear the reflections of a man who had recovered his physical vigor while he, himself, remained largely immobile. The king acerbically responded that had the Aramco executive been a

Muslim, he would have known this all of his life and not just in his later years.[7]

By November 1953, King Abdul Aziz seemed sufficiently healthy that Crown Prince Saud decided to take a short trip to nearby Jeddah for a public appearance. It was important, he believed, for the people to see him as the future leader of the kingdom. On November 8, Saud was received by the Saudi military, with a brass band at the parade they staged for his arrival. The next day, King Abdul Aziz relapsed. Despite his careful consideration, Saud had miscalculated. The palace immediately sent word to Saud to return to his father's bedside at once, but it was too late. There are differing accounts about how the king died. According to one history, the founding king of Saudi Arabia died in the arms of his son Feisal before his heir, Saud, could return to Taif.[8] According to another, the king died of a heart attack in his sleep on November 9, 1953.[9]

The royal family and state ministers waited tensely for Saud's return after the king's death. All wondered if Feisal would yield to his older brother when the latter returned. They did not know how Saud would handle the situation knowing that his own arrogance had kept him from his father's final moments. No one knew what the other brothers, some of them powerful governors of Saudi provinces, would do when the time arrived to pledge loyalty to the new king.[10]

As Saud approached the palace, Feisal rose from where his father's body lay and greeted his brother. According to several accounts, Feisal welcomed Saud back from Jeddah as the king. Feisal then took his brother to their father's body, removed a ring from the dead king's hand, and offered it to the new king. Saud took the ring, signaling his acceptance of the position, and then offered it back to his brother as a sign that Feisal would be the heir and Crown Prince of Saudi Arabia. Feisal's fealty, given immediately and without hesitation, set an example for the entire court. *Al Saud*, with perhaps only one exception, pledged loyalty to Saud as King of Saudi Arabia.[11]

Abdul Aziz did not have a funeral. Foreign dignitaries, prominent tribesmen, wealthy oil executives, and jealous Arab strongmen did not come to pay their respects. Funeral prayers were recited in Taif and then Abdul Aziz was buried without fanfare in an essentially unmarked grave in Riyadh.[12] Feisal flew back to the capital with the body and oversaw the king's burial.[13] According to their Islamic tradition, he was buried in a white shroud with his feet facing Mecca.[14] According to biographer David Howarth, writing only eleven years later in 1964, "Few people now in Riyadh remember where [his grave] is, and nobody visits it."[15] Today the area is a formal cemetery in which several of Abdul Aziz's sons, including at least one other Saudi king, are also buried. The graves of the royal members of *al Saud*, including King Abdul Aziz, remain unmarked and are scattered between those of common men and unidentified bodies.[16]

This humble memorial was in accordance with Abdul Aziz's strict faith in Wahhabi Islamic custom.[17] Wahhabi practitioners were careful not to venerate the graves of men who had lived great lives. Abdul Aziz ibn Saud was a man—a man who had accomplished great things—but just a man. He was, in accordance with his religious beliefs, buried and mourned as such. The Saudi flag was not even lowered to half-staff, because the flag is inscribed with the *shahadah,* or Islamic declaration of faith. The country's *ulama* declared that the flag should never be flown at half-staff. There was no formal national mourning for the man who had built a kingdom out of warring provinces and tribes.[18]

◆

Many scholars and chroniclers of King Abdul Aziz described him as a simple man. They did not mean he was simple in thought or ambition, but that he enjoyed the simple pleasures of life—women, his children, physical exploits, good food, strong coffee, and belief in his God. The trappings of modernity and wealth did not entice him personally, but they came to his country nonetheless. In fact, he had invited them in.

In 1933, he, along with Abdullah Sulaiman, sat in Jeddah with the American representative from the California Standard Oil Company. King Abdul Aziz allowed his finance minister to review the concession agreement they had spent weeks negotiating, article by article, before he asked for Sulaiman's final opinion. Sulaiman was satisfied. King Abdul Aziz looked at him and said, in Arabic, "Put your trust in God, and sign."[19] Sulaiman did so, marking the beginning of the American presence in Saudi Arabia and opening the door to modernity for Abdul Aziz's people.

King Abdul Aziz had been skeptical that the Americans would ever find oil in his kingdom. The money the oil company paid him upon signing the concession agreement helped with his immediate financial needs. When the company found oil, however, the small groups of geologists hunting for fossils in the desert or drilling deep into the sand on his eastern coast became his country's lifeline. The oil they pumped from the ground was turned into roads, hospitals, electricity, plumbing, education, and a professional future for his people. The Americans of Aramco were "his partners in development," as King Abdul Aziz often referred to them.[20]

King Abdul Aziz might have personally preferred the pastoral lifestyle of the early days of his kingdom. He might have derided the effect material wealth had on some members of his family and felt more than a little uneasy at the pace at which his people's traditional lifestyle was changing. He undoubtedly struggled with the effects of the fast-paced modernization. It was evident from those who spoke with the founding king in his later years that those changes bewildered him.[21]

Even though he was king of a country that was quickly becoming vital to Western industrialized nations, King Abdul Aziz, at the time of his death, was in many ways the same Bedouin sheikh who had slipped into the city of his birthright under cover of darkness and fought his way to victory. He brought his family of refugees back to their ancestral home and then spread his rule across the peninsula. He took a gamble when he signed an agreement with the American oil company, but he did so in order to provide a better future for his people.

When he died, Aramco's newspaper, *Sun & Flare*, published a moving memorial to the king, mentioning "the social and economic improvement" he had brought, through the company, to his people. "His Majesty had modern airports built . . . a wireless [radio] communications network spread across the country and telephone systems. . . . Roads were built, and harbors . . . transformed into deep water ports. . . . Historic mosques [were] strengthened and repaired and new mosques built. Hospitals . . . were provided [and] many schools were opened for the education of Saudi youth."[22]

The unified kingdom, the emergence of Aramco, and the oil export business provided new opportunities for young Saudi men. Ihsan Bu-Hulaiga, a Saudi from the Dhahran region, explained the impact Aramco had on his community and family. "I'm from the Eastern Province, from al-Hasa," he said. The al-Hasa region, close to the Persian Gulf, was a well-known oasis area even before Aramco arrived. "Al-Hasa is the largest oasis globally," Bu-Hulaiga said softly as he described a hometown in which men generally took on the profession of their fathers and worked within the family and community. "Aramco meant a great deal to us, as kids," he said. "They built schools, they offered summer employment for the pupil and university students and they created lots of jobs. They used to come to the villages, everywhere, to attract Saudis, to convince them to work."

Bu-Hulaiga described his own family's first encounter with Aramco as a positive experience. In the early 1970s, his cousin decided to drop out of school because "he came from a family that needed support." After ninth grade, the cousin joined the Aramco workforce. Mr. Bu-Hulaiga recalls his cousin leaving the community during the week but returning on weekends. "He was speaking English [and] always neat" was Bu-Hulaiga's childhood impression. Able to earn money to help support his family as well as continue his education, his cousin ultimately received a scholarship from the company and went to a college in Texas, where he earned a bachelor of science degree. "He came back and worked in contracting," Bu-Hulaiga explained. "He had a very successful career. He was the first one in his family to work for money."

Reflecting back on the time when Aramco was a "wholly American enterprise," Bu-Hulaiga said, "I think having Aramco there made wonders, really, to the generation. . . . In the 1940s and 1950s, Aramco managed to assemble a small army of Saudis, in total maybe fifteen or seventeen thousand Saudis, working for Aramco. [They were] Bedouins and farmers and first-time employees—the first generation ever working for a payroll and a monthly payment." He recalls the pride his community, still largely agricultural and pastoral in the 1970s, felt when a man from their hometown was promoted to Aramco vice president. "He was among the earliest wave of Saudis being promoted to senior positions, like to top management positions in Aramco."[23]

Aramco certainly changed the lives of many poor Saudis in the kingdom, but the ambition and perseverance of the men who strove for more should not be understated, and neither should the role the Saudi government played in assisting them. Othman Alkhowaiter was fourteen when he heard about Aramco. He had only a fourth grade education and worked on his parents' small farm. "I was born with Aramco," he said, in 1933. In 1949, at age fifteen, Alkhowaiter left his family and went "to Aramco to try my luck." He traveled for six straight days to get to Dhahran but he failed Aramco's tests twice due to poor vision in his left eye. Through persistence, he found a position working as a laborer on Tapline and did a variety of jobs until his twenties when he decided to finish his education.

By the time he was ready for intermediate school and high school, in 1954, the Saudi government had decided to provide stipends for men to finish their educations. Alkhowaiter completed a six-year course in four years. In 1959, the government started a small scholarship program for Saudis to attend the University of Texas to study petroleum engineering. Alkhowaiter was selected. When he returned with his degree, Aramco "accepted me immediately as an engineer." He worked for the company until he retired at age sixty as a vice president.[24]

Perhaps the clearest example of how Saudi lives were changed by Abdul Aziz's decision to invite Aramco into his kingdom is that of a young Bedouin boy who was born three years before oil was discovered at Dammam Well Number 7. At the age of four he lived with his divorced mother and her family and tended the family's baby lambs in the desert. He did not own a pair of shoes until he turned nine. When he was eight, his mother sent him to live with his father on the coast near Dhahran. There, his elder half brother was attending an Aramco-run school for young Saudis and brought him along. The young men studied in the morning and worked as office boys for the company in the afternoon. Previously illiterate, the boy learned to read and write both Arabic and English and studied mathematics and science.

When he graduated, Aramco sent the young man to Lebanon for secondary school and ultimately to the United States for college and graduate school, where he earned two degrees in geology. He returned to Saudi Arabia to rejoin Aramco, this time as a professional geologist. This man, Ali al-Naimi, rose through the company's ranks to become its first Saudi CEO. He later became oil minister of Saudi Arabia—one of the most powerful positions in the country open to people outside *al Saud*.[25] It was possible for a desert shepherd boy from a broken home to grow up to run one of the world's largest companies and achieve global prominence because Abdul Aziz ibn Saud had brought peace and stability to the peninsula, had taken a chance on Aramco, and had driven a hard bargain with his American partners for a better outcome for his country.

In return for the founding king's protection and beneficence, his people gave loyalty. Abdul Aziz had won the loyalty of the warring tribes, cities, and regional sheikhs through military might, strategic marriages, and political patronage. He had not formed an imagined community or collective ideology, as many other peoples in the modern era had used as a basis for unity. Rather, the threat of the king's military might and his largesse held the country together. This was part of the bargain that legitimized Abdul Aziz's rule—he won his crown by force but kept his crown by showing his people that he had the wealth and power to provide for them. They were his subjects for as long as he could show them he had the ability to care for them as king.

Without any real industry, Saudi Arabia's population could never muster enough in taxes to support this deal. A constant stream of income from oil, however, could provide King Abdul Aziz and his sons with the funds they needed to prove they could take care of their subjects. *Al Saud*'s sovereignty over that natural resource was Abdul Aziz's lasting legacy to his family. He had provided for his family, expanded his tribe, and created a country. His treasury had serious debt when he died, but he had set *al Saud* on a path to future riches and his people on the path to modernity. At the time of the king's death, Saudi Arabia's future looked promising. The king had met his duty. King Abdul Aziz's sons knew, however, that it was their duty to maintain and increase *al Saud*'s wealth and power for their own children. Their stewardship over the kingdom and the gift from God under its sand were vital to the future of their family.

◆

The vicious transition of power that many Saudis—and not a few Americans—worried about did not materialize after King Abdul Aziz's death. Whereas bloody coups gripped Egypt, Iraq, Syria, and Iran in the 1950s, power changed hands swiftly and simply in Saudi Arabia. Just as Abdul Aziz had ordained, Saud became king, and his brother Feisal became Crown Prince. However, Saud was not the same type of ruler his father was. "Saud lacked the touch of greatness," a biographer explained, "and it often seemed that he knew he lacked it." The man "was tall but not quite so tall, sometimes charming but never quite so charming, commanding but never quite able to command the same uncritical obedience."[26]

Saud was born in 1902, purportedly on the same day that King Abdul Aziz captured the city of Riyadh.[27] He was, according to Ambassador Hart, "a big, jovial extrovert with a reputation for generosity among the tribes."[28] He kept the Bedouin tribes appeased with money and marriages, sometimes taking a new wife offered by the tribe at the time of a visit. As a manager, Saud would "assent to whatever seemed the line of least resistance," a quality the Aramco executives who dealt with him discovered even before he became king. Saud wore thick glasses, walked with an odd gait, and was described as "slightly clumsy."[29]

In 1955, it became evident that despite laws banning the sale of alcohol in Saudi Arabia and the Islamic proscription against consuming it, Saud regularly drank alcohol. Though members of Saud's inner circle might have thought it was a "well-kept secret," even foreign businessmen knew of the king's penchant for Cointreau. This not only impaired his abilities but also took a toll on his health. He was not yet sixty, but the new king suffered from poor circulation, high blood pressure, and a variety of "stomach troubles" no doubt compounded by his lifestyle.[30]

When it came to affairs of state, he spent lavishly and without care—on palaces that were never used and left to decay in the desert and yachts that sat at port because no one knew how to sail them.[31] Even before Saud became king, his spending habits were evident. In 1951, despite Saudi Arabia's mounting bills to Bechtel for public development projects, then Crown Prince Saud ordered an opulent trailer from the company. He used this trailer, or a similar one, on his trips to visit Bedouin tribes in the desert. Reportedly, Bedouin families seeking his favor would offer him young girls as brides, and he frequently took them to "a velvet bed placed beneath wall to ceiling mirrors" in his trailer. It was noted, however, "that he did not always consummate the marriages."[32]

His brother Feisal was the opposite of Saud in almost every way. Ambassador Hart described Feisal as "a worldly man," who "preferred the simple life and was not known for his cars and palaces, nor for his amorous escapades." During his life, Feisal had only three wives or possibly four, in contrast to his brother Saud, who had forty-one wives, according to the King Saud Foundation.[33] Feisal spoke "excellent, if limited English," though he spoke Arabic almost exclusively when interacting with American diplomats.[34] His face was "lean and drawn," and his body seemed "an emaciated shadow" next to his elder brother's.[35] Many of the Americans who interacted with him described him as a master at hiding his true thoughts. According to Robert Lacey, a historian who spent significant time in Feisal's court, the man "never allowed his chiseled features to betray what he was really thinking."[36] Frank Jungers, the president and CEO of Aramco for much of the 1970s, wrote that the only way he could tell if Feisal was truly "irritated about something" was when he saw him pick at his camelhair robe.[37]

According to Jungers, "Feisal was known for his masterful personal and political skills," but the public rarely experienced this powerful leader because he mistrusted journalists and "rarely allowed himself to be interviewed."[38] Feisal was personally thrifty to the point of austerity, though he did not withhold on his sons' educations. Appearing "taciturn and severe," Feisal was also known to hold grudges and was a man of habit, to the point of obsession. According to Ahmed Zaki Yamani, who served as Saudi oil minister for over two decades, Feisal peeled and ate an apple after meals in precisely seven minutes, every single time.[39] Many of the key players in the Saudi government also turned over during the generational transition. Saud had been compelled by his father to retain longtime finance minister Abdullah Sulaiman after the king's death, but the finance minister resigned in 1954.[40] Details of the incident that led to his resignation and disappearance from public life are hazy, but it apparently followed a fight with Feisal over Saudi Arabia's budget.[41] After his resignation, Sulaiman seems to have focused his attention on agricultural pursuits from his home at an oasis in the Nejd region. His son, Ahmed Sulaiman, according to Ambassador Hart, went on to run a "plantation of vegetables and wheat" in the fertile Qasim sector and became "one of the great businessmen of Saudi Arabia."[42]

Saud elevated Sulaiman's deputy, Mohammad Suroor, to the finance minister position. Suroor essentially gave Saud carte blanche to spend as he wished—both personally and for the state. Over the next four years, Saudi spending ballooned while oil revenues stagnated. Saud sought to rule in the style and manner of his father. He wanted to preside, render decisions, and command allegiance. In Saudi Arabia's tribal society, however, loyalty had to be earned. It could not be inherited. Saud came across as generally unintelligent and most often resorted to winning favor by buying it. He sought love and admiration, as opposed to respect. Within the family, Saud eschewed the policy and religious debates Feisal and his other brothers enjoyed, because he could not stomach discord and disagreement. Some of those around him suspected he avoided them because he could not hold his own against Feisal.

Before Abdul Aziz died, the old king had decreed the establishment of a council of ministers. Saud presided over the council's formation and even named Feisal president of this body but then rarely consulted its members on matters of state. Feisal was trapped by Saud's lack of engagement. His father had envisioned the two of them governing as partners, but of course, Saud was king and Feisal just Crown Prince. There was no opportunity to challenge Saud's financial management, because there was no room for debate in the monarchy. Saud had quickly surrounded himself with sycophants who, in turn, benefitted handsomely from Saud's spending habits.[43]

By early 1958, the kingdom was on the brink of a serious financial crisis. The country was in debt, and Saud had directed the treasury to print currency to pay for the new government buildings he had decreed should be built. There was rapid inflation.[44] The State Department learned from King Saud's special envoy that it would take an immediate infusion of $50 million just to stabilize the riyal.[45] In addition, the Saudi government owed more than $92 million to Chase Manhattan bank and other US financial institutions.

There was a growing sense among *al Saud* that the lack of fiscal discipline Saud showed was not only leading the country into a financial crisis but also disgracing the country in the eyes of the Arab world. Neither the country's civil servants nor its military had been paid for several months, and, though no one seemed to know how much money was in the treasury, it looked like the government employees would not be receiving their regular bonuses for Ramadan.[46] In a country where the royal family's power was built on its ability to provide for its people, abandoning contractual obligations could lead to drastic political upheaval.

Fear must have been growing among some of the brothers about the family's ability to maintain its power and control, particularly as they observed the political shifts taking place around them in the Arab world. Monarchies were crumbling and nationalist republics were taking their places. Beginning with Egyptian army colonel Gamal Abdul Nasser's overthrow of King Farouk in 1952, monarchies across the Middle East were being challenged by nationalist strongmen. In 1954, Mohammad Mossadeq, the nationalist prime minister of Iran, successfully forced the shah into retreat. The Iranian monarch's rule was only restored with the help of the CIA. In February 1958, Nasser's influence extended to Syria, where new Arab nationalist leaders joined with Nasser in establishing the United Arab Republic. Finally, on Saudi Arabia's northern border, the army was preparing to capitalize on public dissatisfaction with Iraqi king Faisal II's rule and stage a coup.

Several of the younger, more concerned brothers gathered in March 1958 at the home of Prince Talal. Born approximately twenty-nine years after Saud, Talal was a young man in 1958. He would eventually outlive almost all of his brothers. In the 1960s, Talal became known for his outspoken support of liberal reforms, but in 1958, he was just a former minister of communications. King Abdul Aziz had appointed him to the post before his death, but the prince resigned in 1955 after a dispute with his brother Mishaal over which ministry, his or Mishaal's, should control the Saudi national airlines. Of the members of *al Saud* gathered at Talal's residence in 1958, the only senior brother present was Abdullah, who would later become the sixth king of Saudi Arabia. The discussion that night led to a resolution to speak with Saud and try to convince him to change his wasteful ways. Talal, with the blessing of his older brother Abdullah, left immediately in his new private plane and flew across the country to meet the king in Medina, where he was staying.

Talal made absolutely no headway during his conversation with Saud and promptly returned across the country in his plane. When he arrived back in Riyadh, he sought out Crown Prince Feisal that same day. Feisal was hardly in a position to deal with matters of state at that juncture, much less a potential insurrection from within. He had recently returned to Saudi Arabia from almost a year in the United States, where he had undergone a series of medical procedures to remove a benign tumor from his stomach. When Talal came looking for him that March night, Feisal was relaxing with his hawks at a desert encampment outside the city. Despite his recent malady, Feisal accompanied Talal back to the younger brother's palace, where the other brothers had remained throughout the evening.

With the Crown Prince now present, the nine brothers discussed potential reforms. One of Talal's ideas was to create a formal *Majlis al Shura*, or consultative council, for the family, which would facilitate important discussions and assist in decision making. More brothers, he suggested, should be brought into the government and included in the decision-making process. Unlike his father's Council of Ministers, the *Majlis al Shura* would invite more brothers to participate. Saudi Arabia's problems, Talal argued, could be traced to Saud's exclusion of his brothers from the government and concentration of power in his hands. The plan the brothers put together that night, however, relied heavily on the participation and goodwill of Feisal. Feisal, as Crown Prince, had to be the one to lead the government reforms, and he was the only one who might have been able to convince Saud to acquiesce. Despite his recent surgeries, Feisal was so distraught over the state of affairs when he had returned to Saudi Arabia that he agreed to champion the reforms.[47]

The following day, Feisal discussed the matter with Saud, and, to everyone's relief, the king agreed to the brothers' suggestions. According to the plan, Saud retained his crown but essentially delegated governing the country to Feisal. This was accomplished through a decree, issued by Saud, which, according to a US State Department analysis, "implicitly acknowledged the failure of his own policy." Saud's power remained contained to the Royal Guard Regiment and the influence he had carefully cultivated and maintained with the Bedouin tribes.[48] When Feisal took control of the government, he found the financial situation much more dire than he had expected. The story told later was that the state treasury contained the equivalent of barely $100 in cash.

The Crown Prince quickly fired Mohammad Suroor. Feisal himself took over the responsibilities of the finance minister position, and he placed an uncle in the former role to serve as a buffer against citizens, family members, and other elements of the government seeking funds. Then Feisal went one step further and recruited Zaki Saad, an Egyptian economist from the International Monetary Fund, to serve as his financial advisor.[49]

With great difficulty, and through sheer force of personality, Feisal managed to secure a loan from a Saudi bank that he could use to pay the military and civil employees their back wages and the expected Ramadan bonus. By paying the military and civil servants what they were owed as quickly as possible, Feisal negated a potential political grievance before it could become a serious threat to the monarchy. He convinced Aramco to underwrite the debt Saudi Arabia already owed to American banks and to guarantee additional loans so that the kingdom could borrow enough to keep the country out of bankruptcy while he brought spending under control and worked on a new budget.[50]

By the end of the year, Saudi Arabia had a legitimate budget for 1959, which severely limited spending. In fact, for the first time ever, the budget distinguished between government spending and royal family expenses. What truly made a difference, however, was that Feisal and the uncle to whom he entrusted control of the treasury enforced the prescribed limits on family spending too. After a year of austerity, by 1960 Saudi Arabia was close to finally balancing its budget.[51]

It seemed as though Feisal had successfully managed to bring the country back from the brink of bankruptcy, but the relatively smooth sailing depended entirely on King Saud's continued acquiescence to the financial decisions of his younger brother. Saud, however, saw the improvements his brothers made and felt not just resentment over the austerity but jealousy as well. He wanted to do more than just sign off on the yearly budget Feisal presented. Even the Americans at the embassy in Jeddah saw Saud's dissatisfaction. In fact, an attaché asked Feisal directly about reports of growing discord between the Crown Prince and the king. "I wish to assure you," Feisal responded, "there are no differences between myself and the king. As is the case among friends we sometimes do not see eye to eye, but we are never at loggerheads with each other. The day will never come when I stand in one place and the king in another."[52]

It is quite possible that Feisal was simply trying to reassure the Americans of Saudi Arabia's political stability. However, it is well documented that Feisal suffered personal distress at the idea of challenging his brother's rule. Given Feisal's overwhelming sense of duty, allegiance, and responsibility, it is far more likely that he was distraught at the growing fractures between Saud and him, and between Saud and the other brothers. But Saud was the king. And the king was not happy.

SIX

PUTTING THE HOUSE IN ORDER

According to tradition, Mohammad, the final prophet of Islam, died in 632 C.E. in the arms of his wife, Aisha, at her home in Medina. He passed away after a short illness that struck him at the apex of his religious and political quest. His armies had conquered the religious and commercial center of the Arabian Peninsula, known as Mecca, a short time earlier. Just as the military, political, and theological might of the Islamic community, or *umma*, was beginning to influence lands outside the desert peninsula, its leader passed away. According to many accounts, Mohammad's death came as a shock to his followers, who saw their military successes as merely a prelude to even greater victories.[1]

Mohammad accomplished more than the spread of monotheism through the Arabian Peninsula. Both Judaism and Christianity had been introduced with limited success before Mohammad's brand of monotheism arrived. Scholars have argued that his historical legacy was formidable and reflected a unique synthesis of monotheistic religious beliefs and Arabian tribal politics.[2] The concept of ultimate faithfulness and allegiance to an all-powerful, single God, rather than to just a tribe or family, had a significant impact on the social and political development of Arabia. One scholar explained that even after Mohammad's death, "tribal, regional, and ethnic obligations had now become, at least theoretically, subject to the greater claims of a divine and universal law."[3]

With no living sons, four daughters, and no clear indication of who might succeed him, a crisis loomed.[4] Mohammad's earliest converts would determine their prophet's successor according to time-honored Bedouin traditions. According to Bernard Lewis, a preeminent Western scholar on early Islam, "The concept of legitimate succession was foreign to the Arabs at the time, and it is probable that even if Mohammad had left a son the sequence of events would not have been different." Arab tradition "had only one precedent to guide them—the election of a new tribal chief." Mohammad's closest and earliest adherents—Abu Bakr, Umar, and Abu Ubayda—chose a new leader from among themselves. Abu Bakr was chosen as the *khalifa,* or caliph. *Caliph* is best translated as 'deputy,' because Abu Bakr led the *umma* as Mohammad's deputy, not as a replacement.[5] When Abu Bakr died, the council selected Umar as the next caliph, and succession continued this way until a controversy emerged over the successor to the fourth caliph. Mohammad's son-in-law, Ali, had been selected as the fourth caliph, but he was murdered shortly after. One faction of the *umma* wanted Muawiya, a man from a prominent Damascus family, to succeed Ali as caliph, and another faction of the *umma* wanted one of Ali's sons to succeed him as caliph. This political and religious controversy ultimately split the *umma* in two—in what came to be called the Sunni-Shi'a split.

More than thirteen hundred years later, another powerful Arabian family grappled with the death of a founding leader. Once again, they would come to lean on the customs of the tribal Bedouin society of the peninsula to safeguard their family's enduring rule and future prosperity.

◆

By 1960, Saudi Arabia seemed well on its way to fixing the fiscal troubles that had plagued it since the days of Abdul Aziz. According to Ambassador Hart, Feisal "reduced the amount of royal take from oil income [from] something like 60% to about 14%." Feisal's control of the country's finances was absolute. Hart said that even though Feisal had installed ministers "in whom he had confidence," he still kept a tight leash on ministerial expenditures.

"He once showed me a piece of paper," Hart explained, "which he kept in the pocket of his *thobe*, which showed every minister's budget. Every time he would meet them, and he would meet them often, he would say, 'What have you done with this money? I want an accounting for your part of the budget.'"[6]

Feisal's austerity was a welcome antidote to Saud's excesses, but the second son of Abdul Aziz was not a perfect steward of his father's legacy. In order to balance the budget, Feisal reined in the personal spending of the royal family and cut almost all government-financed development work in Saudi Arabia. Two years into his reforms, the dramatic drop in government spending triggered a recession. Feisal insisted on saving money instead of funding economic development, and some of the other brothers, Talal included, were growing concerned.

After two years of necessary tightfistedness, the Saudi economy needed an infusion of cash and perhaps even some deficit spending. Talal saw both economic and political possibilities for development in Saudi Arabia at this juncture. Talal hoped *al Saud* would adopt policies to accelerate Saudi Arabia's economic growth, and he also believed that it was imperative for the government to incorporate democratic elements. Talal was technically from the same generation as Saud and Feisal, but he was born at a different time. Though birthdates of the princes are often disputed, it is believed Talal was only twenty-nine in 1960, while Saud was fifty-eight and Feisal was fifty-six. Talal worked with several brothers who were similar in age, including Abdul Muhsin (thirty-five), Fawwaz (twenty-six), Badr (twenty-eight), and his full brother Nawwaf (twenty-eight). These "Liberal Princes," as they were called, drew up a plan that included an elected legislative body, a limited monarch, and a draft constitution.[7] Talal came to believe that he could maneuver Saud into accepting the liberal-minded reforms he and his group sought. He therefore lent his support to the king when Saud decided to take back executive authority in December 1960.[8]

According to the State Department, the exact timing of Saud's resumption of power was a surprise, but the move "was not unexpected since the King had resented the delegation of authority to Prince Feisal which had been forced upon him more than two years ago and had been waiting for an opportunity to regain full royal powers."[9] Saud had tried twice before to reassert himself by denying requests from Feisal, but on each "of those occasions, Feisal submitted his resignation which was refused."[10] Finally, in December, Feisal submitted the 1961 budget for Saud's approval, and Saud refused to sign. According to Ambassador Hart's account, "When Faisal heard that it had been rejected by his half-brother, Faisal got up and left the meeting and his position as Prime Minister."[11] Saud accepted this as his brother's resignation. Back in Washington, the State Department jocularly noted the situation with the following line: "*Moral:* Don't submit your resignation unless you really want to quit."[12]

To Feisal, however, governing with the knowledge that his brother's fickle whim could upend carefully crafted state budgets was not governing at all. Likely, he meant it every time he submitted his resignation to the King, but Saud had not been able to bring himself to dismiss his brother. Saud likely knew that he could not or did not want to do the things Feisal took care of. Feisal was not ostracized and continued to serve as foreign minister, but he refused to deal with the government in any other capacity. After his abrupt resignation, Feisal "went out and took some members of his family and camped in the desert," which was, Ambassador Hart noted, "the way his father always did things." There he refused to see anyone from his brother's court, even though "messengers went out and people tried to get him to come back." Feisal always responded that he would not return unless Saud completely changed his attitude. "He realized," Ambassador Hart said, that Saud would not, "and so said that he was not going to have anything more to do with him [and] that without authority he did not want the position of Prime Minister."[13]

Talal assumed control of the Ministry of Finance and brought in two princes who supported his liberal reforms to serve as ministers of interior and communications. Talal's plans called for expanding the Saudi government to include more nonroyals and, eventually, he hoped, introducing a constitution. Saud, however, quickly lost interest in Talal's liberalization plans and even lost interest in the fiscal responsibility he had promised to exercise. Saud never really committed to financial responsibility. He made a show of firing half of the palace chefs, but he did little else. It did not take Talal long to realize his mistake that Saud would never really support his ideas or his plans for reforms. After a fight with the king, Talal resigned as well in September 1961.[14]

◆

In late 1961, Saud suddenly began bleeding from the stomach. He was immediately rushed to an Aramco hospital, where doctors feared he might not live.[15] After he was stabilized, however, the severity of his malady forced the king to seek treatment in Boston, Massachusetts, and then later, for an extended period of time, in Europe.[16] Before he left, the entire clan assembled at the hospital to say good-bye to their king. Ambassador Hart, who grew up in the Boston area and helped arrange Saud's transfer to a local hospital, watched as even Feisal stepped forward to kiss Saud on both cheeks in the traditional Arab farewell. Of Feisal, Hart observed, "He did his duty like everybody else and left at once without saying a single word to the King."[17]

In Saud's absence, Feisal resumed control over all state affairs. Feisal found that during his time away from executive authority—less than a year—Saud had not seriously damaged Saudi Arabia's financial standing. Nevertheless, Feisal had retribution to exact. Feisal's own brother, Talal, who had previously undermined the Crown Prince in favor of Saud in 1960, found himself the object of Feisal's ire. When Talal had called for *al Saud* to introduce liberal political reforms, he might have thought he was acting with the best intentions for Saudi Arabia. However, Feisal thought his advocacy for a constitution was too much; it undermined both the monarchy and fundamental Islamic tenets. In 1962, even though Talal had already resigned from Saud's government, Feisal had his passport revoked for showing sympathy toward Nasser. Talal and the other supporters of the liberalization movement, such as Princes Fawwaz and Badr, left Saudi Arabia to live in exile in Cairo and Beirut. In retaliation, Feisal froze Talal's Saudi assets, but after that the two reached an acceptable impasse from afar. Four years later, Talal and the other so-called Liberal Princes who supported him were forgiven and allowed to return to Saudi Arabia.[18]

Another casualty of Feisal's return to power was Abdullah Tariki, the general director of petroleum and mineral resources. Tariki is a well-known figure in global oil politics, mostly because in 1960 he cofounded, along with Venezuelan oil minister Juan Perez Alfonso, the Organization of Petroleum Exporting Countries, better known as the OPEC cartel.

Tariki, also called the "Red Sheikh," was one of the first American-educated Saudis to work for the Saudi government. After completing his undergraduate studies in Cairo, he obtained a master's degree in geology at the University of Texas in 1947. While in the United States, he worked for Texaco, one of Aramco's parent companies. Upon returning to Saudi Arabia, Tariki was appointed to be a petroleum advisor in the Finance Ministry, under Abdullah Sulaiman. The first time Tariki appeared on the State Department's radar was in September 1951, when, at a stop in Mexico on his way to a petroleum conference in Venezuela, he caught the eye of the American attaché for economic affairs at the US embassy.

It was at this early date that the Americans became aware—even if the Saudis were not—of Tariki's "radical attitude." According to the attaché at the Mexican embassy, during his visit to Mexico, Tariki "associated almost continuously with PEMEX [the Mexican national oil company] officials, who filled him with the glories and success of oil nationalization. He appeared . . . strongly impressed by the advantage of nationalizing oil." According to the attaché's informant, "Tariki evidenced intense nationalism amounting almost to anti-foreign antagonism."[19] Only a month later, the Americans in Saudi Arabia—both diplomats and Aramco executives—would experience Tariki's style of blunt confrontation firsthand. Tariki drew their attention when he took up the cause of Aramco's Saudi workers during a labor dispute.

Tariki considered the lack of Aramco housing for Saudi families an injustice against Arabs. At that time Aramco was building new barrack-style housing for Saudi men who worked for the company in Dhahran, but Aramco reserved family-style housing in the Dhahran compound for American and other Western employees.[20] Tariki took it upon himself to investigate the conditions at the Saudi facilities in Dhahran, incite some small-scale worker protests, and then push Aramco to provide better housing. Tariki, himself, was the first Saudi to gain access to American housing facilities in Dhahran, where he lived with his first wife, an American, from 1952 until their divorce in 1954.[21]

The Americans' early assessment of Tariki, made in Mexico, proved accurate. Tariki's goals were the nationalization of Saudi Arabia's oil assets and the nationalization of Aramco. He drew significant guidance from examples of countries that appropriated foreign-owned resources or companies and placed them under government control. Of particular appeal to Tariki were events such as the nationalization of all Mexican subsoil resources in 1917 and the Egyptian revolution of 1952, which removed King Farouk and brought the Arab nationalist Gamal Abdel Nasser to power.[22] He watched the shah of Iran stand by, powerless, as Mohammad Mossadeq nationalized Iran's oil industry in 1954, and he saw Nasser nationalize the Suez Canal Company from British and French control and get away with it in 1956.

In 1954, the Saudis decided that they had the right to form their own national shipping company and ship Aramco's oil on their own oil tankers. To this end, the Saudis contracted with the Greek shipping magnate Aristotle Onassis to lease tankers for a Saudi national shipping company. Yet Aramco argued that this violated the concession agreement in which shipping rights were given to the company.[23] Aramco firmly believed that Tariki, as a petroleum advisor in the Finance Ministry, was involved in this scheme.[24] The issue went to international arbitration, where it was not resolved for several years.

Tariki tried to assert Saudi national control over its oil resources again in 1958, when he arranged for a Japanese consortium of companies to acquire offshore drilling rights near Saudi Arabia's border with Kuwait, called the "neutral zone."[25] Both countries split oil rights in that small area. Tariki played a major role in negotiating a concession agreement that favored Saudi Arabia. Instead of the 50-50 profit-sharing arrangement that had become the standard arrangement between oil companies and oil-rich states, Tariki negotiated the Japanese into a 56-45 deal favoring the Saudis, with an additional clause for the Saudis to acquire equity in the company if it found oil. Despite protests from the United States and Great Britain, the deal remained in place.[26]

In 1959, Aramco won its arbitration case against Saudi Arabia in the Onassis shipping dispute, but the prolonged fight had embittered Crown Prince Feisal toward the Aramco executives.[27] Even the State Department thought Aramco could have been more conciliatory and less hostile in its legal battle, though Aramco was clearly in the right according to accepted contract law.[28] The company took the State Department's advice to heart and offered the Saudis two seats on the board of directors as a consolation gift to repair their relationship. The Saudis accepted the offer and, to Aramco's surprise and chagrin, decided to appoint Abdullah Tariki and Hafiz Wabha as their representatives to the Aramco board.[29] Hafiz Wabha, a former Saudi ambassador to the UK and a close confidant of *al Saud*, was not threatening, but Tariki's anti-Aramco views were well known. Officially, Aramco said that "the Saudi members of the Board are most welcome," but, privately, "management [recognized] that their appointment [posed] many problems for the future." When Aramco offered the Saudis the chance to select their own representatives, it apparently did not occur to the executives that the Saudis would choose government officials, and "particularly not that Tariki would be one of them."[30]

Aramco officials assumed that the Saudi board members would vote with Saudi Arabia's interests—not Aramco's interests—in mind, particularly when dealing with "problems to be negotiated with the Saudi Arabian Government." The real concerns were that Tariki would impede the operations of the board with his anti-Western rantings and, most importantly, that his dual positions of board member and oil minister of Saudi Arabia represented a clear conflict of interest. As a board member, he would have access to sensitive information about Aramco, but as oil minister he was the primary negotiator across the table from Aramco. Aramco's parent companies—Standard Oil of New Jersey (Exxon), Standard Oil of California (Chevron), Texaco, and Standard Oil of New York (Mobil)—decided they were not willing to complain about Tariki's appointment to the king or Crown Prince. Instead, they shifted more responsibilities so the Aramco board became even less influential and more power was given to the shareholders (the parent companies).[31]

As the new president of Aramco, Tom Barger flew to Riyadh in the spring of 1959 to meet with the king and the Crown Prince. Barger was the same geologist who, as a young man, had participated in early Aramco expeditions in the Arabian desert that looked for fossilized fish as signs of petroleum deposits and longed to reunite with his young wife who stayed behind in the United States. In a way, Barger grew up with Aramco and Saudi Arabia. He would later become CEO and chairman of the board before retiring in 1969.

When Barger arrived in Riyadh, he "spent about five minutes in a purely formal call on the king." The next day, he visited Crown Prince Feisal, who took the time to assure Barger that the relationship between Saudi Arabia and Aramco was healthy. Aramco's gesture seemed to have overcome any residual acrimony from the shipping dispute. Feisal told Barger that "there were actually no real problems between [Saudi Arabia and Aramco]—that respect for the rights of one another erased all problems." According to Feisal, the appointment of Tariki and Wabha to the board demonstrated Aramco's respect for Saudi Arabia. The Crown Prince continued, "In a long life together differences of opinion may arise—even in a family—even between brothers." Feisal paused and smiled. "Such differences can be adjusted," he finished.[32] This was Feisal's circuitous way of reassuring Barger that Aramco and Saudi Arabia were still partners in the oil business and that Saudi Arabia was not rushing to separate itself from the Americans.

Despite Feisal's words of reassurance, Tom Barger and other Aramco executives were right to be concerned about Abdullah Tariki. They described him as "fanatically obeying political and ideological motives." The US ambassador in the late 1950s, Donald Heath, said that he was "personally friendly with Tariki and [admired] his honesty" but found "him filled with implacable, irrational hostility toward Aramco."[33] However, for all of Tariki's talk about the "ill-treatment" of oil-rich countries like Saudi Arabia at the hands of oil companies, Tariki did not use his voting power on the board to challenge Aramco.[34] In fact, the Aramco board members were surprised at how easily Tariki went along with the proceedings at Aramco's annual meeting.[35] Perhaps he knew that with only two votes, board meetings were not how he would achieve his goals. Nevertheless, the Americans simply accepted his relative silence. There is no evidence that the Americans in Aramco wondered about Tariki's plans to pursue Saudi control and Arab nationalism.

In fact, Tariki was largely occupied with the concern of how oil-rich countries like Saudi Arabia could defend their share of oil revenues when their operations were being run through partnerships with international oil companies (IOCs), such as British Petroleum, Royal Dutch Shell, CFP, and the parent companies of Aramco.[36] Tariki was always an Arab nationalist at heart who wanted the state to control Aramco and the country's oil industry. However, he found little support for nationalization within Saudi Arabia, because *al Saud* did not want to disrupt its strategy for long-term revenue. Outside Saudi Arabia, Tariki found a more sympathetic ally in Venezuelan oil minister Juan Perez Alfonso. Alfonso had spent a great deal of time considering how producing countries could wrest control from the IOCs. During a brief period in which he lived in exile in the United States, Alfonso studied the Texas Railroad Commission, a government body in Texas that regulated oil production in that state. Specifically, he reviewed the commission's efforts to raise depressed oil prices in the region in the 1920s and 1930s by controlling oil production. His examination led him to believe that an international cartel of oil-producing countries could be effective in raising prices on a global scale.[37]

In an oft-told story, Wanda Jablonski, the popular American petroleum journalist and founder of *Petroleum Intelligence Weekly*, introduced Alfonso and Tariki at a petroleum conference in the Middle East in 1958. Wanda Jablonski's friendship with Tariki is well documented and also a subject of great speculation. Some surmised that the journalist and the oil minister were having an affair, since they often spent time together, alone, at each other's residences. The two even appeared together publicly at a cocktail party hosted by BP at the World Petroleum Congress in New York in 1959. Jablonski always denied the rumors that she and Tariki had any relationship other than as friends.[38] Although Jablonski was not as close with Juan Perez Alfonso, she also had a personal relationship with the Venezuelan minister and had written an in-depth profile of him for her publication. According to Jablonski's story, she was with Alfonso at the Hilton hotel in Cairo when she noticed Tariki sitting in the lobby and went to speak with him. She then invited both men to her room for drinks.[39] It is worth noting that in later years, scholars such as Juan Carlos Boue have suggested that this story is not entirely correct and that Tariki and Alfonso actually knew each other long before Jablonski's introduction. This contention is logical, since the US embassy in Mexico first noticed Tariki in 1951 as he stopped on his way to a conference in Venezuela.[40]

In 1960, Tariki and Alfonso invited the petroleum ministers from other oil-rich countries to a meeting in Baghdad. Kuwait, Iraq, and Iran joined Saudi Arabia and Venezuela. This meeting led to the formation of OPEC. The organization's mission was twofold: to "defend the price of oil" through limits on oil production and to promote the control of native governments over their oil resources. In 1960, the IOCs did not see OPEC as a significant force despite the fact that OPEC members owned about 80 percent of the world's exported oil. During the first decade of its existence, the cartel was unable to make noteworthy progress toward either of its goals.[41]

Abdullah Tariki made little headway in promoting his Arab nationalist causes in the 1950s and early 1960s. Tariki and his fellow OPEC oil ministers knew that their countries still depended on the expertise, equipment, and marketing outlets of the IOCs to produce and sell their oil. OPEC was reluctant to pressure the IOCs too much, but Tariki continued to express his nationalist beliefs in Saudi Arabia. These activities, rather than his involvement in OPEC, ultimately ended his career at home.

Tariki's oil policies grew from his fervent ideological beliefs and were most accurately described in the slogan he adopted for a petroleum publication he started in the mid-1960s that proclaimed, "Arab petroleum is for the Arabs." The Saudi royal family, however, was satisfied with its arrangement with Aramco, especially as oil production—and therefore Saudi revenue—continued its steady rise. Tariki continued in his job as oil minister because he was smart, American educated, experienced in the petroleum industry, and a native of the same Nejd region as the ruling family. However,

Tariki's ideas were dangerous for Aramco and dangerous for US and other Western interests that relied on Saudi oil supplies. Though *al Saud* might not have known it at the time, Tariki's ideas were also dangerous to the royal family. True nationalization in the mode of Nasser and Mossadeq entailed taking the resources for the people, not for the ruling monarch. Taken to its conclusion, nationalization policies included deposing that monarch.

King Saud was not especially bothered by Tariki's politics and allowed Tariki a great deal of freedom in his role. Saud, unlike his father, did not care to know much about the details of the oil industry or even where the kingdom's money came from. Tariki, therefore, had great leeway to express his opinions on the future of the oil industry and even to act on them. He often spoke favorably of Mohammad Mossadeq's actions in Iran to the Americans he dealt with, which they took as either a threat or a warning. Neither was appreciated. But his admiration for Mossadeq could have been seen as a threat to *al Saud* as well.

When Tariki's speeches began openly attacking "the sanctity of concessionary contracts," the American ambassador finally brought the matter to King Saud's attention. Tariki, he said, was scaring away the foreign investors Saudi Arabia desperately needed. When the ambassador explained that Tariki had "mentioned to a member of [his] staff his admiration for Mossadeq and his regrets that the latter had not succeeded in his nationalization plans," the king just "burst into scornful laughter."[42] To the Americans, it was unclear if anyone in the government was watching Tariki.

Saud and Feisal did not share Tariki's radical Arab nationalism. Neither son of Abdul Aziz sympathized with his desire to nationalize Saudi Arabia's oil assets in the manner that Iran and Mexico had. Nevertheless, at least initially, they both recognized the value of Tariki's knowledge, dedication, and long-term vision for the country and its oil. Tariki had proven his worth when he worked with Abdullah Sulaiman in the 1950s to recover millions of dollars of revenue for Saudi Arabia in the oil pricing controversy that followed the 50-50 profit-sharing deal. With Tariki in charge of petroleum relations, however, his brazen and confrontational style stood in stark contrast to Sulaiman's measured scheming and complete devotion to his king.

Feisal saw this, even if he did not let on to the Americans, and he did not approve of Tariki's activism. It was bad for business. Nor did he trust that Tariki had the interests of *al Saud* at heart. When Tariki began openly criticizing the royal family in 1962, Feisal fired him immediately. He had tolerated Tariki's affinity for Nasserite Arab nationalism because Tariki's knowledge of the oil industry had been valuable to Saudi Arabia. What Feisal could not abide were attacks on the family. In Tariki's place, the Crown Prince installed the "moderate and suave" Ahmed Zaki Yamani. Yamani, a 32-year-old lawyer from Mecca, had been an oil advisor to the Saudi government for four years.[43] Yamani proved to be the opposite of Tariki—loyal, respectful, and congenial. He served as minister of petroleum for twenty-six years. Ironically, it would be Yamani who eventually engineered the Saudi'ization of Aramco, but he did it in the way of *al Saud*, not the way of Nasser and Mossadeq or Tariki.

◆

Despite the political turmoil in *al Saud*, Aramco continued to grow throughout the 1960s, and, along with it, the kingdom's economy grew. The 1960s were a crucial period for Aramco in terms of oil development. The price of oil in the 1960s was relatively low and stable, but Aramco, under the leadership of CEO Tom Barger, made several important discoveries in Saudi Arabia. Between 1963 and 1965, Aramco geologists discovered major offshore oil fields and an onshore oil field that ran into the Persian Gulf. Three more offshore oil fields were discovered in 1967, as well. The most important discovery, however, came in 1968, when Aramco finally struck oil in Saudi Arabia's empty quarter, the Rub al'Khali.[44]

Tom Barger and other Aramco geologists had been among the first Americans to explore the region for oil in 1938. Though unsuccessful in their quest in the 1930s, in 1968, Aramco used more advanced methods to locate a massive oil field in an area largely untouched by humans. At the time, the costs were too high to justify developing it, but Aramco determined that the field held over fourteen billion barrels of oil and at least twenty-five trillion cubic feet of natural gas.[45] These discoveries, along with their sensible and well-timed exploitation, set the stage for even greater Aramco success and the profit and power it would bring to the royal family.

◆

After Saud returned to the kingdom, the conflict between the king and the Crown Prince became publicly apparent. Saud was having difficulty dealing with the reality that he was king in name only. He often spent months away from Saudi Arabia seeking medical treatment for his myriad illnesses. During these absences, Feisal would not even bother seeking Saud's approval on major state decisions. Upon returning, Saud would openly express resentment when he witnessed Feisal exercising the king's executive power in his place. Feisal, in turn, resented Saud for continuing to cling to the authority he had failed to use wisely. This led to fights in which Saud would "demand the restoration of his full powers," and Feisal would answer by threatening to resign.[46] This internal strife reflected poorly on Saudi Arabia's image and was exactly what Abdul Aziz had sought to avoid.

In 1963, Mohammad, the next most senior prince after Feisal, tried to mediate between his two older brothers. He arranged for Feisal to receive Saud at the former's home in Taif, the mountainous area near the western coast where the royal family traditionally spent summers. Mohammad accompanied Saud and observed while one of Feisal's sons brought the two brothers coffee. According to the account of Feisal's son, Feisal showed extreme deference to his brother, the king, throughout the entire encounter. Feisal sat on the floor below Saud and kissed his hand, but when Saud demanded Feisal yield control of state affairs back to the king, Feisal quietly refused.[47]

Feisal justified refusing the king for the good of the country, but altruism was not his sole motivation. Feisal, for all his religious devotion, was at heart an ambitious man. At this point, he had all of the evidence he needed to show that his policies were better for the kingdom and for the family. Feisal's usually generous patience had worn thin, as had most of the respect he still had for his brother. If Feisal continued to respect Saud, it was because he was the oldest living son of their father.

Feisal's oldest son explained his father's mind-set with the following story. His father had once told him, "If my brother Saud ordered me to kill you, I would catch hold of you, take you to the steps of his palace, and sacrifice you there for him to see."[48] At that point, Feisal's own allegiance to the office of the king had become the greatest obstacle the brothers faced in putting their own house in order. It was clear that Feisal would neither yield authority to Saud nor directly challenge his brother. It was also clear that for the good of the country and the family, the situation could not continue.

In September 1963, some members of *al Saud* attempted to forestall a confrontation between the king and the Crown Prince. Saud was recuperating in Vienna after having surgery on his stomach. Fearing the inevitable clash when the king returned home and again challenged Feisal, several of the brothers went to visit him at his hospital bed in Europe. They told their king that he had to promise to stop meddling in government affairs when he returned. He had to commit, in writing, not to overspend his allowance and to stop challenging Feisal's decisions. The brothers were clearly surprised when Saud consented and signed the document to that effect.[49]

◆

To the brothers' chagrin, Saud immediately disregarded his promise when he returned to Saudi Arabia. He refused to sign Feisal's budget for the coming year. Feisal reacted by taking the budget straight to the Council of Ministers and winning approval for it there. Saud's reaction to Feisal's defiance was to leave Riyadh for a cross-country trip that was essentially a way for him to rally support from his tribal base. This plan was to culminate in a return to Riyadh with a swell of popularity, which, Saud must have thought, would make it impossible for his brothers to refuse his return to executive authority. This move—taking his case directly to the people in contravention of his brothers—was too much for the brothers to ignore. Never before had any son of Abdul Aziz looked outside of *al Saud* for political support or involved non–family members in internal family disputes. In response to this action, Feisal, with the full support of his brothers, ordered the celebration Saud had arranged for his arrival in Jeddah to be significantly minimized.

When the red carpet was pulled out from under his feet, Saud abandoned his plans and returned to Riyadh. The incident was demoralizing for a man who thrived on the adoration of his people, but Saud was not ready to give in yet. He returned to his palace in the capital and refused all visitors. He ordered fifteen hundred (though some sources say eight hundred) soldiers from the Royal Guard to patrol the walls and guard the palace doors.[50] The presence of men with machine guns on the ramparts was obvious to everyone who drove by. Though Saud might have assigned the guards as a defensive move to protect himself and what was his, the brothers, in particular Sultan and Abdullah (head of the Saudi National Guard), considered this move a threat against the rest of the family. They moved to put the army and the National Guard on alert. Ultimately, Saud failed to make any additional military moves, and his intentions remained a mystery. Anxiety lingered in Riyadh throughout the winter of 1963.

Feisal, on the other hand, continued with business as usual. He maintained his strict work routine, despite the fact that the king had barricaded himself inside his palace and surrounded himself with armed soldiers. As it happened, Feisal rode past this scene each day on his way to carry out his duties. The tension between Saud and the rest of Abdul Aziz's sons rose until, one day, Feisal had his driver stop in front of Saud's palace walls. Feisal got out of the car and approached one of the soldiers. He asked the man, who had been standing outside in the heat with a heavy weapon for some time, if he and his fellow soldiers had received sufficient refreshment. Without waiting for an answer, the Crown Prince told the guards that he would arrange to send over more coffee, then returned to his car.[51]

The move was brilliant. Every day thereafter, when Feisal rode by Saud's palace, the guards stationed on the walls and out front saluted the Crown Prince in his car. Saud grew more furious and reacted with what amounted to a declaration of war. He sent a letter to Feisal that read, "When my enemy has his hands around my neck, I strike at him with all my strength." It is not known how Feisal reacted to this letter, but their brother Mohammad was incensed. Already known as somewhat of a loose cannon, Mohammad immediately went to confront the king. According to family lore, Mohammad threw the letter at Saud and admonished him to "never do anything like this to us again!"[52]

Mohammad deeply objected to Saud's decision to divide the family by sending this letter. Later, when Mohammad was asked about his actions that day, he explained that he had reacted less out of support for Feisal and more out of disgust at Saud's pathetic attempt to sow discord in the family for his own pride. Solidarity within *al Saud*, in Mohammad's conviction, was the top priority, and Saud's threat, as empty as it likely was, evidenced the king's lack of respect for family unity.[53]

Exactly what went on internally within the family between 1963 and 1964 is difficult to piece together because those involved went to great lengths to avoid speaking about it. Eventually, it seems, Saud came out of his palace, and it was decided that he would represent Saudi Arabia at the upcoming Arab League summit. The hope was that this would provide Saud with a means to save face externally, although internally he remained powerless.[54] The maneuver, however, did not work as intended. Saud returned from the summit puffed up with self-importance and demanded the restoration of his full powers. At that point, both Mohammad and

Abdullah wanted to use the National Guard to overthrow Saud. Feisal still counseled restraint.[55]

Instead of relying on force, Feisal looked to religion. In a country with no constitution other than God's word, the *ulama*, or established Islamic clerics, provided legitimacy to the political system. Feisal and the now united sons of Abdul Aziz (which again included Talal, who had by then returned from exile in Egypt and made amends with Feisal) asked the *ulama* to issue a *fatwa*, or statement of religious adjudication. The *ulama*, at this point, were squarely in Feisal's court. According to their interpretation of Islamic legal tradition, Saud had willingly turned over his authority as chief executive to Feisal. The clerics did not consider a demand from Saud to be a reasonable justification to overturn this.[56]

◆

Mohammad took the first step toward removing Saud once and for all. He marshaled support for a motion that would forever strip Saud of any claim to executive authority. His plan called for Saud to be permanently reduced to a ceremonial monarch, while Feisal would govern. Mohammad's uncles—the brothers of Abdul Aziz—brought the proposal to the *ulama*. The majority of the clerics agreed with the brothers and issued a proclamation formally demoting Saud on March 29, 1964. Their ruling made it clear that Feisal would never again need Saud's consent for any state matter.[57]

The day after the *ulama* issued their *fatwa*, the members of *al Saud* closed ranks around Feisal. They gathered at Mohammad's home, described as a palace of white stone in the southwest section of Riyadh. Abdul Aziz's extensive progeny—his sons, their sons, and even various cousins—arrived in a long procession of cars. Seventy princes assembled that day, along with some of Abdul Aziz's closest tribal allies. The formality of this meeting, which differed from the regular and frequent meetings and councils in which various members of *al Saud* gathered to discuss policy and matters of state, was reflected in the name the brothers gave the gathering—The Council of Those Who Bind and Loose.[58]

The practice was traced to an Islamic tradition from the time of the first caliphs in the 7th century and reflected the concept that a gathering of the elite leaders in society possessed the authority to make important political decisions for the *umma* (Islamic community) because of the number of individuals assembled and their roles as leaders. Such an assembly was not designed for regular governance but for extraordinary measures such as installing a new political leader.[59] The council issued its decision to permanently remove Saud from all official duties on March 30, 1964. Immediately, tribesmen from across the peninsula began the journey to Riyadh to pledge *bayah*, or loyalty, to Feisal.

Saud observed these events and saw the last vestiges of his dignity stolen from him by his own kin. There was nothing in Arabian tradition for him to look toward to heal his wounded pride, as there had never been a ceremonial head of state in Bedouin political culture. After several months of enduring the humiliation of his usurped authority, Saud brought his case before the *ulama* and his own family. He appealed their decision on the basis that Arabian tradition had never before had a king who reigned with no power. The Islamic scholars agreed with him, as did the sons of Abdul Aziz. This time they formally deposed him. Saud, their reasoning went, had proven incapable of governing wisely or of exercising restraint.

Several senior princes, including Mohammad and his full brother and the fourth most senior prince, Khaled, met with the *ulama* in Riyadh. All present agreed that the only course of action was to inform Saud that he had to abdicate. Feisal took no part in any of these discussions. The *ulama* were prepared at that point to declare Feisal the king, so a small delegation of princes and clerics was dispatched to inform Feisal. They reached Feisal at his desert retreat outside of Riyadh just as the call for the evening prayer commenced. The group knelt together in prayer as the sun set over the courtyard. After the prayers, his brothers revealed the *ulama*'s decision to Feisal, who immediately questioned the necessity of this drastic move. He feared irreparable damage to the family if Saud did not go quietly. He wanted to know how they planned to convince Saud to acquiesce.

Feisal's skepticism was correct. Saud would not accept his fate easily. Several of the *ulama* tried for three days to convince Saud to step down, but the king, who remained ensconced in his palace, steadfastly refused to speak with them. Finally, when it appeared as though the brothers might have to call in the National Guard to forcefully remove him, Mohammad went to his brother's palace one last time. No one knows what he said to Saud, but when it was over, Saud bin Abdul Aziz left his palace and his title behind. He went straight to the airport in Riyadh, where he found all of the sons of Abdul Aziz waiting for him. They respectfully said their good-byes. Feisal lingered toward the end and kissed his brother's hand—eyes cast downward in respect the entire time. The two said nothing to each other.

After a brief consultation with his doctors at the Aramco hospital in Dhahran, Saud left behind his brothers and his throne. The oldest son of Abdul Aziz lived the rest of his life in exile, along with his sons and immediate family. Five years later, in 1969, he died at his home in Athens, Greece.[60] Following his death, Saud's body was brought back to Saudi Arabia, and Feisal had him buried near their father, Abdul Aziz. Feisal stood respectfully at the graveside and recited verses from the Koran until Saud's body was interred, but after the funeral Feisal tried—and failed—to convince the family to disinherit Saud's sons.[61]

◆

The smooth transfer of power from one leader to the next is one of the greatest challenges to a political system. In modern democracies, the procedures for how power changes hands are often delineated in constitutions and happen at regular intervals. In more authoritarian political systems, the processes are less standardized, happen more infrequently and with greater tension. Even in monarchies, in which succession is tied to the ruler's bloodline, the process is not necessarily as simple as it might appear.

Even in the heyday of the Islamic empires of the Middle East, succession was not standardized and varied greatly across cultures and traditions. In the Umayyad Dynasty, an Islamic caliphate that reigned in the 7th and 8th centuries from Damascus, oldest sons tended to succeed their fathers by birthright. The Turko-Mongols who swept through the Middle East in the 13th century, however, practiced a form of collective sovereignty in which territory was often divided between multiple heirs.

In the Ottoman Empire, which ruled the Middle East from the 14th through the beginning of the 20th century, the sultanate recognized only one legitimate successor, but it was not always clear who that would be. Some sultans, upon assuming the throne, executed all of their brothers in order to ensure that they would face no challenges during their rule. During the 15th and 16th centuries, Ottoman tradition considered each son of the sultan, no matter who his mother was, to have "the dynastic sovereign gene." After the sultan died, his sons would wage a battle for succession, each usually from his own provincial seat of power. Sometimes the previous sultan made his preferences known while he was still alive to quell potential infighting. Sometimes he did not, and the contest for the throne between his sons could go on for some time. This fight for the throne pitted the sons against one another, as they relied on their military strength, political maneuvering, and deceitful scheming. They battled to reach the capital and see who could grab and hold on to their father's throne first. Often, the victor would then execute his remaining brothers.[62]

In 1965, the Saudi monarchy was still new. No formalized method of succession had been instituted. The uncertainty, political machinations, and violence of the early-modern Ottoman Empire were exactly what *al Saud* wanted to avoid. Public displays of internal division and strife, such as Saud's actions, could irreparably damage the family's ability to rule. Rivalries between brothers would split the population and threaten the prosperity that Abdul

Aziz had brought to a unified Saudi Arabia. The ten-year power struggle between Saud and Feisal might have appeared tame in comparison to those of the early-modern Ottoman Empire, but even the appearance of instability was something the ruling family wanted to avoid at all costs.

Al Saud came to realize that the line of succession needed to be settled far in advance of a monarch's ultimate passing. The family also needed a system to ensure that a prince with Saud's failings could not rise to become king. If the king of Saudi Arabia was to rule as chief executive, then the family needed a method to guarantee that future kings would have *al Saud*'s best interests and long-term objectives at heart. The kingship was not a birthright. It was an obligation and a responsibility to the long-term profit and power of the family.

The solution they devised drew, not surprisingly, on the pre-modern traditions of the Arabian desert. In previous times, leadership of the Bedouin tribe was not automatically conferred to the son of a previous leader. Ability, temperament, bases of power within tribal factions, and seniority all played significant roles in the decision-making process. In 1965, *al Saud* adopted a similar process. Feisal officially assumed the throne in November 1964, but the Crown Prince and heir apparent was not announced until March 1965.

Many expected Abdul Aziz's third son, Mohammad, to become Crown Prince. Mohammad's seniority, as well as his influential role in Saud's bloodless removal, made him a natural choice.[63] Mohammad was ambitious, intelligent, and only fifty-four years old at the time. He had played a leading role in assembling the coalition of brothers and Islamic clerics needed to oust Saud, not to mention convincing his brother to go peacefully.[64]

Mohammad was wild—a quality that Abdul Aziz had harnessed in his son's youth by sending him with Feisal to put down a dangerous rebellion of the legendary *Ikhwan* fighters. The violent uprising had been resolved, but Mohammad's fiery temperament had not cooled in the intervening years. Though loyal to the family

King Abdul Aziz ibn Saud. *Copyright © Saudi Aramco Archives/Saudi Aramco World/SAWDIA.*

ABOVE: Harry St. John Bridger Philby, advisor to King Abdul Aziz, interpreter, and adventurer. *Copyright © Saudi Aramco Archives/Saudi Aramco World/SAWDIA.* BELOW: Saudi finance minister Abdullah Sulaiman and Socal representative Lloyd Hamilton signing the original oil concession agreement in 1933. *Copyright © Saudi Aramco.*

ABOVE: Dammam Wells No. 1, foreground, and No. 7. in 1937. This is before Well No. 7 became productive. *Copyright © Saudi Aramco.* BELOW: Oil well in Dhahran in 1938 or 1939. *Copyright © Nestor Sander Collection/Saudi Aramco World/SAWDIA.*

Traditional latticed balconies in Jeddah on the Red Sea coast. For decades, Jeddah was the only city where westerners lived outside of Aramco facilities. *Copyright © Khalil Abou El-Nasr/Saudi Aramco World/SAWDIA.*

ABOVE: Aramco Administration Building, Dhahran 1949. BELOW: International Bechtel Inc. paving a runway for the new Jeddah airport, 1949. *Both images copyright © C. Stribling Snodgrass Papers, American Heritage Center, University of Wyoming.*

ABOVE: View of Riyadh in 1949 and the Masmak Fort. *Copyright © T. F. Walters/Saudi Aramco Archives/Saudi Aramco World/SAWDIA.* BELOW: View of Tapline in 1967, the pipeline built by International Bechtel Inc. that carried Saudi oil to the Mediterranean Sea. *Copyright © Saudi Aramco World/SAWDIA.*

The Aramco board posing in front of Dammam Well No. 7 in 1962. Zaki Yamani is fouth from left, Tom Barger in sixth from right, and Hafiz Wabha is fourth from right. *Copyright © Saudi Aramco.*

LEFT: Aramco offshore operations in 1967. Copyright © Tor Eigeland/Saudi Aramco World/SAWDIA.
BELOW: Portrait of King Feisal. Copyright © Dick Massey/Saudi Aramco World/SAWDIA.

Inside the Grand Mosque in Mecca during the Hajj pilgrimage in 1974. *Copyright © S. M. Amin/Saudi Aramco World/SAWDIA.*

ABOVE: Tankers receiving Aramco oil in the Persian Gulf to be shipped globally in 1975. *Copyright © Tor Eigeland/Saudi Aramco World/SAWDIA.* BELOW: Barrels of Aramco crude oil wait in Galveston, Texas, in 1977. *Copyright © Katrina Thomas/Saudi Aramco World/ SAWDIA.*

ABOVE: Students at the King Fahd College of Petroleum and Minerals in Dhahran in 1980. *Copyright © B. H. Moody/Saudi Aramco World/SAWDIA.* BELOW: Jubail petrochemicals facility in 1982. *Copyright © Saudi Aramco World/SAWDIA.*

ABOVE: Abqaiq oil gas seperation plant in 1984. *Copyright © Saudi Aramco World/SAWDIA.*
BELOW: King Fahd in 1990. *Copyright © Michael Isaac/Saudi Aramco World/SAWDIA.*

ABOVE: Aftermath of Saddam Hussein's intentional oil spill in the Persian Gulf. *Copyright © Ron Johnson/Saudi Aramco World/SAWDIA*. BELOW: Environmental protection team repositioning booms to clean up the oil spill in the aftermath of the Gulf War. *Copyright © Abdulla Y. Al-Dobais/Saudi Aramco World/SAWDIA*.

ABOVE: Renovated Masmak Fort in the midst of modern Riyadh, 1999. *Copyright © Abdulla Y. Al-Dobais/Saudi Aramco World/SAWDIA.* BELOW LEFT: Khalid al Falih, then Saudi Aramco CEO, with Zaki Safar, a young engineer. *Copyright © Zaki Safar.* BELOW RIGHT: Guard outside OPEC headquarters in Vienna, Austria, in November 2016. Security has been a priority since Carlos the Jackal attacked OPEC in 1975. *Copyright © Ellen R. Wald.*

ABOVE: Reporters surround Saudi oil minister Khalid al Falih at the November 2016, OPEC meeting in Vienna, Austria. BELOW: The site of Aramco's first producing well, Dammam Well No. 7, was preserved on the Aramco campus. *Both images copyright © Ellen R. Wald.*

ABOVE: Shaybah crude oil facility in Saudi Arabia's Empty Quarter in 2003. BELOW: Reservoir modeling for the Shaybah oil facility. *Both images copyright © Saudi Aramco.*

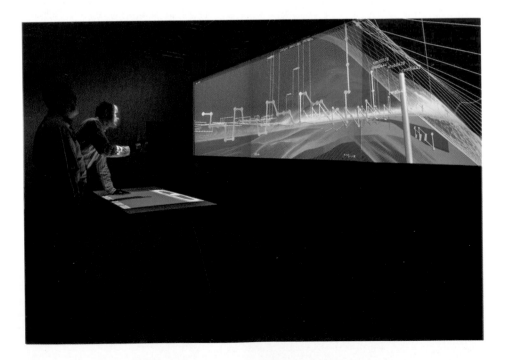

and honorable to the core, he angered easily and either could not or did not wish to control his temper. This had earned him the nickname Abu Sharayn, which is translated as "father of the two evils." The two evils in question referred to his riotous rages and his inclination to drink alcohol—the former amplified when he engaged in the latter.[65] Mohammad's personal life was also problematic for a most public position. The prince frequently traveled to Beirut for rowdy, weekend-long parties that even he admitted were not appropriate for a monarch.[66]

Some in the family wanted Fahd, Abdul Aziz's seventh son, to become Crown Prince. Fahd was also the son of Abdul Aziz's popular and influential wife Hassa Sudairi. The Sudairi family hailed from a prominent *Nejdi* tribe with which *al Saud* had a long history of alliances. Elevating Fahd to Crown Prince, however, would have meant skipping over his more senior half brothers Khaled, Nasser, and Saad. Fahd had shown himself to be intelligent, capable, and ambitious. At the insistence of his ambitious mother, he had served on the royal advisory committee from a young age, and, in 1962, he had assumed the important post of interior minister. Some in the family, however, were wary of his methods. Fahd tended to rely mostly on his own judgment when making decisions and rarely sought the counsel of other family members. His tendency to isolate himself concerned them.[67]

Hassa Sudairi bore eight sons for Abdul Aziz. The first, Saad, died when he was still a child. Three years later, in 1922, Fahd was born. He was followed by six brothers, the last of whom, Ahmad, was born in the early 1940s. Just as Hassa did with Fahd, she ensured that her other sons also took prominent and powerful positions in the government to establish their experience and strength at a young age. Her surviving sons would come to be known as the Sudairi Seven, and the combination of their political influence and numbers would lead observers over the years to assume that the other brothers were wary.

The consensus within *al Saud* was that Mohammad, despite his leadership capabilities, should not become king.[68] Bowing to the wishes of the collective, and ever loyal, Abu Sharayn stepped aside, later admitting that he would probably not have made a good king. Fahd, though promising, had significant critics. In fact, Mohammad refused to step aside unless it was guaranteed that Fahd would not be vaulted ahead of other brothers in the line of succession.[69]

Instead, *al Saud* chose Mohammad's younger brother Khaled as Crown Prince and next in line for the throne of Saudi Arabia. Khaled was a candidate everyone could agree on. He might not have been everyone's favorite, but eventually he became the consensus choice and would help heal family divisions from years of discord. Khaled was Mohammad's full younger brother by two years. He had built a reputation as a pious peacemaker, but he had little desire to rule. He admitted to preferring the simplicity of desert life and his hobby, falconry, to the politics of the palace.

Abdul Aziz had recognized Khaled's talent for conflict resolution and had dispatched him in 1935 to negotiate a settlement with Yemen. As foreign minister, Feisal had continued to rely on Khaled's skills and had frequently brought his brother along on international trips. Despite his talents, Khaled lacked the force of personality that Feisal and Mohammad evinced.[70] Khaled refused Feisal's offer of the Crown Prince position several times before family pressure finally wore him down. *Al Saud* needed a peacemaker. Once Khaled became Crown Prince, he spent many long hours overseeing the family *majlis*, where he listened to disputes and adjudicated them in Feisal's stead. Khaled disliked the demands of his position and, on more than one occasion, asked Feisal to relieve him of his duties and remove him from the line of succession. However, he was convinced to continue when confronted with the reality that his presence kept peace between the ambitions of Mohammad, on the one hand, and those of Fahd, on the other.[71]

By 1965, *al Saud* had worked out a system of governance in which sovereignty would be passed not through primogeniture but instead through a system reminiscent of that used by the ancient Arabian tribes. The brothers would gather and decide through consensus who would best further the family's long-term objectives as king and which government positions the other brothers should assume. Royal succession would not be based on seniority alone. Rather, *al Saud* would determine succession with significant weight placed on ability, talent, and experience, in addition to seniority. Consensus and harmony among brothers also became priorities. After the very public fights between Feisal and Saud, the family sought to conceal any future infighting from the public eye. The appearance of unity and consensus, *al Saud* learned, was a powerful tool in projecting stability and power. Key family members with the potential to create fissures might be plied with gifts of money or land to harmoniously accept the decisions of the majority.

It was accepted that Abdul Aziz's throne would be passed from brother to brother and stay among the sons of the founding king. Additionally, *al Saud* used the role of Crown Prince, and eventually Deputy Crown Prince, to establish a line of succession in advance and avoid future conflict and tension upon a king's death. More than just next in line, the Crown Prince position developed into an important locus of power within the Saudi government. In many cases, the Crown Prince functioned as a counterpoint to the king, ensuring that different bases of power were represented.

This method, which resembled the boardroom of a business more than a European-style monarchy or a modern democracy, ensured the continuation of agreed-upon principles and goals, no matter who ruled. Fifty years of relative political stability for the family followed the difficulties of Saud's reign. This is not to say that *al Saud* was always in agreement on policy or on succession. Indeed, lingering concerns threatened to interfere with *al Saud*'s stability, wealth, and power. The family would have to accommodate the many surviving sons of Abdul Aziz who would be excluded from the line of succession. Eventually, the family would have to determine how the line of succession would transition from Abdul Aziz's sons to the next generation of rulers.

SEVEN

WAHHABISM, WOMEN, WESTERNERS, AND RIYALS

B y 1965, Riyadh looked more like downtown Miami than the Saudi stronghold that Harry St. John Philby described in 1922. Philby wrote about the "clay towers of the Wahhabi capital," which "showed dimly through a screen of palms."[1] Even in 1943, when a *Life* magazine photographer visited King Abdul Aziz for a feature on his kingdom, Riyadh still looked much as it had when the king conquered it in 1902. A rare photograph of the Riyadh city marketplace reveals an unpaved, dusty square with crowds of robed men milling in front of squat, mud-walled buildings. The caption reads, "Main street Riad. This is the city marketplace, and on the lamppost in background the heads of beheaded criminals are suspended for some days as an example. The beheading would take place here too. Photographer Landry got permission from the King to photograph the streets of Riad [for] only one day at 5:30, [and he] was not allowed to get out of the car for fear Wahhabis might assault him."[2]

Pictures of the capital in 1965 show short palm trees lining a newly paved boulevard flanked on either side by large buildings built in the brutalist style and painted white or yellow. The street is filled with period cars in red, turquoise blue, and various shades of white. Riyadh in 1965 was a modern—if poorly planned—city. The city's population growth also attested to the massive physical changes in Saudi Arabia during the second half of the 20th century. In 1944, Riyadh had a population of approximately 50,000. In 1952, that number had increased to 80,000. By 1965, the population was estimated at an astounding 225,000. Less than ten years later, in 1972, that number had doubled. Nearly half a million individuals called the city their home.[3]

This kind of population growth and concentration in urban areas resembles the population shift that occurred in Britain and the United States during the Industrial Revolution. In Saudi Arabia, however, the changes were based on an influx of wealth from oil, not job opportunities from manufacturing. As people settled in cities, whether inland in Riyadh, in Jeddah on the western coast, or in one of the newer industrial cities built for the oil industry, life became more cosmopolitan. By the early 1980s, in fact, Saudi Arabia had become one of the most urbanized countries in the Middle East.[4] New infrastructure, technology, and travel all contributed to a current of social modernization running through Saudi Arabia in the 1960s and 1970s.

When the oilmen first came to Saudi Arabia, Abdul Aziz did his best to separate the Westerners from his traditional people. He and the religious *ulama* who ruled the social sphere did not want Western culture to change the Arabian way of life or to interfere with the control wielded by the monarch and the *ulama*. Separation proved untenable, because even with limited physical contact, modernity reached the Saudi people. Oilmen, global business,

Western educations, and new communication technologies were vital to *al Saud*'s reach for more profit, but they also brought modernizing social influences. Abdul Aziz's sons came to see a connection to, and partnership with, traditional forces in Arabia as essential to maintaining power, a strategy that would be enforced when emergency struck the country at the heart of its religious heritage. Tension between modernity and tradition—between profit and power—would become inevitable.

◆

Saudi Arabia, particularly the interior of the country where *al Saud* originated, maintained a largely traditional, pastoral, and religious culture even through the 1940s. Political order was maintained through a tribal system, in which individuals, families, and clans all belonged to a larger tribal unit that governed relations with other tribes and adjudicated problems through violent or nonviolent means. There is a common misperception that only nomadic Bedouins organized themselves according to tribe and subtribe. In fact, tribal lineage played an important role in both Bedouin and settled lifestyles in Arabia. The Saudi royal family hails from one of the seven largest tribes, the *Anaza*, but there are at least twenty-five tribes of note in the region, some of which stretch in geographical reach as far as northern Iraq and Syria.[5]

Both in and out of cities, Arabians raised livestock or worked in agriculture, fishing, pearl diving, marauding, or small-scale commercial activities. Such was the lifestyle through the first half of the 20th century. King Abdul Aziz considered powerful, nomadic, marauding tribesmen a threat to his rule. After subduing them militarily, he forced them to pledge permanent loyalty to him. They could fight only upon his order and against enemies he identified. In return, the king provided for their material well-being.[6] In many cases, he accomplished this by redistributing the tribal lands he had conquered back to the tribes, with the constant threat that the lands could be repossessed if the tribes challenged him. He also convinced many of the marauding tribes to settle in oasis villages and towns and accept an agricultural lifestyle. Periodically, in the early days of his rule, the king had to send his sons and their forces to quell an uprising, but most were satisfied with the exchange.

For Saudi Arabia and *al Saud*, the meeting of traditional life and modernity was not always easy to navigate. Four particular areas in which the tensions were most glaring, and in which the monarchy had to make difficult choices, were religion, education, women, and terrorism.

In addition to a pastoral lifestyle, the overriding component of premodern Arabian life was religion—particularly a brand of Sunni Islam called Wahhabism. Wahhabism originated in the 1700s in Abdul Aziz's native Nejd region. Wahhabism has often been described as a fundamentalist and puritanical form of Islamic practice. These portrayals are not necessarily false, but they do not entirely explain the movement's rationale. Mohammad ibn Abd al-Wahhab, the founder, lived during an overall period of "renewal and reform" in the Islamic world. Born at the turn of the 18th century to a family of great religious scholars and jurisprudents, Abd al-Wahhab was deeply disturbed by what he saw as a general decline in belief and practice among Muslims in his region. For Abd al-Wahhab, his coreligionists appeared to have abandoned the principle of *tawhid*, or monotheism. This included engaging in practices such as wearing charms to ward off evil spirits, praying at the tombs of important individuals, engaging in animism, and employing other superstitious practices.[7]

Abd al-Wahhab's style appeared drastic to other religious scholars at the time. He did not just recommend the destruction of tombs and monuments where Muslims flocked to pray; he actually toppled these monuments himself. However, his ideas appealed to a local political and tribal leader, Mohammad ibn Saud, particularly since Abd al-Wahhab seems to have assured the leader that if he promoted Wahhabi beliefs, God would favor his rule and that of his descendants. In 1744, Mohammad ibn Saud and Mohammad ibn

Abd al-Wahhab formalized their relationship in an alliance marked by each party swearing an oath of loyalty to the other.

Abd al-Wahhab exercised control over religious issues, while Ibn Saud led military and political activities. As Ibn Saud conquered more territory, Abd al-Wahhab expanded his area of religious influence and won more adherents to his approach.[8] The alliance was so successful that Ibn Saud conquered most of the peninsula and established the short-lived first Saudi state, with Abd al-Wahhab at his side. Through Abd al-Wahhab's alliance with Ibn Saud, his brand of religious practice and thought, with its strict adherence to the written words of the Koran and *hadiths* (saying or action attributed to the Muslim prophet Mohammad), penetrated most of what would, in less than two hundred years, become the modern Kingdom of Saudi Arabia.

When Abdul Aziz spread his rule throughout Arabia in the first half of the 20th century, he too made a bargain with religious leaders. Wahhabi practices had always remained strong in the Nejd region of the country, and as Abdul Aziz moved westward he also used Islamic, and specifically Wahhabi, principles to legitimize his rule. In the Saudi kingdom, Abdul Aziz and his successors predicated their rule on the protection of Islamic values and practices. Abdul Aziz physically controlled the important Islamic cities of Mecca and Medina, along with the holy places within. He also made a bargain with the Wahhabi religious authorities that further solidified his legitimacy.

Like his ancestor before him, Abdul Aziz entered into a mutually beneficial relationship with the *ulama*. The religious authorities were co-opted into the state by placing them on the government payroll and giving them authority over judicial, social, and some educational matters. In this way, he kept the *ulama* out of the political, economic, foreign policy, and military spheres while simultaneously turning a potentially powerful enemy into an ally. The *ulama* benefitted financially from their incorporation into the state bureaucracy, and they recognized the right of *al Saud* to rule.[9] To a large extent, the *ulama* were given authority over certain policy areas, including the judicial, social, and educational. However, while *al Saud* often consulted with the *ulama*, the king and his subordinates were always the ultimate arbiters of all other policy. The *ulama* at times publicly questioned the Islamic legitimacy of certain policies set by *al Saud*, and did so on issues ranging from television to the education of girls, but they never acted in contravention of royal decrees.[10]

The US ambassador to Saudi Arabia from 2009 to 2013, James B. Smith, commented on the relationship between *al Saud* and the Wahhabi clerical establishment. "If you go back to the original agreement between *al Saud* and Mohammad ibn Abd al-Wahhab, *al Saud* runs the government, the [clerics] run the religion. So, these guys deal with the laws of God and these guys deal with the laws of man. And they always support each other. That's the agreement."[11]

At a basic level, the Saudi royal family supported the Wahhabi religious traditions and practices because the family members themselves were religious men. By all accounts, Abdul Aziz was deeply devout and adhered to the principles and practices of his religion throughout his life. Feisal and Khaled, the third and fourth kings, were both known as deeply religious men who prioritized the beliefs and practices of Wahhabi Islam. Khaled, it is said, routinely consulted a small, pocket-sized Koran that he kept in his *thobe* throughout his daily duties as king.[12] Other brothers, such as Mohammad, who did not become king but held an important role as the most senior living brother for many years, and Fahd, who did become king, were more lax in their personal observance of Islamic precepts. Both Mohammad and Fahd are said to have gambled, frequented nightclubs, and hosted extravagant parties when abroad. However, in their public roles within the family and as ministers of the Saudi state, they adhered to the principles and tenets of their father's faith. When Fahd became Crown Prince he stopped gambling, and when he became king he stopped visiting his massive palace in Marbella, Spain, where he and his guests reportedly used to funnel "$10 million per day to the resort's hedonistic economy."[13] *Al Saud*, as a collective, presented itself to the public as a family of devout believers regardless of what the kings and princes might have believed or practiced on an individual level.

Support for the religious authorities in Saudi Arabia was also an important strategy for *al Saud* to legitimize and maintain power. Active support and connection with the *ulama* played a key role in the regime of nearly every *al Saud* monarch. Abdul Aziz, of course, brokered the initial bargain with the *ulama* that legitimized his ascension on religious grounds. This bargain, in turn, was maintained and nurtured by Abdul Aziz's sons. The brothers never considered transitioning the throne from Saud to Feisal without a *fatwa* from the *ulama*. Khaled met with the state religious authorities every Tuesday of his reign, and Fahd, his successor, continued that tradition despite feeling hemmed in on some policy issues by the more conservative *ulama*.

Introducing new technologies into society also required approval and negotiation with the *ulama*. The debate over television in 1963 was particularly rancorous. In 1962, as Crown Prince, Feisal announced a development program for Saudi Arabia. One component was the introduction of television. From the start, the *ulama* opposed television on the grounds that it would bring "lewdness" into the home.[14] Feisal chose to bring television to Saudi society regardless of the objections of the *ulama*, but he made a bargain with them to secure their approval. Feisal granted the *ulama* ultimate authority to "monitor" the content of the programming and censor anything deemed inappropriate or contrary to Islamic beliefs and values.[15] The *ulama* censored romantic scenes from foreign films and even parts of animated Disney films where Mickey Mouse pecked Minnie on the cheek.[16]

Despite the careful censorship of television programming in the kingdom, Feisal's decision was challenged by one of *al Saud*'s own. Khaled bin Musaid, a prince and grandson of Abdul Aziz, participated along with a group of zealots in an ill-conceived campaign against television. Khaled bin Musaid had been deemed mentally ill and had received treatment at a facility in Vienna in 1961 and 1963. For years, however, he had fought against King Feisal's plan to bring television to the people of Saudi Arabia. Khaled bin Musaid considered the technology antithetical to Islamic values and spoke widely about it as "the work of the devil."[17] In 1966, he and other similarly minded believers attacked a television station, aiming to destroy the antenna. The group was captured by the police, and authorities shot and killed Khaled bin Musaid as he reached for a gun.[18] Broadcasting content continued to be subject to approval by the *ulama*, although in later years satellite dishes enabled Saudis to access Arabic and foreign-language television programming from stations not subject to content approval by religious authorities. In this and other ways, *al Saud* continued the bargain the patriarch made with the *ulama*. The brothers used the *ulama* as a source of legitimacy, but in return they also ceded to the religious leaders control over certain aspects of Saudi life and society.

The *ulama* were afforded a unique privilege in a monarchy: they were permitted open criticism and stances in contravention of government policies. However, the *ulama* never were allowed to engage in sedition. The *ulama* early on took the position that criticism of the established government and opposition to its rule "was a cardinal sin."[19]

In 1979, while Saudi Arabia was in the midst of a process of liberalization, a group of religious fanatics seized the Grand Mosque in Mecca. The Masjid al-Haram houses the *kaaba*, considered the holiest site for Muslims. This incident was a national trauma and transformative for *al Saud*, who reacted to it with an increased religious traditionalism enforced by the government and spearheaded by the *ulama*. Ambassador Smith credited a clear transformation to what occurred in 1979. "Saudi Arabia started going ultraconservative after the takeover of the Holy Mosque."[20]

The seizure of the Grand Mosque was planned and orchestrated by a Saudi man named Juhayman al-Utaybi. Juhayman, whose name meant "scowler," came from a family steeped in antagonism for *al Saud*. His father had fought against *al Saud* in a 1929 uprising of *Ikhwan* forces. Although the Saudis put down the rebellion and killed many of the *Ikhwan*, Juhayman's father escaped and made a life for himself on the outskirts of Riyadh. Juhayman grew up to become a particularly skilled sharpshooter. After a stint in the National Guard, Juhayman moved to Medina in 1973, to be near the New Islamic University, though he never formally enrolled.

The dean of the university, a highly esteemed cleric named Sheikh Bin Baz, was known for his conservative speeches that castigated modern technologies, women newscasters, and visual venerations of the king in government offices.[21] Blind since his youth, Sheikh Bin Baz gained some infamy in the West when he issued a statement that supposedly declared the Earth was flat. In fact, he was cautioning Muslims to question claims without evidence, in this case the American claim to have landed on a moon that he, himself, could not see. However, in 1985, Sheikh Bin Baz eagerly listened to Prince Sultan bin Salman's account of his own travel to space. The prince served as payload engineer on a NASA mission aboard the space shuttle *Discovery*, and, after returning to Saudi Arabia, he described the appearance of the Earth from space for the blind sheikh. Though excited to hear about the mission and its technological marvels, Sheikh Bin Baz never issued any further rulings that would have put the controversy to rest.[22] Sheikh Bin Baz might not have seen a place for modernity and space technology in his own life, but it seemed he could reconcile with it and accommodate its presence.

Though Sheikh Bin Baz's commentary on social policy in Saudi Arabia seemed perilously close to criticism of the monarchy, *al Saud* was not alarmed by Sheikh Bin Baz's sermons. King Khaled, Crown Prince Fahd, and the other princes felt secure in their rule and in the balance of their bargain at that time. However, in the 1970s, Sheikh Bin Baz was deeply troubled by the creeping modernity he noticed in Saudi society. As dean of the New Islamic University in Medina, a position for which he received a government salary, Sheikh Bin Baz started a group called Dawa Salafiya al Muhtasiba, loosely translated as "Islamic outreach that follows the ways of the Prophet's companions, and that is carried out with charitable goals."[23] The group was essentially a missionary organization designed to send Islamic emissaries to the Saudi people to reinvigorate the Islamic precepts and Wahhabi beliefs that Bin Baz promoted. Juhayman was recruited for this group.

Juhayman listened to the *ulama* who opposed royal portraits, cinemas, magazine photographs of women, and television shows, but to him these formed an impetus to oppose the royal regime itself. In 1977, the clerics became aware of Juhayman's particular ideology and that he was attracting a following among "disaffected young students." They formally cut ties with him. Juhayman's anti-Saudi ideology only grew more radical after his connection with the *ulama* ended. He openly called the Saudis illegitimate rulers and called on his followers to oppose Saudi rule by, for example, destroying the national identification cards that the government required all Saudi citizens to carry.[24] To Juhayman, *al Saud* was an illegitimate ruling dynasty because it permitted violations of his own norms.

While recruiting followers at the Imam Muhammad ibn Saud Islamic University of Riyadh, Juhayman met a student in his early twenties who would become the center of his radical mission. Mohammad Abdullah al Qahtani grew up in a small, poor, Bedouin town in the southern part of the country. He had an unusual appearance for an Arabian—pale skin, straight hair, and light brown eyes. He was a precocious student of religion and distinguished himself by delivering sermons at a local mosque in the poor neighborhood of Riyadh.[25]

By 1978, Juhayman became obsessed with the idea of the *Mahdi*, a concept in Islamic tradition of a redeemer sent by God to bring "peace and justice" to earth. The concept is not directly mentioned in the Koran, but some *hadiths* contain specific qualifications and descriptions of the *Mahdi*, including his lineage, name, and looks. Mohammad Abdullah al Qahtani fit, or manipulated his heritage to fit, those descriptions.[26] Only a year later, in 1979, Juhayman and his followers had taken up semi-permanent residence at the Grand Mosque in Mecca. Juhayman began to prepare his followers for a fight against the Saudi regime that, he believed, should happen soon. He was convinced absolutely that Mohammad Abdullah al Qahtani was, in fact, the *Mahdi*. Juhayman even divorced his wife and married al Qahtani's sister in preparation so the two could be related.

Juhayman decided that just as Islamic year 1399 came to an end and year 1400 began in November 1979, he would stand in the Grand Mosque in Mecca and declare that al Qahtani was the *Mahdi*. On November 20, 1979, Juhayman and his followers smuggled themselves, along with weapons, ammunition, food, and other supplies, into the mosque. They hid inside the open-air pallets used to transport the dead. Just after the 5:18 A.M. call to prayer, they took over the PA system. Juhayman stood at the loudspeaker and declared to all of Mecca that Mohammad Abdullah al Qahtani was the *Mahdi*. At that point the rest of Juhayman's men, who were hidden among the throngs of worshippers, revealed their weapons and took control of the mosque, barricading themselves inside.[27]

Juhaymen sent snipers to the mosque's minarets and dispatched guards to patrol the walls. The news quickly reached King Khaled in Riyadh. Crown Prince Fahd was away, at an important Arab League summit with his nephew, Turki al-Feisal, head of the Saudi foreign intelligence agency. Turki immediately returned to the kingdom, where he joined Fahd's Sudairi brothers Sultan (defense minister), Nayef (interior minister), and Ahmad (deputy interior minister). As they discovered who had taken control of the Grand Mosque, the royal brothers were dismayed to learn that Juhayman and many of his cohort were known subversives. Not only did Sheikh Bin Baz—who, by 1979, had risen to become the Grand Mufti (chief cleric) of the Saudi *ulama*—know about Juhayman's dangerous ideology but the authorities had on several prior occasions arrested Juhayman and his followers, only to release them later.

Soon both the military and the National Guard surrounded the mosque, but they could not attack. Islamic tradition dictated that no weapons could be used, nor acts of violence perpetrated, in the Grand Mosque. Despite the fact that Juhayman and his followers had broken that proscription first, King Khaled and Princes Sultan, Nayef, and Turki would not send soldiers into the mosque without approval from the Saudi *ulama*. That permission was quickly granted in the form of an "emergency *fatwa*" that allowed *al Saud* to utilize "all necessary measures" to break the siege but still required the military to "protect the lives of Muslims inside the Mosque."[28]

At 3:30 A.M., on the day following Juhayman's attack, the Saudi government counterattacked the mosque. The military used shells designed to minimize structural damage. As the military attempted to break down one of the doors to the mosque, Juhayman's forces fired on the soldiers and killed many. The raid failed, and the military was forced to retreat and reconsider the strategy, given the extreme firepower Juhayman's group had demonstrated.[29] Three days in, on November 23, the *ulama* issued a second *fatwa*, which granted the government much broader powers to fight inside the mosque. The only condition was that the government had to first offer Juhayman and his followers the opportunity to surrender. The military broadcast this message from a truck that drove around and around the mosque for several hours. Not a single person surrendered.[30]

The second Saudi attack began the same day, with missiles shot at the minarets to kill the snipers. The military then used a motor-powered battering ram to enter the building. Fighting inside the mosque was intense. Even Juhayman's scholarly *"Mahdi"* entered the battle, picking up grenades launched by Saudi forces before they detonated and throwing them back at the military. This lasted until a grenade finally exploded in his face and killed him.

It took two days for Saudi forces to regain control of the aboveground portions of the Grand Mosque. Juhayman and what was left of his group moved underground, where they had stashed supplies in the prayer rooms and catacombs. After nearly two weeks, the Saudi military finally drilled holes in the ground and flooded the underground rooms with CS gas, a paralytic agent they had flown in from France. The Saudi troops descended into the basement areas wearing gas masks and arrested or killed the remainder of Juhayman's followers. None of them surrendered willingly. Juhayman himself was finally taken prisoner on December 4, 1979.[31]

Ultimately, the Saudi military suffered 588 casualties, with 127 dead. Of Juhayman's rebels, 117 were killed, while 12 innocent worshippers were killed as well. The 63 captured perpetrators, including Juhayman himself, were executed. The executions were held publicly in various cities across the kingdom to send a message. Prince Salman, who was governor of Riyadh in 1980 and would become king thirty-five years later, ensured that each execution in the capital was not only witnessed by the fellow tribesmen of the condemned but also carried out by one as well. The message was clear—these men were not heroes but traitors to the country and to the religion.[32] Tribalism was subservient to loyalty to *al Saud*.

After the punishments had been meted out, the king and other members of *al Saud* reviewed their kingdom's relationship with religion. Though Khaled had been meeting with the *ulama* every week, he still missed the religious groundswell that had resulted in Juhayman's radical movement. The *ulama* told Khaled that the cause of this violent episode lay in the proliferation of exactly the "un-Islamic practices" Juhayman had campaigned against before he became obsessed with notions of the *Mahdi* and a doomsday scenario. Crown Prince Fahd had been in the midst of pursuing a series of liberal reforms, but following the seizure, King Khaled became resolute with a new response. *Al Saud* would move toward religion.[33]

The changes were immediate and swift. The government prohibited magazines from printing photographs of women. The time allotted for Islamic studies in schools was increased, even in schools like the College of Petroleum and Minerals. Subjects like international relations and psychology were eliminated, pages with objectionable material were ripped out of college textbooks, and enforcement of social "morality" practices was noticeably increased. For example, even in Jeddah, the coastal city in which foreigners had always been permitted to live and in which men and women had always been permitted to mix in public, coffee shops were forced to place dividers to separate the sexes.[34]

Male guardianship laws, which had always been on the books, were suddenly enforced with surprising frequency. Saudi women, who had been accustomed to easily going out with their husbands, found themselves stymied by police if they did not have documentation proving, beyond a doubt, their relationship to the men they were with. In this post-Juhayman world, a woman had to carry her national identification card to prove that the man she was with at a hotel was her husband. Without appropriate documentation, both husband and wife could find themselves stuck in limbo at a police station for hours, a situation that not only inconvenienced many but also brought great embarrassment.[35] Flush with new funding from the government and broad discretionary powers from the *ulama*, the police and the *mutawa'a* (the morality police, or the Committee for the Promotion of Virtue and the Prevention of Vice) flexed their muscles.[36] Before Juhayman, the *mutawa'a* prowled the streets ensuring businesses closed during times of prayer. After Juhayman, the *mutawa'a* began corralling men into the mosque for prayer.[37]

The change in the social fabric of the country was noticeable, even to Westerners. Tim Barger, the son of the Aramco geologist and CEO Tom Barger, who was born and reared in Saudi Arabia and lived and worked there as an adult, recalled that "right before the siege [on the Grand Mosque] they were seriously talking about opening up bars in hotels. Everything was headed in a liberal direction." Afterwards, he said, "Everything made a big U-turn then, and the road to liberalism was closed."[38]

Though the particular events of late 1979 have been seen as a turning point toward conservatism, some observed that Saudi society had begun to gravitate toward greater religious influence in everyday life even before Juhayman's attack. Linda Porter, an American woman, described Saudi Arabia as a much freer place in the 1960s. She and her husband, Dr. J. Winston Porter, first moved to Saudi Arabia in 1964, when he accepted a job teaching chemistry at the new King Abdullah College for Petroleum and Minerals.

Linda Porter, who had a degree in public health and microbiology, worked in a laboratory at a hospital in nearby Dammam at the time. "In the 1960s, I covered my head. I had to wear a little white shawl and I wore a skirt," she recalled. The Porters moved back to the United States but returned to Saudi Arabia in 1974. They lived in al Khobar, a city close to Jubail, where her husband was the project manager for industrial facilities under construction. "Coming back in the 1970s," she said, "I covered myself from head to toe."[39]

Nevertheless, most evidence indicates that Saudi Arabia was seemingly on the path of general liberalization in the 1960s and 1970s until the Saudi monarchy made an abrupt change in the 1980s. Another reason to choose traditionalism could be found on the other side of the Persian Gulf, where the Iranian monarch had been deposed by crowds of angry Iranians shouting, "Death to America." The Iranian revolution had surprised much of the world in January and February 1979, only months before the seizure of the Grand Mosque. The shah was a cultivated, sophisticated monarch who had just shared a New Year's toast with President Jimmy Carter. Underneath Iran's veneer of European-style modernity, however, lay a population simmering with economic resentment, religious fervor, and fury at the injustices perpetrated by the shah's secret police against Communists and clerics alike. The Saudis watched as the shah and his family fled for the United States, and they saw a mass of students (black-robed women among them) storm the US embassy and take the Americans hostage. Much like the shah, *al Saud* owed a great deal to the Americans and Western influence.

Although the Saudi kings and princes had always displayed religious devotion that was surely lacking in the shah, they came to believe that they might have mistaken complacency for security. They had become flexible with certain Islamic traditions in favor of modernity. Following the Juhayman incident, many believed that King Khaled, known for his personal faith, was responsible for the "fundamentally religious" response. Crown Prince Fahd also believed it was necessary to increase Islamic strictures in society. Fahd worried that he might be "on the wrong side of the mosque," as the shah of Iran had been. "He could not," said Adnan Khashoggi, the billionaire arms dealer and Fahd's close friend, "get over what had happened to the Shah."[40] The responses to the seizure of the Grand Mosque, particularly in light of the Iranian revolution, were remarkable because they shifted the balance between modernity and traditionalism, between profit and power.

◆

Alongside the turn to religious orthodoxy, Saudi society did continue its path toward modernization in other areas. The massive growth in education speaks to this. In 1960, Saudi Arabia did not have compulsory education, and only 12 percent of Saudi youth were enrolled in primary school.[41] By 1986, that number had grown to 52 percent.[42] In 2007, with school attendance compulsory, almost 95% of primary age children were enrolled in school. Even though Saudi law only required students to attend up to age fourteen, the number of children attending secondary school grew as well. In 1970, only about 15,000 Saudis were enrolled in secondary education. By 1980 that number had increased to 100,000 pupils, and as of 2007, 90 percent of secondary age children were enrolled in school.[43]

In 1974, only 4.1 percent of 20- to 24-year-olds in Saudi Arabia (men and women) were enrolled in institutions of higher education. By 1986, that number increased to almost 14 percent.[44] Almost two decades later, however, that number had barely doubled.[45] For twenty-five years following the seizure of the Grand Mosque, foreign study (which once had been encouraged by the kingdom and enjoyed by princes as well as promising citizens) was barely supported. Finally, in 2005, King Abdullah established a scholarship under his name to promote higher education. This program awarded full scholarships, along with travel and living expenses, to any Saudi student pursing higher education outside the country. The program proved extremely popular, and by 2014, almost 200,000 Saudi students were attending American universities at the undergraduate and graduate level.[46] Increased funding for higher education within the kingdom also helped send more students to colleges and universities in Saudi Arabia—for both Islamic and secular educations. In 2015, Saudi Arabia reported that 63 percent of 20- to 24-year-old youth were enrolled in higher education.[47]

The implications from this explosion in education—particularly higher education and higher education obtained abroad—were significant. The primary benefit for *al Saud* was a growing resource of technocrats, professionals, engineers, and even entrepreneurs. On the other hand, the rapid expansion in higher education led to a growing number of professionals seeking high-paying jobs in the kingdom, which the job market could not fully accommodate. As a result of Aramco, the modern Saudi economy had always been dominated by the oil and gas sector. The Saudi government also invested heavily in related industries such as petrochemicals and mining. Other areas, such as communications, tourism, health-care, retail, and non-petroleum-related manufacturing have lagged behind the energy sector.[48] By the 1990s and 2000s, the government had become the largest employer, employing 70 percent of Saudis in the workforce.[49] This unequal growth created an imbalance in the Saudi economy that, along with a lack of private sector jobs, frustrated young, educated job seekers.

International students returned to Saudi Arabia exposed to other cultures and societies significantly less conservative than Saudi Arabia. Dr. Janet Breslin-Smith, the wife of former Ambassador James B. Smith, said that Saudi Arabia is "socially conservative, culturally conservative in ways that [are] hard for us to even get our arms around. . . . [But] at the same time, it still boggles my mind that they made this incredible commitment to not just education in general but these scholarships." Of the Saudi youth who studied abroad, she observed that "in some ways they are more confident, more aware, more professional."[50]

With the focus on education, more students learned foreign languages, especially English. As a result, they were able to consume media from outside the kingdom at the same time that media became more easily accessible due to rapid advancement of wireless data networks. In fact, Saudi Arabia's data network, both cellular and wireless Internet, became more advanced, with better coverage than those in the United States.[51] Saudis have become some of the most active social media users in the world.[52] With educational opportunities encouraged by the state and communication infrastructure built by the state, Saudis could not be kept separate from other cultures anymore, even within the borders of Saudi Arabia.

In the spring of 2017, Mohammad al Sheikh, a Saudi minister of state and former World Bank lawyer, spoke with Fox News Channel anchor Bret Baier. "You know," he said in nearly unaccented English, "I received a degree from a US university." He paused briefly. "My wife actually graduated from a US university," he added. The American anchor raised his eyebrows. "Hundreds of thousands of Saudis were actually educated in the US, and they experience the US culture, and they're coming back. And if you look at the youth and their connection to the world today, it truly is a different world for everybody. Anybody who's been coming to Saudi Arabia over the last ten, fifteen years can really see the change that we have achieved over the last decade. But hopefully over the next decade they'll see significantly more change, and it's going to be positive change."[53]

The Saudi minister hoped to use evidence of the global, and particularly American, education of Saudi youth as evidence that Saudi Arabia would be moving toward social and political liberalization. Ambassador Smith discussed this issue with King Abdullah, who, more than anyone else, was responsible for a generation of Saudis receiving educations in liberal societies outside the kingdom. "I remember a meeting with King Abdullah," Ambassador Smith said. "Somebody asked him what would be the impact of all the education. And he said, 'I don't know. But if you educate everyone that's got to be good.'"[54]

◆

Nothing illustrates the conflict between profit and power and modern and traditional in Saudi society like the issue of women. It is not unreasonable to say that women in Saudi Arabia have not been treated equally to men. Legally, women have not been considered "competent witnesses" in court. Women's testimony has only been accepted at the judge's discretion.[55] Civil proceedings concerning marriage, divorce, and custody arrangements have all favored men. The law has permitted men to practice polygamy, and Saudi labor laws have stated that men and women must be separated at work.[56] Saudi women have been governed by a strict guardianship system that has generally given men (either a father, brother, or husband) control over many aspects of their lives. Women have been required to obtain written permission from their male guardians for travel outside the kingdom, enrollment in higher education, employment (until 2008, when King Abdullah abolished this requirement), and some medical procedures.[57]

Iffat al Thunayan, the wife of Feisal, opened the first school for nonroyal girls in Saudi Arabia. In 1952, after sending her own sons abroad to continue their educations, Iffat turned her attention to the education of girls. Iffat believed strongly that the government should provide education for girls and women, and though she couched her support in terms of the advantages an educated mother brings to raising devout sons, it is clear she wanted girls to learn science and other secular subjects. She found an ally when Saud became king. He had started a school for his own daughters. In 1960, Saudi Arabia established a national committee to oversee women's education, with participation by some of the *ulama*. Iffat thought this was not enough, and with her own funds she opened a teacher's college for women to train the female teachers needed to educate Saudi Arabia's girls.[58]

Despite Iffat's devotion, education for girls was met with strong backlash in some of the most conservative areas of the kingdom. Even though members of the *ulama* were heavily involved in all aspects of women's education, the town of Buraida, for example, organized a large demonstration against the opening of a school for girls there in 1963.[59] Educational opportunities for women grew rapidly in the 1970s and 1980s, although all education took place in single-sex environments. The government encouraged women to attend college by providing free tuition, stipends, and even gifts of money or land when women graduated. By 1989, twelve colleges for women in Saudi Arabia had graduated sixteen thousand students. However, women were still prohibited from studying certain subjects that would lead to collaboration with men, such as engineering and architecture.[60]

By the 1990s, Saudi Arabia had over seventy-eight thousand women college graduates, many of whom sought professional careers. Although the Saudi workforce remained male dominated, the 1990s saw an influx of women into new professional areas such as marketing, advertising, journalism, and even broadcasting. Saudi women began taking jobs that required them to work at home to avoid working collaboratively with men. Women had always worked in education and medicine—professions in which they could deal solely with other women. It was clear that the entrance of more women into the workforce was causing tension in the balance between modern and traditional. In 1995, in a nod to power over profit, the Ministry of Commerce took a position that would limit the opportunities for women in entrepreneurial pursuits. The ministry decided to stop issuing business licenses to women for businesses in which the women would be supervising foreign workers, meeting with male clients, or regularly engaging with male government officials.[61] This policy was later reversed.

At the same time, however, the government continued to promote women joining the workforce. In 1999, then Crown Prince Abdullah explicitly stated *al Saud*'s commitment to creating a professional class of women in Saudi Arabia. "The most important thing is [women's] full participation in the life of society," he said. "Issues like driving cars by women and women [obtaining] ID cards are comparatively simple."[62] While the guardianship system was not abolished and women were not allowed to drive, some women flourished professionally. Several princesses rose to top roles in government agencies. In 2014, Sarah Al-Suhaimi, not a member of *al Saud*, became the CEO of NCB Capital, the investment arm of the National Commercial Bank, and in 2017, she became the chairperson of Tadawul, the Saudi national stock exchange.[63] When Saudi Arabia held its first elections for municipal councils, women were permitted to vote, as well as run for office. Despite limited registration locations and restrictions that prohibited women candidates from speaking directly to male voters, seventeen women were elected to serve on municipal councils in 2015.[64]

Yet the guardianship laws continued. During his tenure as king, from 2005 to 2015, Abdullah did promote women's education with the royal scholarship program that offered full scholarships to women, as well as men, to travel abroad for university degrees. However, he did not end the prohibition against women driving or relax many other restrictions on women. Only two and a half years after King Abdullah's death, his brother, King Salman, assisted by his 32-year-old son, Crown Prince Mohammad bin Salman, decreed that Saudi women would be permitted to obtain driver's licenses starting in June 2018.[65] Other restrictions that hindered women from accessing government services without a guardian's permission were also relaxed a few months earlier.[66]

Samah, a Saudi-born millennial seeking asylum in the United States, traveled to the States as a student. According to Samah, speaking in 2017, she was admitted to a master's program in creative writing at Notre Dame de Namur University in Belmont, California. The Saudi government gave her a scholarship covering tuition and expenses. She eventually convinced her father to sign the forms as her guardian, permitting her to go. A month into her first semester, however, her father changed his mind and asked the government to revoke her scholarship. The government obliged. Eventually, she was able to change her father's mind again, but the bureaucrats said he would need to travel to the Saudi embassy in Washington, D.C., to reapprove. He refused to make the trip, so she was unable to recover her scholarship. The university and several charities and businesses in the San Francisco, California, area came to her aid and allowed her to complete her studies and graduate.[67]

The Saudi guardianship system has meant that women like Samah have not been able to pursue their own dreams, let alone some basic daily activities, without the permission of a male guardian. It is hard to reconcile the strict guardianship system that has limited women within Saudi Arabia with the generous gift and liberty that young women have received from their government when they have traveled across the world—often alone—for free educations in liberal societies. The government has sent Saudis abroad for education with the intention that they would return, benefit the Saudi economy, and create profit. However, this has heightened the tension with traditionalism, especially in the case of female students.

Despite the Western media's focus on the oppressive nature of the Saudi guardianship system, women outsiders who have visited the kingdom have expressed varying opinions. *New York Times* columnist Maureen Dowd was invited in 2010 by the Saudi ministry of tourism. She wrote extensively about her mostly negative impressions in a *Vanity Fair* article titled A GIRLS' GUIDE TO SAUDI ARABIA. Saudi Arabia, she wrote, is "a country that legally, sexually, and sartorially buries its women alive." Saudi Arabia, Dowd explained to readers, "didn't abolish slavery until the 1960s. Restrictions on mingling between unrelated members of the opposite sex remain severe." Her irritation began on the flight to Riyadh. "The in-flight movies offer a taste of things to come. If you order *The Proposal*, you get a blurry blob over Sandra Bullock's modest décolletage." About the *abaya* and headscarf the Ministry of Tourism presented her with, Dowd said they "make you look like a mummy and feel like a pizza oven."[68]

In contrast, Brid Beeler, who accompanied her husband, an American government employee, to live in Riyadh in the late 1980s and then returned regularly, relayed more positive impressions. Although she had not lived in Saudi Arabia for decades, Beeler became a travel consultant and regularly arranged and accompanied tours of the country for foreigners. She explained that even though much had changed for women professionally in Saudi Arabia since the 1980s and 1990s, there had been many myths perpetuated about Saudi women. When she first arrived in the kingdom, she said, "people tried to indicate that women weren't working," but, in fact, they were working—just separately from men. To avoid the possibility of men, even foreigners, disturbing the women, "on the door in Arabic it would say . . . 'Women's section. Keep out.' But in English it would just say, 'Please keep the doors closed for air conditioning purposes.'"

Technology, Beeler said, made it much easier for women to work in Saudi Arabia. "You have Saudi women who hop in an Uber car today and they go to work. And they're not accompanied by a guardian." According to Beeler, Saudi women did not "really announce to the world at large what it is they're doing in society. They just quietly went on with their work, whatever their work might be, whether they're fashion designers, whether they're artists, whether they're in the graphic design business, whether they're in the IT business.

"Over the years," she explained, she came "to realize that the women rule the roost" and that Saudi men had to handle many extra family obligations because women were prohibited from driving. In her opinion, "most people in the West don't really realize the pressures on . . . Saudi men, in the society and how good Saudi women had it."[69]

On the other hand, the guardianship system has had very real consequences for women in Saudi Arabia. Some women have been lucky to have fathers, husbands, or brothers with liberal mind-sets who have supported their independence. For other women, the guardianship laws have been stifling or even dangerous. A Saudi woman in her midthirties, who uses the name Laura, sought refuge in Canada to escape an abusive family. According to Laura, her father was abusive to her as a child. After an arranged marriage to a drug addict and a subsequent divorce, she returned to her father's home, where the abuse continued. She went to an NGO for assistance, but when they told her that they could not help her without her father's knowledge, she realized that was too dangerous. She felt she could not go to the police, because she had witnessed friends who were betrayed by the authorities and returned to abusive men. Because she could not leave the country without a male guardian's permission, she convinced family members to travel with her to Bahrain. From Bahrain, she fled on a direct flight to London and then to Canada, where she had a lawyer already hired to help her apply for asylum.[70]

Laura, who fled in 2012, explained that when much of the civil paperwork in Saudi Arabia went online and smartphones became accessible, women could more easily circumvent the male guardian requirement. The Saudi civic documentation process was put online through a portal on iPhone and Android apps called *Absher*. As Laura explained, "One of my friends, she stole her dad's cell phone when he was sleeping. She went on *Absher*. She logged in with the activation code, and then she set up an acceptance for her, a permission to travel, and then after that she changed the cell phone number to her cell phone number so he [wouldn't] notice whenever she flees [*sic*] the country. . . . She's not the only one who did it."[71] Once again, traditionalism met modernization in Saudi Arabia.

◆

Religious Islamic terrorist organizations in the Middle East have presented themselves as the harbingers of Islamic traditionalism. *Al Saud*, which includes many extremely traditional and devout family members, has disagreed with this. Global observers have judged Saudi Arabia for supporting terrorism—directly or indirectly—but Saudi Arabia has seen itself as a longtime victim of Islamic terrorism and on the front lines of the fight against it.

The perception in the West has been that Saudi Arabia has been one of the premier sponsors of Islamic-based terrorism. For example, an October 2002, a Council on Foreign Relations Task Force report read, "It is worth stating clearly and unambiguously what official U.S. government spokespersons have not: For years, individuals and charities based in Saudi Arabia have been the most important source of funds for al Qaeda; and for years, Saudi officials have turned a blind eye to this problem."[72]

Opinion pieces and prominent media commentators labeled Saudi oil money as "the main source of financing for terrorism and religious fanaticism throughout the Islamic world."[73] Prominent politicians in the West called on leaders to have "difficult conversations" with "Saudi Arabia and the Gulf states [which] have funded extremist ideology."[74] Al Qaeda founder Osama bin Laden and the 9/11 pilots were Saudi Arabian citizens. This has provided support to the argument that the Saudi people and the Saudi government supported a radical Islamic agenda that sanctioned the killing of civilians and provided monetary support to terrorists.

In fact, *al Saud* has feared terrorism and has considered it a threat to the monarchy's power and profit. Religion, as expressed by the Wahhabi clerical establishment, legitimized *al Saud*'s right to rule the country, but at the same time, the family has also understood the power of the concept of violent *jihad* and how it could be a powerful organizing tool for revolutionary movements. While Abdul Aziz used the concept to rally support during his conquest of the peninsula in the early 20th century, terrorists have used the concept of a violent *jihad*, translated as 'struggle,' to gain support in attacks. For this reason, *al Saud* has prioritized the fight against terrorism.

Saudi Arabia has been the subject of numerous terrorist attacks. For Americans, the most memorable terrorist attack in Saudi Arabia was the bombing of the Khobar Towers in 1996. The building housed American airmen stationed in Saudi Arabia, and nineteen of them were killed when a truck bomb destroyed it. In the years since the Khobar Towers bombing, some have blamed al Qaeda, and others have blamed Iranian-led and -affiliated groups.[75] In 2003, al Qaeda operatives were responsible for a host of terrorist attacks in cities across Saudi Arabia that targeted the Saudi government and Westerners. In 2004 alone there were over thirty terrorist incidents in Saudi Arabia, including one against the American consulate in

Jeddah.[76] Aramco's oil facilities have also been targeted. In 2006, security forces thwarted an al Qaeda attack on Abqaiq, an Aramco oil processing facility about thirty-six miles south of Dhahran.[77]

In the 2017 interview with Fox News host Bret Baier, Mohammad al Sheikh, the minister of state, addressed *al Saud*'s position on fighting terrorism. "We've actually been fighting and combatting terrorism for a very long time. We had had, unfortunately, hundreds of events. We've thwarted hundreds of events more over the last couple of decades and we've been the victims—the whole world has been the victim of terrorism, so we are very serious about this."[78] Then Crown Prince Mohammad bin Nayef, who ran counterterrorism efforts in Saudi Arabia, received a medal from the CIA in 2017 for his success in fighting terrorism. His methods included "targeted and selective" manhunts for terrorists, "merciless" suppression of all forms of dissent, and a program of incarceration and rehabilitation for former al Qaeda agents.[79] Though *al Saud*'s response, particularly since 2003, has been severe, the threat of terrorism from organizations like Islamic State has persisted.

It is no secret that Saudi Arabia—through the government, individual royal family members, clerics, or private citizens—funded Muslim religious institutions around the world. It is also clear that *al Saud* prioritized support for the fundamentalist view of Islam that Wahhabism conveys. It is critical, however, to distinguish between a fundamentalist view of religion and a radical one. Fundamentalist views support strict interpretations and traditional forms of practice, whereas radicalism supports upheaval, revolt, and political change. As the powerful ruling family of a preeminent Middle Eastern country, *al Saud* has resisted change. The family has always prioritized political stability in order to maintain power for future generations. Radicalism has only threatened this goal. It is an altogether different question whether global religious institutions funded by Saudis or Saudi Arabia for the purpose of promoting conservative Islamic practices have been foci of radicalism. The point is that at least since 2001, it has not been in the interest of *al*

Saud to support radicalism or political Islamic movements that can serve as nothing but a threat to the ruling family.

Still, serious questions about Saudi Arabia's role in the larger network of terrorism have remained unanswered, even after the US government's 9/11 report and even after the 2016 declassification of twenty-eight pages that were assumed to have addressed this subject.[80] Did Saudi Arabia or Saudi citizens knowingly contribute to terrorist organizations, especially before September 11, 2001? Did Saudi Arabia or Saudi citizens knowingly contribute to or assist radical Islamic institutions, including mosques? Should *al Saud* have known about or more thoroughly investigated the institutions that received public and private Saudi funds? Since the September 11 attacks revealed the extent of some Saudi citizens' involvement in radical Islamic terrorism, has the Saudi government taken sufficient steps to ensure that public and private Saudi money would not fund terrorism?

The best analysis can come from examining Saudi priorities to determine the country's rational motivation. *Al Saud* has always feared destabilization, and the country's *ulama* generally have come to fear this as well, as they have enjoyed a comfortable position of authority in the kingdom due to *al Saud*. Radical Islamic organizations like the Muslim Brotherhood, Hamas, Hezbollah, al Qaeda, and Islamic State were all labeled by the Saudi government as threats to its power, stability, and legitimacy in the 21st century. All of these organizations have promoted fundamentalist Islamic practices similar, in many ways, to Wahhabi ideology, but they have also promoted the kind of radical political change that *al Saud* has never tolerated. It is for these reasons that *al Saud* has designated these and other offshoots as terrorist organizations and banned Saudis from participating in them. Some prominent Saudi *ulama* have also spoken out against the groups and instructed Saudis not to join them. The world of the radical Islamists differs drastically from that envisaged by *al Saud* or its Wahhabi *ulama*. After all, Saudi traditionalism means Saudi royals and Saudi clerics in power—not someone else.

◆

"Saudi Arabia is a religious country," Roba explained to her American university classmates in a modern Middle East history course. Even though she hailed from Jeddah, the cosmopolitan coastal city on the Red Sea, she explained that women were still required to wear a black or dark-colored *abaya* (a long dress-coat over their clothes) and *hijab* (headscarf) in public.[81] There is one place in Saudi Arabia, however, where these conservative dress codes never applied: women always drove cars, and families always sought entertainment at the local cinema. Unmarried and unrelated men and women always sat together in coffee shops and collaborated freely in the office. This is Saudi Aramco, in the city of Dhahran.

Lesley Stahl, in a 2008 *60 Minutes* television report on Saudi Arabia called "The Oil Kingdom," described the difference to viewers. "To western eyes, [Saudi Arabia] is a paradox. Skyscrapers, traffic jams, and shopping malls coexist with ancient tribal customs. The King and the Koran reign supreme and women everywhere are required to cover themselves in black from head to toe." Stahl herself donned an *abaya*, but not a headscarf, for part of the television segment. "The rules apply everywhere, it seems," she narrated incredulously, "except for the women at Saudi Aramco."[82] There, an American lifestyle always predominated and was never affected by the difficult balance between modernity and traditionalism that *al Saud* has struggled to protect.

Aramco has been *al Saud's* greatest source of profit and has functioned, as Stahl described it, "like a little country." Regardless of how the modern and the traditional have clashed inside the kingdom, *al Saud* has never allowed these conflicts to interfere with its greatest source of profit. Saudi Arabia has always segregated its religious and traditional heritage from its primary business—the oil industry.

Back when the kingdom was young, the king permitted non-Arabs to reside only in Jeddah. Abdul Aziz did not want his people corrupted by un-Islamic, Western influences. Aramco was the exception to this rule. Tim Barger, the son of Aramco geologist Tom Barger, was the seventh American born in Saudi Arabia. He explained that Dhahran, Aramco's headquarters located in the region where oil was originally found, was "deliberately placed there, away from society" because "the King didn't really want Americans to mingle with Saudis anyway." His impression of Abdul Aziz was that the king "just wanted Americans to go there, stay out of his hair, and produce oil and make him rich."

The king's desire for Aramco to be left to its own devices to "make him rich" ran deeper than simple isolation. In fact, the governor of the al-Hasa region, where Aramco was located, had far-reaching authority to ensure that the Americans were protected and left alone. The governor of the region, Saud bin Jalawi, was a cousin of King Abdul Aziz and, according to Tim Barger, "the strictest man on earth." The governor "had a reputation for cutting people's heads off" largely because he had to rule an area that stretched from the borders of Oman and Kuwait on the east to two thirds of the way to Riyadh in the west. The area contained an "unruly population of Bedouins and bandits and pirates, smugglers and just normal citizens gone wrong," in additional to the American oilmen. Bin Jalawi's response to the king's directive was to make "it known that no one would lay a finger on any American, ever, for any reason." Though others have referred to bin Jalawi as the "Head Chopper," Barger was grateful that he and *al Saud* were protective of the Americans and the oil business. "There were a lot of people that could have done harm or would have wanted to do harm to the Americans, but bin Jalawi was the guardian. He was the guardian angel."

Life in Dhahran meant that the Americans celebrated Christmas, drank alcohol, and even, in the early years, bought pork products in the Aramco supermarkets. Barger recalled from his childhood that when he "went down to [the nearby town of] Khobar, looking for a Christmas present for my parents . . . every store had Christmas displays—a tree. They loved trees. The snowmen puzzled the hell out them . . . especially Santa Claus."[83]

Lee Ingham, a retired Aramco employee who also grew up in Saudi Arabia, recalled drinking home-brewed alcohol with his friends, many of whom were Saudi. He had grown up alongside them as a child and returned, like them, after college, to work for the same company as their parents.[84] According to Ingham, the Western lifestyle at Aramco continued even as the company grew increasingly Saudi. During the 1980s, even after Aramco transitioned to Saudi ownership, Americans and other expats remained the predominant employees for some time. During the 1990s, however, the balance between Saudi employees and American employees began to shift in favor of the Saudis. Yet even though Saudis eventually came to occupy the senior management positions in the company, Aramco remained an oasis of Western culture and business standards within the conservative and traditional kingdom. Nothing, *al Saud* believed, should get in the way of profit and power.

PART III

EIGHT

"MASTERS OF OUR OWN COMMODITY"

Ahmed Zaki Yamani did not know that King Feisal had been following his legal career long before the two ever met. In 1958, Yamani, who went by his middle name, Zaki, had just opened "the first real law office in Saudi Arabia" in the city of Jeddah. Yamani came from a prominent family in Mecca and received most of his education abroad, first in Egypt and then at New York University and Harvard University, where he obtained a law degree and an LLM, respectively. In Jeddah, he built his practice by gaining a reputation as a skilled advocate in Saudi Arabia's Shariah law courts and as a newspaper columnist. One of his columns, concerning the Council of Ministers, caught Feisal's attention.[1]

"I didn't know it then," Yamani said in an interview in the 1980s, "but [Feisal] was reading my articles very carefully. I later discovered that he used to read everything I wrote."[2] Feisal appointed him minister of petroleum in 1962, just after firing Tariki. Aramco's Division of Arabian Affairs, a department responsible for gathering and disseminating information on important Saudis, described Yamani as a "personable young lawyer of thirty-one years old, with considerable legal background and some practical experience in public administration." Yamani, who took Tariki's place on the Aramco board of directors, was unlike his predecessor in almost every way. While Tariki was brash and confrontational, Yamani was "moderate and friendly." Yamani was a devout Muslim who took special care to eschew alcohol and non-Halal meat when traveling abroad.[3] "In spite of his youthful appearance," Aramco explained, Yamani demonstrated "social poise and a courteous manner which put others at ease." His appointment was a welcome change for Aramco compared to Tariki's aggressive and nationalistic stance.[4]

Yamani spent most of the 1960s cultivating personal relationships with the IOCs and with Aramco executives and board members. He participated in OPEC meetings and negotiations, though the group accomplished little to further its goals.[5] Yamani did not reveal his vision for Saudi Arabia's oil industry until a conference in Beirut in 1968, where he openly declared that Saudi Arabia desired a 50 percent share in Aramco. He explained this desire not in terms of Tariki's Arab nationalism but rather as "the best way" for Aramco shareholders to guarantee their long-term interests.[6] The shareholders he was referring to were Aramco's four American parent companies. To Yamani, ownership in Aramco was not a matter of what Saudi Arabia or Arabs deserved; it was a matter of what was in the best business interest of Saudi Arabia and what he could convince the Americans was in their interest as well.

Yamani's public declaration of Saudi Arabia's goal in 1968 was a bold opening bid that the Aramco parent companies chose to ignore at the time. In 1968, the parent companies felt secure enough in their position in Saudi Arabia to overlook Yamani's comment.

Yamani and King Feisal, like Sulaiman before them, had patience and were content to wait—leaving their opening offer on the table. Yamani's temperament became an asset. Whereas Tariki would likely have complained to the Aramco executives as well as the media about unanswered negotiations, Yamani approached the situation more subtly. He told a British journalist in an interview at the time, "Time is on our side. We don't fight. We believe that our case is so strong that we can get what we want eventually."[7] "Eventually" meant a decade or more, he explained to the journalist. Just like Sulaiman, Yamani saw oil as a long-term asset. The Saudis did not need to accomplish everything immediately, but their goals were immutable.

As it turned out, the time soon came to press forward with negotiations for Saudi Arabia to gain partial ownership—or "participation," in their words—in Aramco. The Saudis found leverage in spare capacity, which marks the amount of oil a producer could add to its daily production numbers if it ramped up production to full capacity. In 1970, the oil exporting countries of the world found themselves in a very different situation than in the 1960s. Prior to 1970, the United States had always been able to increase domestic oil production to satisfy any growth in demand. In 1970, however, production from key Texas oil fields began to decline. At the same time, global demand continued to rise, and the United States soon found itself without any spare production capacity. Global spare capacity, which was about four million barrels per day at the time, was heavily concentrated in the hands of oil-rich countries that belonged to OPEC.[8]

In 1971, OPEC engaged in successful negotiations with the IOCs to raise the posted price of oil by 35 cents per barrel. This victory was small but significant in that it marked the first real negotiating victory of OPEC as a cartel.[9] After that success, Yamani decided to take a more aggressive stance in his negotiation tactics. He sought to use the OPEC cartel, which up to that point had largely focused on collective price negotiation, to further member nations' interests. OPEC, he reasoned, would help the countries gain partial ownership in the IOCs operating on their soil. Qatar, Kuwait, and Abu Dhabi agreed with Yamani and decided to negotiate as a unit.[10] Of course, Yamani was selected to lead the negotiations on behalf of the Persian Gulf OPEC members.[11] Despite this new collective stance, Yamani made little progress in bringing the companies to the negotiating table. Still the Saudis knew the advantages they held. Ultimately, Saudi Arabia owned the oil. More importantly, for the first time, the United States had little to no spare capacity left. Saudi Arabia and OPEC were prepared to push the oil companies if the need arose.

Seeing little progress, King Feisal issued a statement. In February 1972, King Feisal directed the Saudi Press Agency to issue the following: "Gentlemen, the implementation of effective participation is imperative, and we expect the companies to co-operate with us with a view to reaching a satisfactory settlement. They should not oblige us to take measures to put into effect the implementation of participation."[12] He made clear that Saudi Arabia felt it necessary that it achieve a minimum level of ownership in Aramco, and he left a vague threat that he would achieve that end one way or another. As he was not talking about a controlling stake at this time, it seems unlikely that he was actually referring to nationalization. Feisal's statement worked.

As an OPEC meeting approached one month later, and before the OPEC members could discuss in person, Aramco accepted in principle that Saudi Arabia could purchase a 20 percent participation in the company. Feisal's statement had indeed made the difference, as Aramco's primary goal was to "ensure access to as much oil as possible" in the future.[13] Aramco was not going to risk the ire of the king over 20 percent of the company, because, after all, the American oil companies would still have access to Aramco oil, which was the primary concern. Also, it cannot be understated that Saudi Arabia would be purchasing that 20 percent. It was not a gift.

The 20 percent offer was significantly below Yamani's opening of 50 percent participation, but after several rounds of negotiations, Yamani was able to convince Aramco to agree on 25 percent with a provision that the government be able to purchase up to 51 percent by 1981.[14] The agreement ensured that by 1981, Saudi Arabia would be able to purchase a majority share in the oil company on which it had staked its future. This deal, called the General Agreement on Participation, was reached on October 2, 1972. It also applied to Kuwait, Abu Dhabi, and Qatar. This was not nationalization at gunpoint, like Iran's nationalization of the Anglo-Iranian Oil Company in 1954, nor was it acquiescence by Aramco. In testimony before Congress, an executive from one of the Aramco shareholder companies explained that "Saudi Arabia paid for [its shares.]"[15] None of the participants would reveal how much the Saudis paid for their 25 percent share, except to say that they settled on a formula known as "updated book value" to determine the amount the various Gulf countries would pay. The most conservative valuation would have been "net book value," an estimate made based on assets minus liabilities. According to several participants in the negotiations, the "updated book value" increased that valuation somewhat.[16] Reporters deduced after the fact that Saudi Arabia likely paid $500 million for that original 25 percent of Aramco.[17]

The American shareholders of Aramco actually emerged from these negotiations in a much better position than some of the other IOCs in the Middle East. The Iraqi government abruptly nationalized the Iraq Petroleum Company, a consortium of several IOCs, in 1972. Colonel Muammar Qaddafi nationalized British Petroleum's assets in Libya in 1971. Whether anyone at Aramco was willing to explicitly acknowledge this, its parent companies were lucky in the 1970s that they partnered with Saudi Arabia and not one of the more radical regimes. Saudi Arabia was not prepared to use its police-state powers or its authoritarian rule to nationalize the oil industry by fiat or by force. More than ownership, the Saudi government wanted profit, and Yamani and the king saw better avenues for optimizing Saudi profit and power for the long term. They were patient and willing to pursue a traditional business avenue if it would achieve their goals—perhaps not for themselves but for the generations of *al Saud* to come.

◆

Almost exactly a year after his success in negotiating the participation agreement, Yamani prepared to lead the full OPEC team in negotiations with the IOCs. For more than a decade, the oil-rich countries and the IOCs had operated under a system called "posted price," in which the companies calculated the proportion of revenue paid to the countries, generally through taxes, based on a fixed posted price instead of the price for which they actually sold the oil. When the market price of oil fluctuated significantly downward, the IOCs adjusted the posted price unilaterally. As a result, the oil-rich countries would receive less revenue. A dispute over the posted price in 1959 and 1960 was a particular impetus for the original formation of OPEC by Tariki and Alfonso, but OPEC proved fairly impotent and incapable of protecting its members' interests at that time.[18]

Once again, in 1973, the issue was the price of oil. In the 1970s, oil demand rose steeply, and the IOCs began to sell oil at market prices that exceeded the posted price. This meant that the companies earned more per barrel of oil than the countries, a situation the oil ministers of OPEC sought to rectify by inviting representatives of the IOCs to a meeting in October 1973.[19]

The meeting took place at OPEC's permanent headquarters in Vienna, Austria. Yamani, along with Iranian oil minister Jamshid Amouzegar, represented OPEC.[20] The talks began on October 8. The oil companies were represented by Andre Bénard for Shell and George Piercy, a friend of Yamani's, for Exxon. Piercy, as an American working for an American company, should have been restricted from colluding with other IOCs in price-related issues, but he had received a particular exemption from antitrust laws from the Department of Justice, as he and colleagues had before.[21]

Two days before the talks in Vienna, the 1973 war between Israel and the Arab countries of Egypt and Syria had begun.

The discussions centered around a new posted price. Both sides understood that if the posted price rose, the market price would necessarily rise as well. Bénard and Piercy opened negotiations with an offer to increase the posted price of oil by 15 percent (around 45 cents more per barrel). Yamani responded that OPEC was looking for a 100 percent increase (around $3 more per barrel).[22] The two parties were clearly very far apart. Yamani and Amouzegar would negotiate only from their starting point, and Piercy and Bénard were not authorized to agree to any increase above $1 per barrel.[23] The IOCs they represented wanted more time and said they needed to consult with the governments of major oil-importing countries, such as the United States, the United Kingdom, France, and Japan.[24]

The meeting stretched to almost a week, and Yamani and Amouzegar would not wait any longer. As a result of the 1973 war, OPEC had scheduled an additional meeting on October 16, in Kuwait. By October 14, Yamani and Amouzegar knew that if they did not reach an agreement with the oil companies on a new posted price, their fellow ministers in Kuwait would demand a unilateral price increase without any input from the oil companies. The countries would simply increase their tax bills to make the IOCs pay. Even though Saudi Arabia and other countries had negotiated taxes with IOCs in the past, it is a sovereign right of a country to change its tax bill without negotiation. Yamani also knew that the Arab nationalist leaders of Iraq and Libya would pressure the Arab members of OPEC to take sides in the ongoing 1973 war.[25] The Saudi oil minister made clear that he did not want to involve the 1973 war in the oil business. He said he "didn't want to mix prices with politics," but unless Bénard and Piercy could negotiate an agreement, that seemed an inevitable conclusion.[26]

Late on the night of October 14, Bénard and Piercy met Yamani in his hotel suite. There was nothing they could do, they explained.

The IOCs needed more time. Yamani thought that perhaps they did not understand that the balance of the global oil market had swung in OPEC's favor. He tried to convince them to stay.[27] Perhaps Bénard and Piercy had not taken him seriously when he had threatened to unilaterally raise taxes and "exercise our rights on our own."[28] If OPEC and the IOCs did not settle the issue of oil prices immediately, then OPEC would take unilateral action at its Kuwait meeting on October 16.

Piercy did not take his friend's warning lightly. He had an idea of what might happen if he and Bénard left Vienna without an agreement on price, but he felt hamstrung by the inability of the other IOCs to take decisive action. Piercy also understood that the IOCs could face backlash from their home countries for agreeing to such a large increase. The home countries wanted to keep the price of oil low for consumers. Middle East oil was significantly underpriced in the 1960s and early 1970s. Even though the price had increased to around $2 per barrel in 1970, in inflation-adjusted dollars, oil was still below the price it had been in 1958.[29] Yamani thought these facts would have an impact on his negotiating partners, and he was surprised when they did not. Yamani figured that the oil companies could agree to his price hike. In his mind, they simply did not want their governments and customers to blame them for it. "They were happy with the higher prices," Yamani said years later, "because that meant higher profits for them, but they didn't want to be the ones to say yes."[30] Bénard and Piercy left Vienna the following day, and Yamani and Amouzegar headed for Kuwait.[31] That was the last time OPEC and the IOCs negotiated over oil prices. From then on, OPEC would set prices on its own. It is unclear if Bénard and Piercy knew it yet, but they had already lost the negotiation.

On October 16, OPEC reassembled in Kuwait for two purposes. The first, which involved the full OPEC contingent, was to decide a new posted price for oil. In Kuwait, OPEC determined a posted price unilaterally without comment from the IOCs. The second involved only the Arab members of OPEC, in a separate organization they called the Organization of Arab Petroleum Exporting Countries (OAPEC). OAPEC met to discuss a political response to the 1973 Arab-Israel war. The following day, OAPEC considered an oil embargo against countries supporting Israel. Egyptian president Anwar Sadat had called on Arab oil-rich countries to pressure the United States with the threat of oil supply cuts. Egypt had wanted the United States to halt military aid to Israel before the war had even started. At the time, the Soviet Union was supplying both Egypt and Syria with weaponry comparable to what the United States supplied to Israel.[32]

Saudi Arabia's position was complicated. On the one hand, Feisal and Yamani expressed that they felt pressure from their neighboring countries to participate in any political action. On the other hand, they did not believe in using oil as a political tool. They had both said so publicly.[33] Neither one wanted to lose Aramco's customers. They believed cutting off oil supplies would hurt revenue.[34] It seemed there was little to gain in manipulating oil supplies for politics. Profit came before regional or ethnic affinity, as it almost always had for Saudi Arabia. But, if the Saudis could use the political situation to increase profit and power, they could succeed in both regards.

After all, in 1947, King Abdul Aziz had not been willing to forgo profit for regional politics. At the time, he had told Ambassador Childs and the State Department that the United States' policies toward the Jews in Palestine, while not his preference, would not jeopardize his business relationship with Aramco.[35] Even though King Abdul Aziz had expressed concern about the situation of the Arabs in Palestine before, most notably in an interview with *Life* magazine in 1943 and when he met with US president Franklin Roosevelt in 1945, he made it clear to the Americans that their support for the Jews in Palestine would not threaten the US-Saudi relationship.[36] Similarly, before the 1973 war, King Feisal did express concern for his Arab neighbors and for US policy supporting Israel. In fact, he asked Aramco's American shareholders to lobby the Nixon administration on behalf of the Arabs.[37] Nevertheless, like his father, Feisal's priority was profit. In Feisal's case, events aligned in a way that made it possible to use regional politics to increase his wealth and the wealth of Saudi Arabia.

By the end of 1973, *al Saud* believed it had accumulated enough leverage to influence the oil market, improve its financial situation, and increase its own economic power. In just three years, the share of the global oil market controlled by Aramco and Saudi Arabia had risen considerably. In July 1972, Saudi Arabia produced an average of 5.4 million barrels per day. One year later, in July 1973, production was up 56 percent to 8.4 million barrels per day. Saudi Arabia's share of global oil exports was 21 percent, a growth of 8 percent in just three years.[38] If Saudi Arabia could regulate its own domestic production and exports, it could set its own prices and establish a precedent of control. The 1973 Arab-Israel war presented the Saudis with an opportunity to accomplish this business goal under the cover of geopolitical maneuvering.

If Saudi Arabia and its OPEC partners could restrict production, far greater profit could be made and in a way that satisfied regional political alliances and worked in favor of the long-term health of Saudi Arabia's energy industry. There were actually two sincere technical arguments for decreasing Saudi production at that time. There were many in the Saudi government who thought pumping as much oil as they were was detrimental to Saudi Arabia's long-term finances. Saudi Arabia, at the time, was taking in more dollars than it could spend. The dollar had been devalued several times, so the Saudi finance ministry was unhappy leaving the oil profits in the bank.[39]

Production cuts were also seen as valuable from an engineering perspective. Some Aramco engineers had expressed concern that the rapid increase in oil production would harm Saudi Arabia's oil fields if not curtailed. A top Socal engineer who dealt with Aramco engineering issues, William Messick, told Congress that the oil companies "'were taken off the hook' by the embargo, that is without the embargo Aramco would have had to cut back production or risk permanent injury to the fields." As he explained it, pumping so much oil so quickly from the Saudi oil fields was causing the pressure in the fields to drop. Unless Aramco pumped in another substance (most commonly water), the pressure would collapse and the field would be permanently damaged. Aramco did not have adequate infrastructure to support such high levels of production at that point.[40] In 1973, Aramco needed to cut back on production to improve infrastructure and develop additional spare capacity. These were powerful motivating arguments for Yamani and Feisal when it came time, in Kuwait, for Saudi Arabia to take hold of its power in the oil market. The outbreak of war in the Middle East would facilitate an OPEC consensus that happened to be in line with Saudi Arabia's economic strategy.

OPEC's decision on pricing was quick. The cartel unilaterally decided to raise the posted price of oil by 70 percent, to $5.11 per barrel.[41] After the decision was announced, Yamani told his fellow oil ministers, "This is a moment for which I have been waiting a long time. The moment has come. We are masters of our own commodity."[42] Yamani made two important points in this statement. One, he exalted in what he expected to be a successful attempt to take control of the commodity Saudi Arabia had previously left under the maneuverings of an American corporation. The other was that he had intended to take control for a long time. His actions in Vienna and in Kuwait in October 1973 might not have been predetermined years before, but they were not merely reactions to geopolitical events or newfound opportunity. This was a strategic maneuver.

Yamani's pride was evident, but he and his colleagues needed to address implementation of their intended price hikes and market manipulation. They had already unilaterally increased the posted price. They could do that alone through increased taxation or fees charged to the IOCs because, after all, they were sovereign countries and owned the oil in the ground. The second part of the implementation would be production cuts, which would increase global market prices, independent of the posted price increase. The third part would be an embargo on the United States and allies of Israel and the United States. This would cause pain and panic. An embargo would also increase prices. Most importantly, an embargo would demonstrate to the world who truly controlled the oil market.

Cutting production would not be simple for some OPEC countries, especially Saudi Arabia. In Saudi Arabia, Aramco, not the government, controlled the valves to the oil wells. The Saudi government could not decrease production without cooperation from Aramco or the use of force, and Saudi Arabia had always made it clear that it would not use force against Aramco as a company. Saudi Arabia viewed Aramco as its partner. Iraq, Iran, and Libya, the countries that had nationalized the foreign oil company assets within their borders, did not have this problem. It was left to Yamani to convince Aramco to cooperate, one way or another.

Similarly, Saudi Arabia did not have complete control over the export of oil to implement an embargo. During the 1956 Suez Crisis, when Britain, France, and Israel attacked Egypt, Saudi Arabia blocked oil exports to Britain and France. However, at the time, the United States was cooperating with Saudi Arabia's strategy. Therefore, Aramco was not conflicted; the Americans and the Saudis were on the same side.[43] In 1973, Saudi Arabia would be embargoing the United States, the home country of Aramco and Aramco executives. Aramco owned everything—the wells, the pipelines, the refining facilities, the ships—and controlled all of the logistics. Ultimately Saudi Arabia owned only 25 percent of Aramco, and Saudi Arabia had no control except for the threat of force at its ports and borders. Again, Saudi Arabia had always made it clear that it would not use force against its oil partner. Again, it was left to Yamani to convince Aramco to cooperate, one way or another.

At the OAPEC meeting on October 17, the majority of Arab countries supported the production cuts and embargo. At first, Yamani challenged his colleagues on the need to impose an embargo immediately, arguing to avoid haste. "Washington," he said, "should be given more time to formulate a fair policy towards the Arabs."[44] He was not successful in postponing an embargo, but he did manage to keep the official statement from specifically mentioning the United States and directly challenging Saudi Arabia's longtime partner by name. Member nations retained the authority to determine for themselves which countries they would embargo. OAPEC also issued a statement that member nations would cut production by 5 percent immediately and continue to increase production cuts by similar increments each month until a satisfactory end to the 1973 war was reached.[45]

Successful implementation of the price hikes and market manipulation would demonstrate that the countries, not the IOCs, truly controlled their oil industries. At the same time, the call in the Middle East for Arab unity helped OAPEC states, and Saudi Arabia in particular, justify their actions with ethnic and religious solidarity as opposed to blanket economic interest. If Saudi Arabia disrupted the world economy for deeply held religious and ethnic convictions, the victims could understand its actions to some extent. After all, economic embargoes had become common geopolitical tools in the 20th century. On the other hand, an economic assault of this kind for profit was almost unprecedented in the post–World War II era and would be seen as capricious.

On October 21, several days after other OAPEC countries had announced their embargoes, Yamani called Frank Jungers, who had become CEO of Aramco not long before. Yamani told Jungers that Saudi Arabia had decided to embargo oil headed to the United States and certain American allies. Jungers recalled telling Yamani that he "didn't think they'd be able to do it." That was the extent of Aramco's protest against Saudi Arabia's decision. According to Jungers, Yamani responded, "Oh, yes. We've discussed that. We'll be able to do it because you are going to do it."[46] Yamani proceeded to explain to Jungers that Aramco would cut oil production and that these cuts would come from the oil designated for the United States and its allies.[47] Yamani put the onus on Jungers to embargo his own country.

Jungers did not delay or negotiate with Yamani. On previous occasions when a difficult issue had arisen between Aramco and the Saudi government, the process of resolution had always been slow. Dating to the 1940s, each instance had followed a pattern of deliberate discussions, negotiations, and consultations. Jungers might have had options, at least to delay the implementation, but from his multiple accounts, there is no indication that he chose those avenues. He did not ignore the first request and wait for a second to come. He did not try a counteroffer. He did not extend discussions about production cuts and an embargo. In all of his recollections of these events, Jungers never stated that he relied on the State Department, as his predecessors had when they had involved Childs, Hare, and Hart in intense situations of conflict. The State Department helped the American oilmen in the 1940s and 1950s because oil was then an issue of national security for the United States. Surely it was an issue of national security in 1973.

According to Jungers, he and Aramco went on to develop a precise system in which the company monitored and tracked every barrel of oil that left Saudi Arabia's shores to ensure compliance with Yamani's production cuts and embargo. The production cuts came out of embargoed oil. In fact, Aramco's cuts exceeded Yamani's demands, because, according to Jungers, he and Aramco wanted to be sure to satisfy the Saudis. In fact, in his book, forty years later, Jungers seemed proud of the logistical feat Aramco had accomplished, writing, "In the end, I had to admit to myself that the King had given me the right response when I had insisted this couldn't be done. He knew that Aramco could do it. Aramco had the track record."[48]

On October 22, the United Nations Security Council called for a cease-fire in the 1973 war, but OPEC actions were not the impetus for the UN vote. After all, this was only one day after Yamani spoke to Jungers about the production cuts and embargo. The war ended on October 25. However, OPEC's production cuts and embargo would not fully end for four and a half more months.

Back when OPEC decided to raise the posted price of oil to just over $5 per barrel in Kuwait in mid-October 1973, its members had not imagined that less than a month later it would be possible to sell a barrel of oil at a market price of $16. By mid-November, OPEC countries realized they could make much more money selling their oil at market prices than selling it through IOCs and earning revenues based on posted prices. For example, after selling oil for $17 per barrel, Iran could no longer see any reason to earn only a small fraction of that based on the posted price agreement with the IOCs that regularly marketed its oil. OPEC agreed to meet again on December 23, to settle on a new price for oil that reflected the market.[49]

At the meeting, Iran pushed for a fourfold price increase. Amouzegar wanted to see posted prices rise to $17 to $20 per barrel. Yamani agreed that prices should rise, but he fought against Iran's desired extreme price hike. He argued a price hike of that extent would damage the world economy and, therefore, impair OPEC members' prospects. Yamani proposed a more moderate increase to $7 or $8 per barrel. Yamani and Amouzegar argued throughout the night, until the Iranian oil minister finally called the shah of Iran and convinced him to agree to a posted price of $13.30 per barrel. Yamani then called King Feisal, but at that hour, he was unable to reach the king. Yamani was only able to reach the Deputy Crown Prince, Fahd, who told Yamani that he should support OPEC unity. Yamani went back to the negotiating table and managed to get Amouzegar down to a price of $11.65 per barrel, which the Iranians announced to the waiting media almost immediately.[50]

After the meeting, Yamani made his regret clear. He said, "A lower posted price would have been more equitable and reasonable."[51] When King Feisal heard what had happened, he was angry that OPEC had agreed on such a high price, but apparently he did not blame Yamani. Feisal's greatest concern was that such a high price could lead to unstable economic situations among Aramco's customers. Feisal's focus was on Saudi Arabia's long-term financial goals.[52] The production cuts, along with some aspects of the oil embargo, remained in place until March 12, 1974, when Saudi Arabia officially canceled what remained of the oil embargo.[53] Some historians, like Daniel Yergin, argue that there is no true explanation for why OPEC ended its actions when it did.[54] On the other hand, Robert Lacey argues that Saudi Arabia ended the production cuts and embargo only after the United States agreed to sell the Saudi government sophisticated military equipment.[55] Likely, the Saudis were motivated to end the embargo, at least in part, by profit.

The economic and psychological impacts, as well as the pure inconvenience created by OPEC's actions, were severe. The 1973–1974 oil crisis caused havoc on gasoline supplies in the United States, Europe, and Japan. Not only did the price of oil immediately skyrocket far above OPEC's new posted price of $5.11 per barrel, but shortages also appeared. Americans faced gasoline rationing. Consumers were only permitted to purchase gasoline on alternate days based on the numbers on their license plates. Lines at gas stations grew. OPEC's actions not only impacted American consumer's wallets but also disrupted their daily lives. In Japan, riots broke out as a result of the oil shortages and price hikes. Reports of barrels of oil going for $16 or $22 terrified oil-trading companies and triggered panics that only increased real prices.[56] Writing in 1982, nearly a decade later, Henry Kissinger, the US secretary of state during the oil crisis, explained, "The effects of these convulsions continue to this day. Our economic system has not yet recovered; the political and social consequences are still playing themselves out."[57]

The world came to understand the oil crisis as a political action with economic weapons. The world largely saw oil-rich nations of the Middle East wield their economic influence over the industrialized world to achieve a political purpose concerning the Arab-Israel conflict. However, evidence has indicated that although support for Egypt and Syria was a factor in the oil crisis, it was not OPEC's primary motivation. OPEC countries, and in particular Saudi Arabia, were foremost driven by a desire to increase the price of oil and assert control over their oil resources. The 1973 war provided a convenient political justification for oil-rich countries to seize power over the oil market from IOCs and rapidly increase their profits. OPEC's actions, with the stated goal of pressuring the United States on Israel, did not work.

In fact, the United States, cognizant that the Soviet Union was rapidly resupplying Egypt and Syria, considered it a Cold War imperative to resupply Israel and never stopped its assistance to Israel during the war. Similarly, the OPEC countries that had argued most vociferously in favor of employing oil as an economic weapon in the Middle East war actually took advantage of high prices. During the crisis, both Iraq and Iran violated the production cuts they had supported. They both overproduced oil. The lure of revenue proved stronger than any religious, political, or regional sympathy toward their neighbors.

Saudi Arabia, on the other hand, adhered to the production cuts because this was a business strategy it considered in its best interests. After all, in the period leading up to the oil shocks, both Yamani and Feisal had expressed disdain for using oil for political purposes. Yamani had not wanted to break off negotiations with the IOCs before the Kuwait OPEC meeting because he strongly opposed "[mixing] prices with politics."[58] When Egypt had called for oil-rich countries to use oil to pressure the United States, King Feisal had said that it was "dangerous even to think of that." Feisal and Yamani were always primarily concerned about potential damage to the Saudi oil industry and jeopardizing revenue.[59]

What Yamani and Feisal were both saying was that while they held political views, they were not willing to make business decisions based purely on politics. They were not willing to sacrifice their relationships with American customers or face a potential short-term drop in profitability for the sake of politics. However, Yamani and Feisal were willing to test Saudi Arabia's relationship with the United States and to potentially sacrifice short-term profitability for the sake of the long-term business interests of Saudi

Arabia. In contrast, Iran and Iraq were happy to use oil to make a political statement, and then both countries promptly cheated on the agreement.

This was no different than when Abdul Aziz had reassured a nervous US State Department in 1947 when tensions arose regarding US support for a Jewish state in Palestine. King Abdul Aziz would have preferred that the United States not support a Jewish state, but he had no intention of halting the American-run oil industry in Saudi Arabia over a political preference.[60] Abdul Aziz's primary concern was his economic partnership with the American oil company, and he would not permit his politics or the US government's politics concerning Israel to get in the way of a moneymaking relationship. Abdul Aziz supported the other Arab nations in their cause against the Jewish state but continued to forge a good relationship with the United States diplomatically and financially. In 1973, it was politically expedient for King Feisal and leaders of other oil-rich Arab countries to publicly castigate the Israelis and the Americans. This satisfied the political leanings of their populations, who wanted to see Arab nations stand up to Western powers. It also increased their statures in the Arab League. Most importantly for Saudi Arabia, it provided an ideological cover for an economic assault on the world economy. Manipulating the oil market in order to oppose Israel looked better than manipulating the oil market for profit, which was what these countries were doing.

The narrative of a political embargo and Arab solidarity also benefitted the IOCs, such as BP, Shell, and Aramco and its parent companies. As consumers were hit with skyrocketing gasoline prices, the American executives of Aramco's shareholders were pulled into congressional hearings and questioned by the media to explain and justify the massive energy disruptions sweeping the industrialized world.[61] As consumers suffered, profits for the IOCs rose. Royal Dutch Shell, for example, went from a profit margin of 35 cents per barrel of oil to 70 cents per barrel.[62] This was a public relations nightmare at home for the IOCs.

Frank Jungers, the Aramco CEO, like other IOC executives, was quick to blame King Feisal and American support for Israel for both the shortage and for his own swift capitulation to Yamani's production directives. He never stopped blaming Feisal for four decades. In his testimony to Congress in the midst of the crisis in January 1974, Jungers said that he believed the Saudis would nationalize Aramco if he did not comply with the production cuts and embargo restrictions.[63] However, there is little evidence to support this claim, as both Yamani and Feisal believed that nationalizing the rest of Aramco would do more harm than good to Saudi Arabia's oil industry. In a later interview, after he left the company, Jungers admitted that Yamani never wanted to nationalize but rather wanted the Saudi government to "buy into Aramco and become a true participant and thereby get to know the shareholders' problems intimately."[64]

George M. Keller, who was vice chairman of the board of Socal at the time, also directly contradicted Jungers's assertion that Aramco was forced to act under threat of nationalization. In his testimony before the Senate, Keller said, "We have not been threatened with nationalization in Arabia."[65] He said that Feisal warned Aramco shareholders at a meeting in Geneva in May 1973 that he would have to adopt an anti-Israel stance if hostilities between Israel and its neighbors broke because "Saudi Arabia is in danger of being isolated among its Arab friends," not because of his own ideological convictions.[66] Keller said that he and "any of us who were involved" did not fear that Saudi Arabia would nationalize Aramco, but "rather that we could be restricted in how we might be permitted to operate." He concluded, "I think there is quite a distinction here and to my knowledge, the Saudis have never nationalized anything."[67]

Nevertheless, Jungers always blamed the oil crisis first on Feisal's sentiment toward Israel. When asked about Aramco's involvement in the oil crisis during an interview in 2017, he said, "That was King Feisal's reaction to the American dealings with Israel. That was his decision and his decision only."[68] Yet Jungers also wrote about an incident in his own 2013 book that provided evidence against a purely ideological motivation on the part of the king. At one point during the embargo, Feisal gave Jungers permission to secretly break the embargo and use Saudi oil to fuel US Navy ships in the Persian Gulf.[69] Feisal considered the appearance of the embargo more important than actually denying the United States access to oil.

Jungers had every incentive to blame the oil crisis on an uncontrollable ideological force. He had been CEO for barely a year when Yamani demanded he enforce the production cuts and embargo. It is not surprising that he quickly capitulated to Yamani, nor is it surprising that he blamed King Feisal's politics instead of pointing to the more complicated profit motive. Jungers did not last long as CEO of Aramco. Five years after the oil crisis, the Aramco board fired him. As Tim Barger relayed the story from his father-in-law, then senior vice president at Aramco, Jungers "always casts it that he was fired because he was too strident of an advocate of the Saudis, but, actually, he was fired for malfeasance."[70]

The story of the 1973 oil crisis has been complicated by misinformation, intentional and innocent; simplistic explanations; and self-serving excuses from all sides. However, the result was simple. The profit motive pursued by Saudi Arabia benefitted the Saudis and the American oil companies that still owned a majority of Aramco. Aramco, its parent companies, and Saudi Arabia all came out of the oil crisis significantly wealthier than before. Between October 1973 and October 1974, Aramco's American shareholders saw their revenues increase by 56 percent.[71] More than ten years after OPEC's founding, the cartel could finally claim the power to set oil prices. This had been one of its two original missions. The other was to promote control by its members over the oil itself. Saudi Arabia emerged as a leader in the cartel, both because of Yamani's negotiating skills and also because of the share of global oil exports it controlled. Saudi Arabia and OPEC were indeed "masters of [their] own commodity," as Yamani had said right after the price hikes began. The next step was for Saudi Arabia to become master of its own industry.

◆

Yamani did not waste any time moving toward his goal of owning Aramco. Two months after the end of the oil crisis, in May 1974, he told the US ambassador, James Akins, that "he was thinking of converting Aramco into a purely Saudi company." By this, Yamani did not mean nationalization. "The American officials would stay on the job," he told Akins. "The parent companies [in the same 30-30-30-10 ratio . . .] would take crude on long-term contracts." Yamani wanted the Americans to understand that it was his desire and the king's desire to avoid disrupting an operation that was very successful for everyone involved. Yamani reiterated that he "is the world's foremost advocate of capitalism . . . [and] believes in the profit motive and knows that if the American companies are to stay on the job, if they are to do good work, they will have to be allowed reasonable profits."[72]

Specifically, Yamani said that "he has no intention whatsoever of following the lead of Iraq or Iran in trying to eliminate or even reduce rapidly [sic] the foreign role in oil production. He said the Americans must have a major role for the foreseeable future in Saudi oil production and in joint ventures with Saudi Arabia at home and abroad."[73] If all the Saudis wanted was ownership, they could have followed Tariki's vision and taken the nationalization path of Iraq, Iran, and Mexico. That, however, would have interfered with a very profitable enterprise. Yamani's desire to achieve Saudi ownership at that juncture did not come from a groundswell of anti-Western, nationalistic, or even religious fervor. Similarly, when Yamani declared himself a capitalist, it was not out of conviction but out of practical belief that capitalism would maximize Saudi Arabia's profit.

Yamani was, according to Socal vice chairman Keller, "a superb negotiator; he tosses every claim you can imagine on the table and then adds them all up and says we ought to settle for that."[74] Thus, Yamani set the stage for these final negotiations with the Americans carefully. He began by inviting the American shareholders to his house in the mountains near Jeddah for talks. By June 11, 1974, the shareholders and Yamani had reached an agreement to increase Saudi ownership of Aramco to 60 percent, which was, in effect, an acceleration of the previous agreement.[75] The *New York Times* reported this would be retroactive for January 1, 1974.[76] Once again, the parties negotiated a price—never disclosed.

Further negotiations took place in August 1974, but according to Yamani, this "long awaited discussion with the Aramco officials was short and sour." Yamani was disappointed that the Aramco parent companies did not come to the meeting with a plan to facilitate increased Saudi ownership. "Not even a new idea," he strategically complained to Ambassador Akins. "Nothing . . . but an offer to discuss buy-back prices." Yamani was prepared to be patient. He told Akins that Saudi Arabia would "live with the 60-40 arrangement until Kuwait nationalizes." In the interim, he said that the "parent companies would still stay, but it [would] 'not be as favorable for them as the arrangement we could have worked out now.'"[77]

Unlike Sulaiman, who almost always began with an extreme set of demands from Aramco, Yamani's strategy was to push the Americans into showing their hand first.[78] In November 1974, OPEC held a meeting to discuss a new formula for oil prices and invited oil company executives as observers but not participants. There, Yamani tried to pressure the American oil companies. He told the US ambassador (with the implication that Akins would tell the oil executives) that "the [American] companies were in for a 'big surprise' soon." He would not reveal what that was, of course.[79]

His tactic worked, because shortly thereafter the American companies told Akins that they "were considering sending a letter to Yamani, accepting in principle, 100% Saudi ownership of Aramco, pending resolution of certain well-defined problems."[80] Yamani,

who received the information later in the month, "was elated."
He told Akins that "the situation had changed entirely," and
that an "agreement in principle had been reached on all important points and he was sure details could be worked out."[81] By
December 1974, however, the process stalled and talks broke off.
According to the *New York Times*, "The stumbling block was said
to be the demand of the oil companies for oil price concessions as
part of the takeover package."[82] The oil companies wanted Saudi
Arabia to commit to selling oil to them at a discounted price. The
issue remained unresolved when trauma and tragedy struck the
kingdom and then OPEC, both in 1975.

NINE

"NATIONALIZATION WAS NOT THE THING AT ALL"

Prince Musaid bin Abdul Aziz was the half brother of King Feisal and nineteen years his junior. He is most remembered for the notoriety of two of his sons. One, Khaled, was the prince who was shot and killed while storming a television station during the anti-TV protests in 1965. Another son, named Feisal, like the king, was twenty-six years old in 1975. He went to college in the United States and attended several schools, including the University of California Berkeley, but performed poorly at all.[1] After Feisal bin Musaid had been arrested several times for fighting and "barroom brawls," he returned to the kingdom, where *al Saud* determined that "he had disgraced the family with his escapades abroad" and was not allowed to leave.[2]

On March 24, 1975, Feisal bin Musaid spent the evening with friends and his brother Bandar. The group drank whiskey, played cards, and smoked throughout the night, although the others later observed that Feisal drank little. The next morning, at 10:00 A.M., Feisal bin Musaid appeared at the king's palace and waited in the room outside King Feisal's personal office. Typically, family members sought audiences with the king at his home, not the palace. At that time, a delegation from Kuwait arrived to meet with the king and discuss oil policy with King Feisal and Yamani, who was already inside the office with the king. By happenstance, Feisal bin Musaid recognized a member of the delegation and struck up a conversation. When the Kuwaitis were admitted to the office, the king's nephew walked in with them.

King Feisal recognized his nephew immediately and walked over to welcome him. Feisal bin Musaid pulled out a small gun and shot the king three times. Yamani, the Kuwaiti delegation, and a television crew that had planned to film the greetings between the Saudis and the Kuwaitis saw everything. King Feisal was hit in the neck under his chin and in his ear. A third bullet grazed his forehead. The king was rushed to the hospital immediately, and Ahmed Abdul Wahhab, the king's protocol officer, who also witnessed the attack, called Frank Jungers in Dhahran. According to Jungers, Wahhab said, "Something terrible has happened. We urgently need Aramco's help." Wahhab would not divulge any details, but he told Jungers to "think of the most terrible thing you can imagine." He said they required medical assistance, in surgery specifically. Aramco's top doctors arrived in Riyadh two hours later, but they were unable to save King Feisal.[3] He was seventy-one years old when he died.

Mohammad bin Abdul Aziz, or Abu Sharayn, as he was called, was camping in the desert outside of Riyadh when he heard the news of his brother's death. He became the oldest living son of Abdul Aziz, but he had renounced his claim to the throne during the succession crisis a decade earlier. He was still a leader among *al Saud*. He rushed back to the city to join his brothers, who had gathered in the palace barely an hour after Feisal died. Mohammad immediately walked up to his half brother Khaled and spoke the words of the traditional *bayah* oath of loyalty. He then turned to Fahd, the half brother from the Sudairi line in the family, whose ambitions he had previously tried to suppress, and he swore the same oath to him as Crown Prince. The move was not without controversy, because in choosing Fahd, whom Mohammad had come to view as highly qualified, *al Saud* had bypassed two more senior brothers in the line of succession. But because of Mohammad's seniority, his actions spurred the rest of *al Saud* to come forward in order of seniority. Each brother declared his loyalty to King Khaled and Crown Prince Fahd.[4] There could be no hesitation or uncertainty in the face of such a tragedy.

Al Saud buried King Feisal in the same cemetery as his father. Feisal bin Musaid was arrested and tried in Saudi Arabia's Islamic courts for his crime. He was found guilty and sentenced to a public beheading, which was carried out on June 18, 1975. King Khaled approved the sentence, and Prince Salman, who was at that time the governor of Riyadh, was the only member of the royal family to witness the execution.[5] By many accounts Feisal bin Musaid appeared mentally unstable, but there was no indication he had ever received treatment.[6] There were some in the family who, in looking for a reason for his violent behavior, believed Feisal bin Musaid was irate over the confiscation of his passport.[7]

Feisal was born only two years after Abdul Aziz conquered Riyadh, and he was king of Saudi Arabia for ten years. The new king, Khaled, was born in 1912. He was also the younger full brother of Mohammad. Khaled would die of a heart attack in 1982, so he would be king for only seven years, but those seven years would bring great transformation.

◆

Talks between Saudi Arabia and the American shareholders of Aramco did not resume for some time. Feisal's assassination was not the only event that derailed them. In December 1975, Yamani was taken hostage by terrorists during an OPEC meeting in Vienna. Six terrorists from the Popular Front for the Liberation of Palestine (PFLP), led by the infamous Carlos the Jackal, stormed into the OPEC meeting. After a brief gunfight with Viennese police, the terrorists gained control of the floor where oil ministers had been meeting. The terrorists took Yamani, the other oil ministers, and thirty-one other people from the OPEC headquarters to an airplane. They were flown to Algiers, where the terrorists released all but fifteen of the hostages. The plane continued on to Tripoli. Yamani remained captive. According to Yamani, Carlos spent the entire flight telling Yamani that he was the real target of the attack and that Carlos was going to kill Yamani at the end regardless of whether the terrorists' demands were fulfilled.

Unbeknownst to Yamani, an Aramco jet, which had been standing by at the Vienna airport, was following the terrorists and hostages the entire time.[8] When they landed in Libya, the hostages were released, and Yamani was among them. Yamani immediately boarded the Aramco plane. It remains unclear why the terrorists attacked or why the hostages were released, although there was speculation that Saudi Arabia and Iran quietly paid millions of dollars for the release of their oil ministers. Years later, Yamani remained convinced that his government had never paid for his release. The terrorists abandoned the plane in Libya and fled. Carlos the Jackal was ultimately captured nineteen years later.[9]

After that incident, Yamani always traveled with extensive security. In fact, the security arrangements were how journalists realized on March 6, 1976, that Yamani and executives from the American shareholders were meeting secretly at a sailing club in Panama City, Florida. According to a *New York Times* report, "Private jet planes swooped down on the quiet coastal community; their occupants were whisked away in rented cars [and a] large number of private security guards appeared."[10] The next day, the meeting was confirmed as "guards armed with shotguns patrolled the resort where the negotiations were conducted."[11] After five days of talks, Aramco announced an agreement that Saudi Arabia would purchase the rest of Aramco and eventually fully Saudi'ize the company.

Observers at the time did not understand why the American shareholders were willing to entertain negotiations to sell their shares, either in 1972, 1974, or in 1976. Years later, the parties continued to be secretive about their motives and the details of the negotiations. However, Saudi executives and representatives knew that the Americans were aware of the fast approaching horizon on the concession agreement.[12] In 1959, an arbitration agreement confirmed that the still-valid original concession agreement was set to expire in 1993.[13] Further, the Americans did express trepidation that the Saudis might eventually choose to nationalize like so many other countries had. Though Yamani and Feisal had frequently and publicly rejected nationalization, the Saudis continued to use the notion of it as vague intimidation.[14] Moreover, since the very beginning of Socal's adventure in Arabia, the goal had been access to oil. Aramco was a tool for the American companies to acquire oil. They had partnered because none had sufficient capital to commit to the project alone, and the amount of oil each company received from Aramco was in proportion to that company's initial investment. So long as the Americans could negotiate continued access to Saudi oil for at least a while, they could abide by Saudi ownership. In fact, it is known that one of the points of contention during the various stock purchase negotiations of the 1970s was the contractual guarantee of oil to these companies.[15]

Ali al-Naimi, who would become the company's first Saudi CEO and later the kingdom's oil minister, further highlighted that the separation was "very amicable." According to Naimi, "Yamani was a good lawyer and shrewd [and] wise. So he managed, I think, to convince the four companies that this [was] a good deal for both." Naimi said that the American parent companies knew that "Saudi Arabia did not want to nationalize the company like what others [had] done." The Americans wanted to ensure that Aramco would "continue with the American style" of operations because, after all, the American companies would maintain business relationships with Aramco. As Naimi said, "the buyout was fair," and "there was absolutely no bitterness between the two and that is very important."[16]

When asked, even in 2017, Frank Jungers would not reveal how much the Saudis paid for the company.[17] A *New York Times* report at that time suggested that Saudi Arabia agreed to pay between $1.5 billion and $2 billion to the American oil company shareholders, but the newspaper could not confirm that figure.[18] A report by the petroleum publication *mees* said that "no details whatever" were released about the agreement, but that "information that had filtered through the oil industry at various times since the talks began over 19 months ago" suggested that Aramco's book value was $2 billion, of which Saudi Arabia had already paid $500 million.[19] Ali al Naimi, when asked about the purchase price thirty-one years later said, "I don't know. I really don't know."[20] Likewise, Nassir Ajmi, who served as executive vice president of Aramco shortly after the buyout said, "I really don't know."[21] Regardless of the price, the process was slow, and Saudi Arabia did not take full ownership until 1980. Even then, the company legally remained a Delaware corporation, following Delaware corporate laws until 1988.[22] A confused American diplomat commented that the slow buyout process, as opposed to an abrupt nationalization, led to "a curious arrangement whereby the Saudis legally owned Aramco but [it continued] to operate in accordance with its charter issued by the State of Delaware."[23]

Saudi Arabia negotiated a takeover according to accepted business practices. On this subject, Frank Jungers was clear. He explained, "Nationalization was not the thing at all. It was a takeover. . . . There was no nationalization. No one even talked of nationalization. It was a takeover that they had bought and paid for."[24] This sentiment was echoed by Dr. Majid al Moneef, whose resume includes positions on the Saudi Aramco board of directors, as an Aramco employee, and as an advisor to the Saudi Ministry of Petroleum. Dr. Moneef referred to the event as a "takeover," in which almost every process and procedure in the company remained the same.[25] Naimi agreed. He said, "We in the company did not really sense or feel any difference between ownership. We continued the way we [were]. That was the wisdom in the process of how Aramco became a Saudi company."[26] The Saudi employees within Aramco recognized the benefits of this buyout—as opposed to nationalization—because the buyout ensured continuity of culture and operations. For *al Saud* and Aramco management, a buyout was necessary because it ensured continuity of profits.

Ali al-Naimi wrote that the buyout "was a tribute to sound judgment and good negotiating faith on the part of the country as well as the oil company owners." Yamani and *al Saud* considered the expertise of the American founders and operators to be an asset. They were "aware of the failures other oil producers had made in nationalizing their foreign assets" and did not want to jeopardize Aramco's future success in a hasty takeover.[27] As Naimi explained, the Saudis like himself, who would eventually run Aramco, owed much of their success to "proper education . . . proper training . . . experience [and leadership from] their American colleagues."[28] "There were," Jungers observed, "certain things that remain [in Saudi Aramco] as part of that takeover."[29] What the new Saudi Aramco would make of that legacy over the next thirty-five years, however, was not something the Americans had foreseen.

On March 9, 1980, the Saudi government completed the purchase of Aramco and the company became the property of the king, as the sovereign of the Saudi state. In fact, after that date, Aramco employees often referred to the king of Saudi Arabia as "'the Shareholder,' but not to his face."[30] Aramco executives also referred to the "shareholder" as the ultimate decision-maker for the company, but the company generally avoided stating exactly who the "shareholder" was. When asked in 2017, however, top executives said that the government, not the king, owns the company. As Yasser Mufti, vice president of strategy and markets, said in a 2017 interview, "the company is owned by the Saudi Arabian government." The "Saudi Arabian government purchased the company and [Aramco] has been owned by the Saudi Arabian government ever since."[31] However, the evidence is contradictory. Ali al-Naimi recounted telling King Fahd, in 1993, "I am managing your company."[32] On the other hand, Yasser Mufti explained that the Supreme Petroleum Council ultimately appointed directors for the company and approved major decisions until 2015. According to Mufti, in 2015, the Supreme Petroleum Council was replaced by the Saudi Aramco Supreme Council.[33] The crown prince of the Saudi monarchy was appointed chair of this council.[34] Mufti described the council as acting as the shareholder representative but also said, "it basically is the shareholder."[35]

Ultimately, ownership of the company proved irrelevant to the operations of Aramco for two reasons. First, in Saudi Arabia, a monarchy, the king controlled the government, including any council that would oversee Aramco. Second, Aramco was given almost complete operational independence.

The transfer of ownership did not even make the petroleum and financial newspapers. It remained largely unknown to Americans until the *New York Times* covered it somewhere in the middle of the business section several months later.[36] The contrast with other, often violent, oil company nationalizations was stark and obvious. This buyout was boring.

A decade of volatile oil prices was already underway by the time the Saudis assumed complete ownership of Aramco. The Iranian revolution of 1979, a popular uprising against the Pahlavi dynasty, ultimately led to Ayatollah Khomeini and the religious authorities taking control of Iran. The revolution took the CIA by surprise, but it was actually presaged by wild swings in oil prices that began in 1978. Labor strikes by oil workers in Iran began in 1978 and continued to rock the oil market through the shah's abdication in January 1979. In September 1978, Iran's oil production stood at 4.5 million barrels per day. Two months later it was down to only 1 million barrels per day. By January 1979, not a single barrel was leaving Iranian ports. Prices skyrocketed globally, and Saudi Arabia quickly increased its production from 8.5 million barrels per day to 10.5 million barrels per day to compensate for the supply loss.[37]

As Iran was in the midst of violent transition, Saudi Arabia continued to sell its oil at the low price of $18 per barrel even as spot market prices went through the roof. Yamani believed in maintaining stable oil prices that were neither too high for consumers (what he determined to be around $18 per barrel at that time) nor too low for OPEC members. The Saudi oil minister always feared that sudden price hikes would cause recessions in oil-consuming economies. His fear was that such recessions would, in turn, depress oil demand and strike the Saudi economy.

The oil market proved highly vulnerable to forces outside Yamani's control. When the Iran-Iraq War began in 1980, the global price of oil rose until it hit $40 per barrel in 1981.[38] This geopolitical conflagration caused only a temporary spike in prices, even though the war between Khomeini's Iran and Saddam Hussein's Iraq lasted a total of eight years. In 1982, oil prices began a long, slow decline. That same year, Saudi Arabia also suffered the death of King Khaled of a heart attack at age sixty-nine. He had at one time claimed he never wanted to be king and had several times begged to be relieved of his princely duties so he could spend his old age in the desert with his beloved sporting hawks.[39]

Crown Prince Fahd, the eldest living Sudairi brother, succeeded his half brother and became king at age sixty. Fahd's half brother Abdullah, who was only one year younger than the new king, became Crown Prince. Unlike Khaled, Fahd was not known for religious devotion. In public, however, he acted as deferential to the *ulama* as his predecessors and continued the long tradition of weekly meetings with the most senior Islamic clerics.[40] Fahd was most concerned with his pursuit of economic growth and development for the country. Falling oil prices at the start of his reign reduced the kingdom's revenue and hampered his plans.

Oil from Alaska's North Slope, the Gulf of Mexico, and the North Sea in Europe began to enter the global market at the same time as recession tampered demand. OPEC was desperate to keep oil prices from falling and responded with several production cuts between 1981 and 1983. Still, prices continued to fall under $30 per barrel. At the May 1983 OPEC meeting, the oil ministers set an official price of $29 per barrel. No one knew if OPEC could keep the market at that level.

Yamani wanted to regulate the oil market through the power of Saudi Arabia's influence, and he believed he could. Yamani declared that Saudi Arabia would be a "swing producer."[41] Under this plan, OPEC producers would maintain their production quotas, but Saudi Arabia would raise or lower its production in order to keep prices stable. Saudi Arabia's production would fluctuate to counteract market changes.

The theory behind a swing producer is that a powerful oil producer can impact the market by increasing or decreasing its own production. In truth, a swing producer is most effective—perhaps only effective—when the other producers are producing at their full capacities and supply and demand in the global market is at or near equilibrium. If either of these criteria is not met, the swing producer's attempts at market manipulation will be severely mitigated.

Yamani's strategy seemed like a good idea. However, the reality of swing producing did not accommodate Saudi Arabia or Aramco in the 1980s. Between 1983 and 1985, Saudi Arabia cut production to as low as 2.2 million barrels per day from its height during the Iranian revolution of 10.5 million barrels per day. In 1985, oil revenue was so low that the kingdom ran a budget deficit of 100 percent of GDP.[42] Low oil prices and decreased production also hurt Aramco, which faced financial troubles for the first time since the 1940s. The company delayed work on a massive oil gas separation plant and, as a result, lost many millions of dollars more. The company laid off employees and temporarily decommissioned major oil-producing facilities, a process they referred to as mothballing.[43] Yamani's production policy also hampered Aramco's investment in future expansion and forced the company to cancel or scale back long-term plans for future growth.

In 1973, Saudi Arabia, with its OPEC partners, was able to swing the market because the rest of the world lacked spare capacity and demand was high. In the 1980s, Yamani was not successful largely because there was a global recession and a glut (or oversupply) of oil. Saudi oil was not missed from the market enough to raise prices to the level that Aramco and Saudi Arabia needed.

◆

As Aramco's production remained far below the company's capacity and its revenue suffered, major projects and expansion were delayed. The workforce shrank because of attrition and layoffs. Despite this period of downsizing, the company still planned for the future. Aramco knew it would need a continuous infusion of young, bright, capable employees from Saudi Arabia to succeed as a Saudi company in the long term. Under American ownership and management, the company had helped educate and train many of the Saudi employees who were quickly rising through the ranks to become managers and executives, a phenomenon that the first Saudi-born executives would credit for the company's later success.[44]

The Americans who first came to Saudi Arabia, like Tom Barger, thought it was beneficial to cultivate a steady supply of trained and capable locally born workers. When Saudi Arabia took over the company, this program took on new significance. Under American ownership, Saudis filled important roles at the company. Under Saudi ownership, Aramco filled a vital role for the people of Saudi Arabia as a desirable employer and as an opportunity for Saudis to succeed individually.

During the 1980s, Aramco continued to recruit and train Saudi workers for its oil facilities. Beginning in 1979, the company instituted a "fast track scholarship program" for Saudi high school students across the kingdom. The company looked to recruit the very best Saudi students, male and female. It established a rigorous selection process with high academic standards, particularly in the mastery of the English language. The company provided the students who met these standards with full scholarships and living expenses for college education at schools in the United States. Upon graduation, the young Saudis entered Aramco's workforce. The intention was that they would rise through the ranks to become the company's future managers and executives. Only fifty-seven students qualified the first year of the program, including thirteen women.[45]

With this new focus on recruiting the smartest and most motivated Saudis, Aramco quickly became the kingdom's top employer for Saudi talent. By 2006, a study of national oil companies (NOCs) concluded, "In Saudi Arabia, positions with the NOC are more coveted [than positions in government]. The strict selection process of the best students in the kingdom for entry into Saudi Aramco's training programs harnesses the country's best minds to the oil and gas sector."[46] When the Americans came to Saudi Arabia, the country benefitted primarily from the revenue Aramco provided. Over time—beginning with training, education, and jobs—Aramco itself became a tool to improve Saudi Arabia, its economy, and the lives of its citizens. *Al Saud* considered oil a gift from God, but Aramco under Saudi ownership became the prize and pride of the kingdom.

Zaki Safar, a young Saudi who began working for Aramco in 2008 as an electrical engineer described his experience in the Aramco program almost three decades after it began. Born and raised in Medina, Safar initially sought to attend King Fahd University for Petroleum and Minerals, but when he was eighteen, his brother-in-law suggested that he join Aramco. He applied to the company's college preparation program, along with twelve thousand other applicants. By the time Safar applied, Aramco was accepting two hundred Saudis, including Safar. "The program was very intense," Safar recalled. He moved to Aramco's headquarters in Dhahran for eleven months and focused on studying English, science, and math. Safar remembered being placed in only the second English level, and he "was shocked because I thought that I had pretty good English, considering that I used to ace all of my English scores." The company helped him apply to college in the United States, where Safar studied electrical engineering at Colorado State University.

Since becoming a Saudi company in 1980, Aramco has seen its prestige and esteem grow in the eyes of the Saudi people. Safar said he believed Aramco "is viewed widely as a very professional, probably the only professional enterprise that we have here in the kingdom. Very efficient, gets the job done, whether it has to do with the oil and gas industry or other projects." In Saudi Arabia, he said, a common refrain is that "if you want to get something done, give it to Aramco." Safar, like many young Saudis, has been active on social media and explained that "if you survey social media and you get people's opinion . . . you will find that they think highly of the company." During a period when Saudi Arabia's soccer team performed very badly, he said, "people recommended, jokingly, that Aramco be in charge of the team just to help it win."[47]

Recruiting and retaining talent for the future was important, but it was not nearly the most ambitious of Saudi Arabia's plans for Aramco's future. Saudi Arabia was not content to profit off its massive crude oil reserves. Instead, Saudi Arabia harbored a vision for Aramco to compete globally as a major, fully integrated IOC. The long-since-dismissed former oil minister and rabble-rousing Arab nationalist Abdullah Tariki actually had been the first to conceive of Aramco as a vertically integrated Saudi-owned company, but, at the time, his ideas went largely unheeded. Several decades later, in the 1980s, and after a smooth transition to Saudi ownership, Aramco was ready to take the first steps toward the kind of sweeping, global diversification its long-term vision required.

At first, Aramco still focused on two discrete aspects of its larger diversification plan—transportation and refining. Aramco did have one major refinery in Saudi Arabia, called Ras Tanura, built by the Americans in the 1940s, but its plan in the 1980s was of a much larger scale. During times of low oil prices, when oil companies find crude oil revenues curtailed, refining can help offset those losses, as refining generally does well when crude oil prices are low. Shipping and transportation was another area that could generate revenue for the company while its crude oil sales were depressed.

Aramco's first move, in 1984, was to open a subsidiary called Vela International Marine Company. The company started out with only four used tankers but provided Aramco with significant insight into the business of shipping and transporting oil. Aramco had previously been limited by marketing agreements with its former parent companies, which had prevented the company from gaining insights on the shipping industry. Eight years into the Vela venture, the shipping subsidiary remained small, though it had expanded to include four new tankers, which were among the newest and largest ships available. In 1995, Aramco had more money to invest and expanded the fleet by fifteen ships.[48]

Eventually, Aramco sold a majority share of Vela to the Saudi National Shipping Company, but when it first moved into shipping and marketing, these Saudi maneuvers were noticed by the more attentive people in the oil industry, especially after the failed attempted partnership with Aristotle Onassis in 1954. One of these was Glenn Labhart, who, in 1987, was employed as an oil trader with the German conglomerate Metallgesellschaft, which had a large global presence. He found himself working closely with Saudis in the shipping industry on a project modeling oil trades and said that he was "frankly very impressed for how people in Saudi Arabia were very knowledgeable with . . . what they were doing. [They took] a diverse view of the market in order to achieve for themselves greater growth."[49] Every step of the diversification and expansion was planned, and each step increased the company's abilities and position in the market, as well as its profit.

In 1986, Aramco began its plans to expand the company beyond Saudi Arabia's borders. As a new player on the global refining scene, Aramco began where it had the most experience and familiarity—the United States. Technically, Aramco was still an American corporation. Even though it was owned by Saudi Arabia, it would not transfer its corporate registration from Delaware to the kingdom for another two years. In looking for an American refinery to invest in, Aramco's CEO, John Kelberer, suggested partnering with Texaco, one of Aramco's former parent companies.

For Saudi Arabia, the strategy of partnering with a foreign company with expertise in the field—refining in this case—was familiar. It was a strategy the country had employed and would continue to employ many times to learn and gain expertise in new industries and fields. The country's first dealings with Bechtel thirty-five years earlier had been an early example, and the kingdom came out of that relationship with knowledge of construction, greater understanding of Western business practices and law, and construction equipment—plus new infrastructure.

In 1986, the last American CEO of Aramco, Kelberer, was instrumental in bringing Texaco and Aramco together to form a joint venture called Star Enterprises. Star Enterprises ultimately owned and operated several refineries located in Texas, Delaware, and Louisiana. Eventually, Texaco sold its stake to Royal Dutch Shell, and Aramco and Shell renamed the company Motiva Enterprises.[50] Motiva became the largest refinery in the United States, and in 2017, Aramco became its sole owner.[51] Finally, after thirty years, Aramco took over through a negotiated agreement, as it usually did, because the partner was no longer necessary.

◆

Through the initial steps of the diversification and expansion plan, Aramco continued to struggle with poor revenue and profits from its crude oil sales. In four years, Saudi Arabia's oil revenue declined by $93 billion, from $119 billion in 1981 to a low of $26 billion in 1985. At that point, King Fahd decided it was time to intervene.[52] He had given Yamani's swing producer policy time to work and decided that it had failed. Aramco and Saudi Arabia had not benefitted from oil production cuts. The cuts had not been able to support oil price targets. Other OPEC countries, along with new players like British companies extracting oil in the North Sea, reaped the benefits while

Saudi Arabia lost customers and revenue.[53] King Fahd had made drastic cuts to Saudi Arabia's 1983 and 1984 budgets, but he was losing patience. The kingdom had cash reserves of $100 billion, but if oil prices did not rise, even with the austerity measures, the kingdom would burn through those reserves in only three years. Aramco and Saudi Arabia also maintained ambitious diversification and expansion plans to pursue.[54]

Yamani tried to convince OPEC to adopt across-the-board production cuts, or at least adhere to the quotas already in place, but he was not successful. The cartel was fractured and could not reach a consensus. By mid-1985, Yamani made it clear that Saudi Arabia was "no longer willing or able to" attempt to be a swing producer alone and "carry the burden" for other OPEC countries. Six months went by and still OPEC could not reach a consensus on new production quotas. After the December 1985 OPEC meeting, Yamani followed through with his threat. At the beginning of 1986, Saudi Arabia abandoned its swing producer role entirely. Aramco opened its taps and began selling its oil at discounts to regain customers.[55] Yamani's declaration of unfettered production sent prices into a free fall. In just four months, the price of oil dropped from a hard-fought $32 per barrel to under $10.[56] In retrospect, it was clear that the price crash was largely fueled by panic. OPEC's production had, in fact, increased only by about 10 percent, but the market treated it as though the sudden oversupply was much greater. Ultimately, the cheap oil fueled economic development, demand began to rise, and prices recovered slightly by the end of the 1980s.

However, King Fahd was not able to wait for the market to bring him more revenue. Before the October 1986 OPEC meeting, King Fahd instructed Yamani to seek $18 per barrel along with a higher amount of production by Saudi Arabia. Yamani did not think the market could bear both the higher price and expanded production, but nonetheless he conveyed his king's policy to the OPEC partners. His mistake was that he told the OPEC members that this directive came from the king and that he harbored reservations about it. This less-than-subtle insult to his king turned out to be the final straw in what had become a strained relationship between Yamani and Fahd. A week later, Yamani was at home in Riyadh, eating dinner and watching the news, when the newscaster announced that Yamani had been "relieved" of his duties as oil minister.[57] Yamani might have been surprised to learn of his retirement in this fashion, but he knew the announcement was coming. In fact, months earlier, Yamani had moved many of his personal files to offices he had established in London and Geneva.[58]

The relationship between King Fahd and Yamani had been growing strained for a while before his dismissal. Ahmed Zaki Yamani had been a fixture in the global oil scene for almost a quarter of a century, and his firing came as a shock to many of the industry veterans who knew him. For those in the kingdom's inner circle, however, King Fahd's decision was a long time coming. According to Yamani's official biographer, Jeffrey Robinson, King Fahd never particularly liked Yamani. Yamani refused to speak to his biographer about any of the circumstances around his contentious relationship with the king or his dismissal, but stories came out nonetheless. In Robinson's telling, one of the fractures came when Yamani opposed a plan that King Fahd and his brother Sultan, the defense minister, concocted to barter oil with the British for military aircraft. Yamani pushed back and told Fahd and Sultan that this would dump excess oil on the market and drag down prices even further. *Petroleum Intelligence Weekly* reported that King Fahd ordered Yamani to pump the oil to pay for the aircraft and then lie to OPEC about Saudi Arabia's production.[59] In the end, Fahd went through with the deal, which substantially enriched the Sudairi branch of the family and several of the British companies involved. When Yamani insulted the king in front of OPEC in 1986, his position in the government became untenable.[60] In retrospect, Yamani's strength was his ability to negotiate with the IOCs and with other OPEC ministers. His understanding of the oil market was less sophisticated than that of later oil ministers. Yamani's training and background were in the law, so he was well suited to the major tasks of the 1970s—the OPEC-created oil shocks and buying out the American parent companies. He was less well suited to navigate the oil market of the 1980s, in which OPEC was beset with rising production from the United States, Britain, and Norway. Trying to establish Saudi Arabia as a swing producer at that time was a mistake for the kingdom. Its interests were sacrificed, and other OPEC countries eagerly took advantage of Saudi Arabia by overproducing.

Saudi Arabia's commitment to playing swing producer lasted only a few years and was not particularly successful, but the image of Saudi Arabia as the single producer responsible for determining the market persisted. In fact, Saudi Arabia was generally unsuccessful at supporting oil prices in the 1980s because new discoveries, external economic and geopolitical events, and oil market speculation took over. Saudi Arabia's vast productive capacity could impact the market at times, but, as Yamani and the 1980s proved, there are often too many factors at play in the oil market to say with confidence that a single producer's actions will have the intended effect.

Hisham Nazer, who replaced Yamani, had begun his career as an assistant to Abdullah Tariki. Nazer spent most of his career in the Ministry of Petroleum. Aramco's William Mulligan described Nazer, when he first joined the ministry as a young man, as "a member of Saudi Arabia's younger generation of officials," who "prided himself on his modernity and western tastes and outlook." Specifically, he enjoyed hot dogs and baseball when visiting the United States. In Saudi Arabia, Nazer hosted parties with his wife in which men and women could "mix freely."[61] One colleague from OPEC described Nazer as a tough negotiator who held his "cards in front of himself but close to the chest." Others were more skeptical of the new oil minister. Nazer, another OPEC source predicted, "will be the King's voice . . . unlike Yamani he does not have the depth." Yamani loved the press and often used his relationships with certain reporters to his advantage. Nazer, at his first OPEC meeting as oil minister, refused to speak to any of the reporters waiting in the lobby of his hotel.[62]

◆

1988 saw several significant changes that symbolized the final Saudi'ization of the company. In April 1988, the last American CEO of Aramco retired. John Kelberer, who had taken over after Frank Jungers, had been ill for some years before he officially retired. The board of directors named Ali al-Naimi as CEO. Naimi was one of the first Saudis to rise through Aramco's ranks. He had been executive vice president and was the natural choice to serve as the company's first Saudi CEO.

Seven months after Naimi took over, Saudi Arabia severed the last remaining legal ties between Aramco and the United States. The Council of Ministers approved a decree to establish a new Saudi corporate entity called the Saudi Arabian Oil Company. The Arabian American Oil Company, a Delaware corporation, was merged into the Saudi entity. The Delaware business was essentially replaced by the new Saudi corporation "to assume the responsibilities that had previously been those of Aramco." At first, the Saudis grappled with what to call their national oil company. Why, many argued, should they retain the name "Aramco" when the company was no longer tied to the United States? Oil Minister Hisham Nazer was the strongest proponent of maintaining the name Aramco. "The continuity of the name," he believed, "was important to the company's future success."[63] They settled on a new name, Saudi Aramco. A Saudi-based corporation meant that Aramco no longer was required to follow the structural legal limits of the state of Delaware.

Otherwise, the new legal status had little impact on the day-to-day operations of Aramco. Lee Ingham, a longtime American Aramco employee who was also reared in Saudi Arabia as the child of an Aramco employee, explained that from the perspective of the employees, "everybody knew there was a transition, and that the Saudis would own Aramco, but it had no real impact on the company that way. As far as living there and working, it went by without notice. . . . [The transition to a Saudi company] made little difference in what Aramco did and what was expected of my father and what was expected of me. We just carried on."[64]

Although Aramco became a Saudi-owned company, it still maintained a board of directors, corporate governance, and operating practices typical of its origins as an American company.

However, at one point when "creating Saudi Aramco," the government did try to step in. Naimi recalled a particularly difficult round of negotiations with the Saudi ministry of finance. "What they wanted," he said, "was all the income [from Aramco] to come to the ministry and they dole out our expenditures. I said, 'No way. The income comes to us and we give you royalty, taxes, and dividends from our profits. We cannot have the income come to you directly.'"[65]

It took Aramco two years to convince the Saudi government not to pursue this structure. In the end, Naimi recalled, "the king was sympathetic to our view." To Aramco, maintaining a separation between the company and the government "made sense." Naimi said, "had they controlled the purse we would not have expanded the way we did." He and other managers at Aramco considered Aramco more like an IOC than a national oil company and believed maintaining that distinction was key to Aramco's success. "You can't let the fate of a company [be] in the hands of people outside the company," he explained. "Aramco manages its finances. Finances don't come to it from somewhere else."[66] Naimi was a man driven by goals, and, as for Aramco, those goals necessitated independence.

Several other significant changes took place before this move that symbolized the final Saudi'ization of the company. In April 1988, the last American CEO of Aramco retired. John Kelberer, who had taken over after Frank Jungers was fired, had been ill for some years before he officially retired. The board of directors named Ali al-Naimi as CEO. Naimi was one of the first Saudis to rise through Aramco's ranks. He had been executive vice president and was the natural choice to serve as the company's first Saudi CEO.

Ali al-Naimi, who was born into a Bedouin family in the desert of the eastern province of Saudi Arabia, was in many ways emblematic of the relationship between Saudi Arabia and Aramco. Aramco offered him the chance to rise out of his premodern childhood, and Naimi took advantage of every one of the opportunities Aramco offered him. Naimi undeniably worked for and deserved his accomplishments. When he joined the company as a mail boy, he had no education. After his Aramco-sponsored university education, he returned to the company as an entry-level geologist, learned the oil business and corporate management, and then, with brazen ambition, rose to the very top.[67]

A young relative of Naimi's relayed a story from his father, Ali al-Naimi's nephew. In the late 1970s, Naimi's nephew was studying in Philadelphia when Naimi came to visit. The occasion called for a celebratory barbecue, after which Naimi went into the house to relax. Later in the evening they noticed he had "left a book on the arm chair," titled *How to Get Rich*.[68]

Naimi was an avid hiker, who enjoyed exploring the local terrain wherever his travels as CEO took him. These expeditions, which he included in company functions, also served his business purposes. In his memoir, Naimi wrote about negotiations to enter into a joint refinery venture in China. During one of the initial meetings, in 1992, Naimi expressed interest in hiking along the Great Wall of China with his Aramco team. The Chinese did not think the Saudis would be able to take on that kind of expedition, but Naimi insisted that if they left early the following morning, they would have time to hike and return to Beijing in time for their scheduled afternoon meeting.

The Chinese delegates were surprised to find the Aramco men dressed in boots, hiking attire, and backpacks early the next morning. When they reached the Great Wall, the Chinese offered to take them up along a tourist route, but Naimi chose the more difficult hike for them all, which his team completed without much difficulty. They were so fast, in fact, that the group made it back to Beijing with "plenty of time to shower and change into suits for our lunch at noon." Naimi wrote that the Chinese were impressed with him and his Saudi colleagues.[69]

Naimi must have believed that physical activity in front of others gave him an advantage in business, because he employed a similar approach with reporters and foreign diplomats. Richard Eason, an American Foreign Service officer who was the deputy chief of the Economic Section at the US embassy in Saudi Arabia between 1997 and 1999, described visiting Shaybah, an Aramco oil facility in the Empty Quarter, with Naimi and the US secretary of energy, Bill Richardson. The experience flying down from Riyadh was "like something out of James Bond . . . these enormous dunes, four or five hundred feet high [of] beautiful red sand." The press corps that accompanied the group wanted to ask Naimi questions. According to Eason, Naimi said, "OK, you want to interview me? We're going up there." Naimi "pointed to the top of the sand dune," which he proceeded to run up. "That was also," Eason explained, "where he went to get reception for his cell phone," which, coincidentally, at that time, came from nearby Abu Dhabi because "there was no Saudi signal that was all the way out in the Empty Quarter."[70] The effect of a short, slightly stocky, gray-haired oilman marching up a sand dune and leaving the press behind him was humbling to the reporters. Eason said that he followed Naimi up the sand dune but that Secretary Richardson "didn't quite make it."[71]

At OPEC meetings, held every six months at OPEC's permanent headquarters in Vienna, Naimi's walks would become a fixture for reporters. Herman Wang, a senior writer for *S&P Global Platts*, recalled that "as the junior member of our OPEC team" he was assigned to cover Naimi's daily walk around the city. "You would be down there in the lobby waiting for him at 6:00 in the morning and he would then come out. . . . He usually had a couple members of his delegation with him and then his bodyguards surrounding him and a pack of about, between six to ten journalists trailing him. . . . It was quite a sight as we [would] walk through the pre-dawn hours of downtown Vienna. Occasionally we would come across someone who was commuting to work that early in the morning and [they would look at us] kind of . . . 'What is this? Who are these people?'"[72]

As the first Saudi CEO, Naimi pursued a policy of aggressive expansion and diversification. He brought Aramco out of a Saudi cocoon to become an ambitious player in the global energy scene. He steered the company through a number of highly profitable acquisitions and new ventures. Some of it, however, was luck. Just two years after Naimi became CEO of Aramco, Saudi Arabia found itself at the center of a regional conflict that, when the dust cleared and the armies retreated, left Aramco with great advantages.

TEN

"BARRELS OF OIL AND GIGAWATTS OF POWER"

O n August 2, 1990, Saddam Hussein ordered the Iraqi army to enter Kuwait and annex it. His move surprised many, but Saddam Hussein's campaign to delegitimize Kuwait had been in progress for some time. Iraq's unabashed violation of another sovereign nation's borders originated in both long-standing regional conflicts as well as new grievances. Iraq and Kuwait had a border dispute dating back to when the emir of Kuwait asked the British to make Kuwait a British protectorate in the 1920s. In 1990, Iraq owed a significant amount of money to Kuwait and other Persian Gulf monarchies, including Saudi Arabia, for loans during Iraq's eight-year war with Iran. Iraq had been pressuring Kuwait to forgive its debts, but Kuwait refused. At the same time, Saddam Hussein contended that Kuwait was producing oil in excess of its OPEC quota, as well as overproducing oil from a field it shared with Iraq. Iraq charged that Kuwait's cheating was lowering the global price of oil (then around $12 per barrel) and thereby depressing the oil revenues Iraq desperately needed to recover from its long war with Iran.

Invading Kuwait, which Saddam Hussein called Iraq's twenty-third province, was strategically beneficial for Iraq. In 1990, Iraq and Kuwait's combined oil resources amounted to 20 percent of the world's proved oil resources. Kuwait also had what Iraq did not—easy access to the Persian Gulf for shipping that oil. Saddam Hussein, it seemed, did not think that the United States or anyone in the region would care if he invaded a relatively tiny country. He was wrong. The Saudis learned that Iraq's military had overrun their neighbor when the emir of Kuwait called King Fahd's son, Mohammad, from the small town of Al-Khafji on the border between Saudi Arabia and Kuwait. The emir refused to leave his country, even as Iraqi troops moved closer to Kuwait's border with Saudi Arabia. Mohammad and Fahd tried to persuade him to come over the border, but he would not leave until Mohammad came from Al-Khobar and brought the emir to safety in Saudi Arabia.[1]

Both King Fahd and President Mubarak of Egypt felt personally betrayed by Saddam Hussein's actions in Kuwait. At the last Arab League summit before the invasion, Saddam Hussein had promised them he would not attack Kuwait and made a spectacle of sitting next to the emir of Kuwait and referring to him as "brother." After the invasion, King Fahd took no actions other than to open Saudi Arabia to rich Kuwaiti refugees, who quickly filled up Riyadh's hotels. There was some speculation that because Fahd did not respond immediately, he was content to allow Iraq to retain control of Kuwait.[2] King Fahd had no intention of this, and neither did the United States or Great Britain. In fact, the United States sent a military force of 200,000 to Saudi Arabia as part of Operation Desert Shield to defend the kingdom from Iraq's aggression for five months. After assembling an international

United Nations–backed coalition of forces, and passing resolutions in the UN calling for Iraq to withdraw from Kuwait, the United States attacked in January 1991. Coalition forces bombed Iraq for a month before finally launching a ground invasion that lasted only one hundred hours. As American and coalition tanks rolled into Kuwait, they found most of the Iraqi forces fleeing. The war, referred to as Operation Desert Storm, ended on February 28, 1991, with a negotiated armistice.

Although the military results of this short war on Saudi Arabia were minimal, the Gulf War was a transformational experience for Saudi Arabia and for Aramco. For Saudi Arabia, Operation Desert Storm involved welcoming several hundred thousand foreign troops onto Saudi soil to protect the kingdom from a threat its military could not stop. This decision would have deep and long-term consequences for *al Saud*.

The most well-known story about King Fahd's decision to bring in the American military comes from then Defense Secretary and later Vice President Dick Cheney. In 1990, after Iraq invaded Kuwait, Cheney described the process of convincing the Saudis to allow the American military into the kingdom. Once the George H. W. Bush administration made the decision to compel Iraq to leave Kuwait, it became clear that US troops would be necessary. The American military was the only fighting force Saddam Hussein truly feared. "Saudi Arabia," Cheney explained, "was the logical place" to host US troops. Cheney wrote that the Saudis were "traditionally reluctant to have an American presence on their soil." This despite the obvious fact that Saudi Arabia had played host to a workforce of Americans large enough to fill a city for over fifty years, or that Saudi Arabia had hosted an American military airbase in the 1940s and 1950s.[3] It seemed to Cheney that the Bush administration would have to convince the Saudis.

Cheney explained that he first met with the Saudi ambassador to the United States, Prince Bandar bin Sultan. Bandar had been a fighter pilot in his youth, and Cheney's approach to convincing Bandar to support the deployment of US troops in Saudi Arabia was to reveal everything the United States knew about Iraq's forces and America's plans. Bandar was at first skeptical of Cheney's intentions, because in 1979, President Carter had promised to send American fighter jets to protect Saudi Arabia after the Iranian revolution and did not follow through. This time, however, Bandar was easily convinced of the necessity of bringing American troops to Saudi Arabia, as well as the sincerity of the Americans' promise to send a significant force. Bandar flew to Riyadh that night to speak with King Fahd. Cheney argued in his memoir that although US intelligence was never sure whether Iraq intended to attack Saudi Arabia, there was compelling enough evidence for Cheney to present to Fahd. Cheney, General Norman Schwarzkopf, and their staffs departed for Jeddah on August 5, 1990.[4]

Cheney met with US ambassador Charles Freeman, who cautioned the secretary of defense not to be "too aggressive or talk about too large a force," because this might "scare the Saudis." Freeman also warned Cheney that he might have to wait in Jeddah for quite some time before his audience with the king and to be prepared for the process to take several days because the Saudis "don't make up their minds quickly."[5] In Jeddah, Prince Bandar greeted the Americans. He had, Cheney observed, "undergone a transformation." The usually urbane ambassador, who preferred expensive Italian suits, was "dressed in the traditional robes of a Saudi prince." Bandar told Cheney he should be frank about the number of troops the United States would send and how quickly they could arrive.

Cheney believed it was clear the matter was of utmost importance to King Fahd, because the Americans were welcomed into their meeting on time. The room in the king's Jeddah palace had been lined with chairs in an L shape. Along one side sat the Saudis. King Fahd sat at the intersection of the two sides. Also present was Crown Prince Abdullah, Foreign Minister Saud al Feisal, Bandar, and Deputy Defense Minister Prince Abdul Rahman, who was taking Defense Minister Prince Sultan's place because he was out of the country. Bandar positioned himself in a chair just behind the king so he could interpret. Cheney sat next to the king at the front of the row of chairs designated for the Americans. After everyone was settled, servants emerged and poured tiny cups of Arabic coffee for all. Cheney noted that every servant also carried a holstered gun.[6]

According to Cheney's account, he made his case to the Saudis, revealing evidence of Iraqi troops arrayed on the border with Saudi Arabia who were capable of attacking Saudi Arabia and moving on key oil fields with less than two days' notice.[7] Only "military deterrence," Cheney told King Fahd, would discourage Saddam Hussein from attacking. Cheney, perhaps based on his conversations with Bandar, believed that Fahd needed to be convinced of the seriousness of the existential threat Iraq posed to his kingdom and its oil.

Robert Lacey told a different story of Saudi Arabia's decision based on his interviews with high-ranking Saudi officials and Americans like General Norman Schwarzkopf. According to Lacey's account, Fahd was well aware of the threat his Iraqi neighbor posed to Saudi Arabia and knew his best chance at defending the kingdom and checking Iraq's aggression lay with the Americans. King Fahd, Lacey's sources told him, "did not want to show his hand too early." He acted cautiously after the invasion of Kuwait because he did not want to act without the consensus of the various sources of power in the kingdom—"all his brothers, the main ministers, the military, the tribes, and the religious sheikhs."[8]

The *ulama* would prove most difficult to convince, but, according to Lacey, Fahd began his campaign to convince them even before the Americans called. At first the *ulama* said no, justifying their position with a well-recognized *hadith* that said, "Let there not be two religions in Arabia." This *hadith* was commonly used to justify prohibiting foreigners from entering Saudi Arabia, although clearly exceptions had always been made. The *ulama* never seriously questioned the army of businessmen Abdul Aziz had welcomed into the kingdom years earlier. Fahd was prepared for this answer and sent his brothers Salman and Nayef to work on changing the clerics' minds. Both Salman and Nayef were seen as devout men and had many personal connections with members of the *ulama*. By the time Cheney and his team arrived in Saudi Arabia, the *ulama* were already debating and reconsidering the issue. Fahd took this as an indication that they would change their position.[9]

At this point, according to Lacey, King Fahd had already reached out to Washington. As the *ulama* again debated the issue, the king requested that someone from the Bush administration come and "brief him on the threat to his kingdom." The meeting took place on the shores of the Red Sea at the king's palace in Jeddah, as Cheney wrote. According to Lacey, when General Schwarzkopf stepped forward to present the military evidence of Iraq's forces gathering on the Kuwaiti-Saudi border, he showed the king aerial surveillance photographs of five Iraqi tanks that had crossed the border into Saudi Arabia. Schwarzkopf recalled for Lacey that he told King Fahd that the tanks likely did not know they had violated Saudi sovereignty, because the border was not marked in that area. Nevertheless, King Fahd was visibly upset. "I don't care if it's only one tank!" Fahd responded, according to Schwarzkopf and Lacey.[10]

After Schwarzkopf and Cheney presented, Bandar stopped interpreting and *al Saud* began to discuss among themselves in Arabic. Cheney recalled being surprised that the Saudis did not dismiss the Americans or move to another room while they talked.[11] Cheney never knew exactly what the Saudis said, but Lacey apparently learned of the content of the conversation from his sources in *al Saud*. King Fahd seemed ready to invite the American military in immediately, whereas Crown Prince Abdullah disagreed and urged his brothers and nephews "not to rush into a decision."

Fahd responded heatedly. "Like the Kuwaitis! They did not rush into a decision and now there is no Kuwait."

Abdullah reminded his half brother, "There is still a Kuwait," to which Fahd retorted, "And its territory consists of hotel rooms in London, Cairo, and elsewhere."

Abdullah conceded that point. Riyadh's hotels were overrun with Kuwaitis who had no idea when—or if—they might be able to return home. The other princes agreed with Fahd, who looked over at Cheney and spoke his only word of English that entire visit. "Okay," he said.[12]

Cheney wrote that American planes were flying over the Arabian Peninsula within hours and forces arrived soon after.[13] However, American planes had already been flying over Arabia, notably out of Diego Garcia, an island in the Indian Ocean.[14] Operation Desert Shield had begun. On August 13, as Fahd had expected, the *ulama* reconsidered their position and announced their formal approval for the king of Saudi Arabia to "take every means to deter aggression and the incursion of evil" into the kingdom.[15]

King Fahd had most likely already decided to invite American troops into Saudi Arabia before Cheney arrived. It was not the split-second decision the Americans thought it was. Rather, Fahd used the meeting to achieve the consensus he sought from his brothers, particularly Crown Prince Abdullah. The decision was momentous in its long-term implications. As US forces flowed into the kingdom, their presence became a visible reminder to the Saudis that the Americans were there to protect them. This was different from the Americans in Dhahran or elsewhere in the desert who had pumped Saudi oil for years. Those American oilmen and their families had lived in Western enclaves with other Americans and foreigners and had had very little interaction with Saudis who did not work for Aramco. By September 1990, there were more Americans in Saudi Arabia's eastern province than soldiers in Iraq's Republican Guard.[16]

One individual who was greatly aggrieved by the American military presence in Saudi Arabia was Osama bin Laden. Osama bin Laden knew *al Saud* well. His father had run the largest and most successful Saudi construction company, the Binladin Group, and had educated his sons alongside the sons of Abdul Aziz. Osama bin Laden did not enter the family business. Instead, he used his share of his father's wealth to fund the recruitment and training of Muslims from around the world to fight against the Soviets in Afghanistan in the 1980s.[17] When Iraq invaded Kuwait, Osama bin Laden was back in Saudi Arabia and immediately saw an opportunity to put his vast database (*qaeda* in Arabic) of trained Muslim fighters to work. They would, as Osama bin Laden explained to his friend and journalist Jamal Khashoggi, use their skills to fight in the streets to liberate Kuwait from Iraqi forces. In Osama bin Laden's worldview, Saddam Hussein was a secular dictator whose political party, the Ba'ath Party, drew inspiration from socialism and had perpetrated "un-Islamic aggression" against Kuwait.[18]

When Osama bin Laden brought his concerns to *al Saud*, however, he was rebuffed. He even went so far as to present his plan to wage an urban Islamic guerilla war against Iraqi forces in Kuwait to the youngest Sudairi brother, Ahmad. Ahmad thought that his plan "did not seem practical," nor was it appropriate for "the scale of the problem," and politely rebuffed the offer.[19] Osama bin Laden did not appreciate the rejection and left upset and angry. When he saw that instead of the Muslim fighters he had organized, trained, and indoctrinated in Afghanistan *al Saud* had invited Americans into Saudi Arabia, he was incensed. This was the beginning of his fight against *al Saud*. Osama bin Laden's doctrine evolved to portray Saudi Arabia's ruling family as un-Islamic. He even called the king a polytheist.[20] Though the *ulama* had approved officially, not all in Saudi Arabia supported the decision. Some even spoke out against it at the time. Still others did defend *al Saud*'s position.

After the international coalition drove Iraq out of Kuwait, the US military continued to maintain bases to enforce the sanctions and no-fly zones on Iraq. This became one of Osama bin Laden's primary points of issue against *al Saud*. In Osama bin Laden's "Declaration of War," he wrote, "The [Saudi] regime betrayed the *umma* and joined the infidels, assisting them . . . against the Muslims. . . . By opening the Arabian Peninsula to the crusaders, the regime disobeyed and acted against what had been enjoined by the messenger of God."[21] In his view, *al Saud* had become an illegitimate ruling family and thus its regime, along with the Americans who supported it, could become the target of violent acts of terrorism.[22]

Most of the American military forces left Saudi Arabia after the Gulf War, though the United States maintained a military presence in Saudi Arabia for many years afterwards. The United States built and used the Prince Sultan Air Base near Riyadh to police the no-fly zones established in Iraq. The United States then used it to coordinate the 2001 assault on Afghanistan and to coordinate the 2003 invasion of Iraq. King Abdullah allowed the United States to launch the air assault from Prince Sultan Air Base in 2003, with the caveat that afterwards the Americans had to pack up the base and leave for good. In September 2003, American troops finally left Saudi Arabia and moved to the al Udeid base in nearby Qatar.[23] *Al Saud* had requested this to avoid the kinds of charges leveled at the royal family by Osama bin Laden in the 1990s.[24] Nor was Saudi Arabia part of the coalition supporting US forces in 2003.

Between 1991 and 2002, the Saudi military expanded considerably with the help of American military consultants and large purchases of American fighter jets, tanks, armored vehicles, and ammunition.[25] After the 2003 invasion of Iraq, which Abdullah did not support, Saudi Arabia continued to expand its military while diversifying its defense equipment suppliers. In 2004, as part of an economic mission to Russia, the Saudis purchased weapons and equipment from the Russians while continuing to purchase American defense products.[26] Just like *al Saud*'s approach to other industries, including construction and energy, Saudi Arabia first brought in outside expertise to provide services it could not provide for itself. By 2015, Saudi Arabia became the largest importer of defense-related products, as the country looked to defend itself from threats like Islamic State on its northern border and Houthi groups on its southern border.[27] The Saudis could not and would not rely solely on the United States to protect them anymore.

◆

When the American military arrived in Saudi Arabia for Operations Desert Shield and Desert Storm, Aramco was still pumping significantly less oil than its productive capacity. According to Ali al-Naimi, the company had decommissioned 146 oil wells and 12 gas oil separation plants during the 1980s. In July 1990, Aramco produced 5.4 million barrels per day. This was a significant increase from the company's low of 2.2 million barrels per day under Yamani's swing producer policy but still far below the more than 10 million barrels per day it was capable of pumping.[28]

When Iraq invaded Kuwait, oil prices immediately jumped several dollars per barrel. They continued to rise over the next several months.[29] The UN imposed sanctions on Iraq in January 1991, which resulted in the loss of the combined exports from Iraq and Kuwait from the market. Aramco quickly started to bring its dormant facilities back online. The company was tasked with providing fuel to the American forces stationed in Saudi Arabia and jet fuel for the massive aerial campaign the coalition forces planned to launch on Iraqi troops. According to Robert "Bo" Smith, who as a naval aviator and captain was one of the officers involved in early plans for the air defense in Operation Desert Shield, "All the oil, all the aviation fuel that was being burned [by U.S. troops] was not being paid for by the Americans." Aramco provided it and the Saudis paid for it.[30] This was confirmed by Aramco's executive vice president at the time, Nassir Ajmi. In fact, Mr. Ajmi further explained that Aramco provided the coalition forces with advice, fuel, support, and detailed maps.[31] In addition, Aramco anticipated that a successful sanctions resolution against Iraq would result in a gap in the oil market. Aramco wanted to fill that gap with Saudi oil.[32]

Less than a month after Iraq's invasion of Kuwait, OPEC held an emergency meeting and decided to dispense entirely with production quotas.[33] Between July and December 1990, Aramco increased its oil production by over 3 million barrels per day to bring production up to 8.5 million barrels per day. To do this, the company accomplished an impressive engineering and logistical achievement, particularly considering that it was already understaffed and a portion of its American employees had decided to leave Saudi Arabia in anticipation of war. Aramco's headquarters and oil facilities were closer to the war than most of Saudi Arabia's major population centers. In fact, a processing facility for Aramco's Safaniyah oil field was less than sixty miles away from the only pitched ground battle during Desert Storm, and Dhahran was the target of multiple Iraqi Scud missile attacks.[34] The US Patriot air defense system shot down many of those Scuds, although some found targets, including a building in Dhahran that housed US military forces. Twenty-seven US servicemen died in that attack.[35]

Overall, the Gulf War benefitted Aramco's business. The company was able to increase its production very quickly and take advantage of higher prices caused by crisis. The UN resolution adopted in April 1991 placed significant sanctions on Iraq's oil and essentially cleared the way for Saudi oil to regain its market share.[36] In addition, Aramco gained international recognition for its efforts to contain the massive oil spill unleashed by Saddam's troops into the Persian Gulf.[37] The oil spill threatened both the ecosystem of the Persian Gulf and Aramco's offshore oil production. Aramco had massive desalinization plants and seawater-cooled power plants that would be damaged by water contaminated with even a small amount of crude oil. The desalinated water was crucial for oil production, and it also provided the coalition troops and Aramco employees with drinking water.[38]

Through a coordinated international effort, Aramco was able to protect its offshore facilities by establishing an extensive system of movable booms and sand berms.[39] It is impossible to know how much Kuwaiti oil Iraq spilled into the Persian Gulf, but estimates range from 4 million to 10.7 million barrels.[40] Aramco was able to corral some of that crude oil into natural bays along Saudi Arabia's coastline and decontaminate both the water and the crude oil. The company recovered about 900,000 barrels of oil through these efforts and sold it on the market.[41] Reflecting on Aramco's role in the Gulf War, Naimi assessed that the war helped improve Aramco's and Saudi Arabia's image in the international scene:

> We were once again actors on the world stage, but this time, unlike during the oil embargoes of the 1970s, the

eyes of much of the developed world saw us as the good guys. . . . Saudi Aramco kept the world supplied with oil, and the Kingdom served as the major base of operations through which an international alliance thwarted a vicious dictator's attempt to seize a nation unable to defend itself.[42]

◆

Saddam Hussein's invasion of Kuwait and the Gulf War provided momentum for Aramco to continue to expand its foreign footprint. By 1991, Saudi Arabia, with full ownership of Aramco, had already regained its spot as the world's top oil producer.[43] This was not enough. Saudi Arabia was not content to simply watch its profits accumulate. Like always, its focus was on securing more profit and greater power for future generations. With Aramco, this meant diversifying the company and looking toward more long-term opportunities in energy. Aramco's previous owners, the four American companies, saw Aramco as an entity that produced a guaranteed source of crude oil for them to refine and market around the world. Saudi Arabia, on the other hand, saw Aramco as its greatest source of revenue and innovation. In order for the company to maximize revenue, it could not remain a simple oil producer. Aramco could not endure as just another national oil company, pumping out Saudi Arabia's black gold and selling it at the best market price it could get at the time. To ensure Saudi profit and power, Aramco would need to take its place among the great multinational energy companies of the world.

The oil industry is generally divided into three stages: upstream, midstream, and downstream. Upstream refers to exploration and production, primarily focused on finding crude oil and extracting it. Midstream refers to the initial processing and movement of crude oil, natural gas, and natural gas liquids from the point of extraction. Downstream refers to refineries, petrochemical plants, marketing outlets, and product distributors. Aramco already had vast upstream operations. The kingdom's agreement with the company provided Aramco with exclusive access to all of Saudi Arabia's crude oil resources, and the company was also expanding its domestic downstream footprint. In the profitable decade of the 1990s, Aramco expanded beyond Saudi Arabia.

Aramco directed its attention toward Asia. In 1989, before the Gulf War, Aramco had sent a team to China. According to Naimi, the team reported back that China was "a country filled with bicycles, hundreds and thousands of bicycles." In a country where most of the population traveled by bicycle or rickshaw and the power plants burned coal, Naimi wondered, "Who is going to buy our oil?" Korea, Japan, Indonesia, and the Philippines looked like better prospects. Aramco opened negotiations with South Korea in January 1991 and, within seven months, the company reached an agreement to purchase a 35 percent share of Ssangyong Oil Refining Co. Ltd., later renamed S-OIL.[44]

Aramco's strategy was twofold. The company sought to enter into joint ventures with other companies with greater expertise in the downstream sector so Aramco could gain knowledge and expertise in the industry and in Asia. If the venture proved profitable, Aramco would seek to expand its ownership, perhaps to 100 percent. It was a model already proven successful in dealings with Americans. In addition, with these refineries, Aramco secured sales outlets for Saudi crude oil and diversified Aramco's revenue base. Although the profit margins in the downstream sector were generally lower than in crude oil sales, the addition of downstream investments reduced the revenue volatility typically associated with the crude oil business. Ali al-Naimi later explained that Aramco "wanted to do two things. One, of course, [was] to expand the company." The other, he continued, was to "guarantee a market." Aramco, as co-owner in refineries abroad would be "obligated to provide the feedstock for the refinery." This was "one of the driving forces" behind Aramco's diversification strategy.[45]

Throughout the 1990s and early 2000s, Aramco made other investments similar to its Korean ventures, but in other countries negotiations often took longer.[46] In 1994, Aramco invested in a joint venture with Petron, the largest oil refiner in the Philippines, which Aramco then sold in 2008 for $550 million.[47] Aramco started negotiating with Japanese entities in 1991, but it was not until 2004 that Aramco acquired a 15 percent interest in Showa Shell, a Japanese refining company with multiple facilities throughout Japan.[48] Aramco became the largest supplier of crude oil to Japan.[49] In 2006, Aramco, with the assistance and guidance of King Abdullah, opened negotiations with China for a $3.5 billion refinery.[50] Three years later, Aramco signed an agreement with the Fujian Petrochemical Corporation and ExxonMobil to open a joint venture called the Fujian Refining & Petrochemical Company. In 2010, Aramco and the Japanese government signed an agreement whereby Aramco would supply Japan's strategic crude oil storage facility.[51] In 2017, Aramco signed a joint venture agreement with Petronas to build a new refinery in Malaysia and supply the majority of its feedstock.[52]

Aramco's investments in refining, petrochemicals, and storage facilities in Asia led to long-term contracts to provide Saudi crude oil to the Asian market. The investments also enabled the company to gain knowledge and experience in various downstream sectors. Later, Aramco used some of the connections it made with companies in Asia, as well as the expertise it gained in oil refining and chemical manufacturing, to partner with other companies and expand its downstream sector within Saudi Arabia. In 2011, Aramco and Dow Chemical established the Sadara Chemical Company as a joint venture in Saudi Arabia. In 2013, Aramco and Total (a French oil company) opened SATORP, a joint venture chemical plant in Saudi Arabia, near Dhahran. In 2014, Aramco and Sinopec (the Chinese national oil company) opened Yasref, an oil refinery in Saudi Arabia located on the Red Sea coast.[53]

Saudi Arabia's strategy of learning new technologies and industries from established experts continued to serve Aramco well as it expanded from an oil-producing company to a global energy conglomerate. Ambassador Smith described the advantage this strategy provided the company. "There is an arrogance associated with national oil companies," he said. "But the Saudis, they know what they don't know, and if they don't know something they will partner with somebody who does know it for them to learn it." He had the opportunity to visit a new steam injection facility that Aramco built on the border between Kuwait and Saudi Arabia. To build it, Aramco partnered with Chevron, "who'd been doing this out in California for decades." The process would enhance the amount of oil Aramco could recover in older oil wells. "The Kuwaitis were not active participants" in that partnership, according to Ambassador Smith, because "their assumption was, if Chevron can do it, it must not be that hard. [But Aramco wanted] to learn the technology from Chevron."[54]

Aramco also prepared to take advantage of emerging technologies in oil production, such as hydraulic fracturing techniques being used to extract oil and natural gas from shale rock formations in the United States. This relatively new process, commonly called "fracking," combined horizontal drilling with a method of flushing a chemical and water solution into the rock. This caused shale rock formations to release oil and natural gas, which were then brought up to the surface. Fracking took off in the United States in 2008, and several years later Aramco identified shale rock formations in Saudi Arabia that might produce oil through fracking. At that point, the cost of fracking was still too high for it to be profitable for Aramco, which could produce a barrel of oil in the conventional manner at a cost of less than $10.[55] Nevertheless, Aramco began teaching hydraulic fracturing techniques in its upstream professional development program.[56]

Still, the company was planning for a future when exploiting that oil and gas would be profitable. Aramco hired Dan Arthur, a managing partner from ALL Consulting, to consult on environmental issues related to fracking. According to him, Saudi Arabia had discovered "a significant amount of unconventional oil and gas resources [that it] never took advantage of." Aramco, he said, was "very environmentally sensitive" and wanted "to do things right" when it came to developing these resources. The company had begun to drill some fracking wells and planned on significant expansion in the future but wanted "to be proactive" in developing its own regulations for fracking. "They [wanted] to leverage off of" the fact that American companies had done most of the pioneering work in fracking. Aramco knew that American companies were "the experts. So they brought us in."[57]

◆

As Aramco developed as a Saudi company, sometimes the lines between state and company blurred. The company had inherited a particular structure and organization, as well as a mode of interacting with the Saudi state as part of its legacy as an American company. This included a board of directors that oversaw the company's operations.[58] Aramco developed a business plan every year that incorporated long-term strategy. The board approved this plan, and only then did the government become involved with review by the Supreme Petroleum Council. According to one official in the oil ministry cited in Valerie Marcel's study of Middle Eastern national oil companies, the Saudi government's approval was perfunctory. "There's an unwritten aura, a taboo culture against interference."[59] Unlike some other national oil companies in the region, Aramco, not the state, controlled the sale of oil and collected payment.[60] The company then paid taxes to the Saudi state just as it had under American ownership.[61]

In 1986, the Saudi Ministry of Petroleum attempted to exert its influence over Aramco, but that attempt was met with stiff resistance from Aramco's Saudi executives. In fact, Ali al-Naimi convinced his entire team of executives to threaten to resign from the company if the state continued its efforts to "take over Aramco." Naimi wrote derisively of the managerial abilities of those who worked for the Ministry of Petroleum.[62] Ironically, years later, former Aramco officials would essentially take over the Ministry of Petroleum.

Despite the separation between state and company, over the years Aramco provided much more for the Saudi state than just revenue.

After all, the king was the sovereign of the Saudi state so the barriers were only as necessary as the king desired. Naimi, in a rare conversation with King Fahd about oil policy, once told him, "I am managing your company."[63] For example, Aramco provided crude oil, gasoline, and diesel fuel to Saudi consumers, and oil and natural gas to Saudi utility companies at below market prices.[64] This was a major financial commitment, as the monetary value of this energy was significant to the company, particularly during seasons of high demand.[65] It was also significant to the king and to *al Saud*'s relationship with the Saudi people. Cheap, essentially subsidized, energy was a clear sign of *al Saud*'s continued power and strength, as well as a connection for the people of Saudi Arabia to the Saudis' gift from God. Aramco contributed other projects to Saudi Arabia, including the construction of schools and soccer fields, and Aramco officials were occasionally tapped to handle logistics in times of national need. To Aramco, this was akin to the development of community relations, although the common ownership of both the company and the government made many outside observers question the company's independence.

◆

Continuity of leadership had long been a hallmark of both Saudi Arabia and Aramco, but in 1995, in the midst of Aramco's global downstream expansion, both the kingdom and the company faced change at the top. In 1995, King Fahd, the oldest of the Sudairi Seven, suffered a stroke that incapacitated him. It occurred at a troubling time, shortly after terrorists linked to Osama bin Laden had bombed a training center for the Saudi National Guard in Riyadh. Fahd went on to live for another ten years, but Crown Prince Abdullah assumed full executive responsibilities for the rest of Fahd's reign.[66]

Abdullah was not as austere as King Feisal, but he was said to have displayed some similar characteristics. He kept tight control over the finances of the government institutions he ran and over his own family. He worked tirelessly to improve a stutter until he was able to speak flawlessly. He swam laps every day to improve his personal fitness. He cultivated a stern persona in public, but he enjoyed his family and was known to have taught all of his daughters to swim. He made sure all of his children grew up speaking perfect English.[67]

Abdullah's mother was the widow of a Rashidi chieftain who had been killed in the fighting between Abdul Aziz and the tribe of *al Rashid* during Abdul Aziz's conquest of Arabia. After Abdul Aziz expelled the Rashidis from Riyadh, they sought refuge with their relatives in northern Arabia. In 1921, Abdul Aziz captured their stronghold in the town of Hail. Instead of executing his enemies, Abdul Aziz chose peace and welcomed them to live in Riyadh, under Saudi rule. He took one of the widowed Rashidis, a woman from the Shammar tribe, as his wife. In 1923, she had a son, whom Abdul Aziz named Abdullah.[68]

Abdullah, who had no full brothers, gained power within the family through the close relationship he maintained with Feisal and with the prominent role he had in reuniting the family after Talal's exile. He played peacemaker and appeared neutral in family disagreements, which was one of the reasons he was chosen to be Crown Prince after Khaled's death. Another reason was that he commanded an important sector of Saudi society, the National Guard. He molded the National Guard, which operated through the tribal system, into a solid military force, and he also used it to create a shadow network of social services. The hospitals run by the National Guard were particularly known for their high standards. Under Abdullah's guidance, one of these hospitals became an internationally recognized center for separating conjoined twins.[69]

The royal family was protective of its secrets; few people really knew what the relationship was between the sons of Abdul Aziz. Because Fahd was incapacitated, Abdullah ran the government as the Crown Prince. There were rumors of discontent and conflict between Abdullah and Fahd's Sudairi brothers.[70] The perception was that some sons aligned with their full brothers to take an outsized share of power, but little information has been confirmed. After the scandal with King Saud, *al Saud* tried to keep its secrets.

Before King Fahd suffered his first stroke, he had dismissed Hisham Nazer as oil minister. There had been signs of the king's displeasure with Nazer's performance. In August 1995, it was simply announced that Nazer had been removed as oil minister. As Nazer's replacement, King Fahd bucked tradition and did not choose a government bureaucrat. Instead, he chose Aramco's CEO, Ali al-Naimi. Naimi was in Alaska on vacation when he learned that the king had appointed him minister of petroleum and mineral resources. He was told to return to Saudi Arabia for the official announcement.[71]

Naimi might have been surprised at the timing of his elevation to oil minister, but he had reason to suspect the appointment was coming. A little over a year earlier, Naimi had an unexpected audience with King Fahd to discuss oil policy at length. Naimi quickly realized this was a job interview, so he made sure to supply politically appropriate answers and to let the king know that his primary focus was "managing [the king's] company."[72]

Naimi's appointment as oil minister marked Aramco's dominance over Saudi oil policy. At one time Naimi as CEO had been forced to prevent the finance ministry from taking the company's revenue. Another time, the former oil minister, Yamani, had sought to bring Aramco under the umbrella of an existing corporation called PetroMin, which would have placed Aramco under the control of the oil ministry.[73] Aramco's senior management had been particularly anxious about the PetroMin plan, because it had felt that the oil ministry was poorly managed and put political concerns, not business practices, first. With Naimi in place atop the oil ministry in 1995, Aramco's position and the professionalization of oil policy in Saudi Arabia was secure. With a former longtime Aramco employee at the head of the Ministry of Petroleum and Mineral Resources, the ministry essentially became a political arm that served Aramco's interests. Those interests, of course, were one with those of *al Saud*—a vision of long-term profit and power.

At age sixty, Ali al-Naimi retired as CEO of Aramco to enter government service. He remained on the company's board of directors but no longer managed the business. His focus shifted to managing oil policy and, in particular, the difficult task of setting Saudi oil production levels. It was the oil minister's responsibility to negotiate with fellow OPEC and non-OPEC oil-producing nations.

In Naimi's place, Abdullah Jumah became CEO of Aramco. Jumah was one of the first Aramco CEOs who did not have a background in engineering or geology. His background was in political science and history. He was also a published poet. During the Gulf War, Jumah, then an executive vice president, served as Aramco's primary spokesperson. This role was crucial, and Jumah was responsible for crafting a positive image of Aramco.[74] Jumah's background served Aramco's purposes particularly well in the mid-1990s because Aramco was in the midst of its global expansion and diversification and needed an effective representative as it marketed itself. Jumah's fluency in English, easy smile, and deliberate speech formed the right personality as the Saudis went about selling themselves and their oil products to the world.

◆

In 1933, Harry St. John Bridger Philby published a short monograph describing his travels in a section of Arabia called Rub al'Khali, or the Empty Quarter.[75] Philby was only the second Westerner to traverse this great desert with dunes of red sand that can reach up to 820 feet. The desert borders Yemen and Oman in the south and the United Arab Emirates in the east. It has been described as "hyper-arid," meaning it receives less than one and a half inches of rain a year. It also contains some of the world's largest oil deposits. A portion of Ghawar field, the largest conventional oil field in the world, runs along the Empty Quarter's northern edge.

Tom Barger and his colleagues searched part of the area for oil in 1938 and found nothing.[76] In 1968, on the eastern edge of the

Empty Quarter, near the border with the United Arab Emirates, Aramco geologists discovered oil in a new field, which would come to be known as Shaybah. The oil there was so light, as Richard Eason, an American diplomat, described it, "you could almost put it in your gas tank," unrefined at all.[77] In 1968, the world had plenty of oil, so Aramco did not rush to develop an oil field that was so difficult to reach. In addition, the capital investment needed to pump the oil there was immense, so Aramco left the oil underground.[78] Still, the company remained interested in Shaybah. Further tests in 1974 revealed that Shaybah's oil could be found reasonably close to the surface but would still be challenging to access. Neither Aramco nor its American shareholders were interested.

In the 1990s, Aramco began using horizontal drilling for certain projects. When horizontal drilling was used in conjunction with three-dimensional seismic imaging, the oil trapped beneath Shaybah's great sand dunes became more accessible.[79] Still, the infrastructure costs to tap Shaybah's oil were intimidating. The company would have to move entire sand dunes to build an airport, oil-processing facilities, housing for workers, and roads—all without damaging nearby dunes and the salt flats between them. Even in 1995, the cost to develop Shaybah was estimated at between $5 and $6 billion.[80] Aramco and the Saudi petroleum ministry looked into investment from other oil majors. According to Naimi, both Shell and Mobil were interested in Shaybah's prospects and made preliminary offers. The foreign companies did not "think Aramco [was] up to developing it," but they both believed that they were capable, independently, of completing the project in five years and at a cost of $5 billion.

Naimi was greatly disturbed by the idea that foreign companies could develop Saudi Arabia's oil resources better than Aramco. "This was a case of national pride," he said he told the company's management team, and he convinced them to commit to bring Shaybah online by 1998, at a cost of only $2.5 billion. The project would not only be a technical challenge for Aramco; it would also be showcased to the world as an example of Aramco's capabilities.[81] Aramco teams worked unrelentingly, and three years later Shaybah opened on schedule and under budget. Aramco did not need the oil in 1998, but by making the investment when it did, the company positioned itself for future oil demand. Years later, after a significant expansion, the facility grew to produce 1 million barrels of oil per day.[82]

It was clear that Aramco picked the right place to make a showcase of its world-class engineering and management talents.[83] The massive facility makes for an impressive sight, nestled between rippling dunes of red- and orange-tinged sand. As the sun sets, yellow ground lights blink on and outline the periphery and every building with a warm glow. Where there was once no sign of life, roads of gray asphalt shoot out of the artificially flattened valley in every direction. In the distance, associated facilities also light up, and a few natural gas flares burn in a haze. Aside from Aramco, there is nothing for miles and miles.

◆

As Aramco expanded during the 1990s, so too did another organization. When Osama bin Laden offered to deploy the members of al Qaeda to assist *al Saud* in vanquishing Saddam Hussein, his network of fighters was already formidable. Osama bin Laden was banned from Saudi Arabia in 1991 for outspoken opposition to *al Saud*, but he only continued to expand al Qaeda from new headquarters in Sudan. Al Qaeda planned and executed numerous attacks on Americans during the 1990s, including bombings at the US embassies in Kenya and Tanzania, as well as the 1993 attack on the World Trade Center. In 2000, his terrorist organization blew a hole through the side of the USS *Cole* as it was anchored outside of Aden, killing seventeen and injuring thirty-nine American sailors.

With terrorism a growing concern in the late 1990s the US embassy in Saudi Arabia tasked its economic attaché to conduct a study of Saudi Arabia's oil installations and assess their vulnerability to terrorist attacks. Richard Eason's study concluded that Aramco's oil facilities were not especially vulnerable because "by [their] own nature [they were] spread out." Certain areas were vulnerable to penetration, but "to actually bring down the Saudi oil infrastructure for any length of time you needed to have a couple of divisions attacking multiple nodes." His assessment concluded that the "biggest vulnerability was water." Riyadh received its water through two or three large pipelines that came from Dhahran. "You blow those up in a few places and Riyadh has no water in about forty-eight hours." However, he added, "They're also easy to repair."[84]

Al Qaeda's most notorious assault came not in Saudi Arabia but on US soil. On September 11, 2001, al Qaeda operatives took control of four commercial airplanes and flew them into the World Trade Center towers in New York City, the Pentagon, and an open field in Pennsylvania. All four of the planes were piloted by Saudis. Saudi Arabia received great criticism for the role its citizens played in the attacks, but no available evidence has conclusively shown that *al Saud* or the state knowingly provided any assistance to the attackers. Even the 9/11 report from the US government and the much touted "twenty-eight pages," which were not declassified until 2016, failed to show a direct connection between the terrorists and the Saudi government.[85] *Al Saud* has been accused of an indirect role in fomenting terrorism and terrorist sympathies by funding mosques that have been described as fundamentalist. In parts of the West and particularly in the United States, Wahhabism and these mosques have come to be seen as conduits for radicalism. Within Saudi Arabia, Islamic terrorism, religious fundamentalism, and political Islam all represent potential political threats to the *al Saud* regime. Nevertheless, for many in the West, Saudi Arabia is seen in connection to terrorism. Yet, as for Aramco, neither the 9/11 attacks nor the accusations of indirect terrorism assistance have interfered with the business of energy in any significant way.

◆

The oil market from 2002 to 2008 climbed as briskly and with as much energy as Naimi on a sand dune. The price of a barrel of

West Texas Intermediate (WTI) oil in January 2002 averaged about $19. Six and a half years later, in July 2008, a barrel of oil cost $145. This was not the result of strategic production cuts or an embargo. Oil prices climbed steadily as demand for this commodity rose perilously close to overtaking supply and fears of long-term shortages gripped traders. A *New York Times* article from 2005 painted a bleak situation for the industrialized world if demand were ever to exceed supply. "Global recession . . . exorbitant prices for transport fuels and . . . petrochemicals. The impact on the American way of life would be profound. . . . The suburban and exurban lifestyles, hinged on two-car families and constant trips to work, school and Wal-Mart, might become unaffordable or, if gas rationing is imposed, impossible."[86]

Around the same time, the media picked up on a term that the oil industry had been familiar with for many years—*peak oil*. In 1956, the geologist M. King Hubbert issued a bold prediction. He theorized that oil production in the United States would reach a peak in the early 1970s and then begin to decline. His theory gained credence when the majority of Texas oil fields in operation peaked in 1970.[87] Rising prices, however, led to increased investment in exploration and production. Less than a decade later, US oil production was growing again. In 2005, with oil prices rising and, it seemed, very little supply cushion, peak oil once again appeared as a very real danger.

That year, all eyes were focused on Saudi Arabia. In 2005, Saudi Arabia was considered the "sole oil superpower." It controlled 22 percent of known global oil reserves with self-reported reserves of 263 billion barrels. Aramco was producing very close to its capacity of 10.5 million barrels per day. It seemed the only force standing in the way of an energy shock that might cripple the industrialized world was Saudi Arabia's oil production and reserves.[88] The same year, a provocative book was published that called into question Saudi Arabia's ability to satisfy global oil demand. As a privately held company, Saudi Aramco guarded information about its oil reserves closely. Publicly traded oil companies faced financial disclosure regulations that required them to make information about the size and health of their oil reserves public. Saudi Aramco had no such requirement and released only the information it chose.

The book *Twilight in the Desert* was written by investment banker Matthew R. Simmons. It relied heavily on information about Aramco's oil fields gleaned from technical papers presented to the Society of Petroleum Engineers between 1960 and 2004, and concluded that Saudi Arabia's giant oil fields were likely on the verge of collapse.[89] He wrote that global economies depended on the promise of increased Saudi production. If Simmons was correct, global economies could face an unprecedented danger.[90]

Aramco engineers challenged Simmons's contention and particularly his assertion that the company had not effectively maintained its oil fields and had allowed longtime problems to fester. However, Aramco continually refused to allow any outside parties to inspect its oil reserves and said that this data was "the equivalent of state secrets." Ali al-Naimi explained that "we see ourselves as custodians of our primary natural resource for future generations." For Aramco, "sharing too much proprietary knowledge could very well give other oil producers an advantage in competing with us."[91] An Aramco engineer explained, in contrast to Simmons's argument, the company had been more careful to preserve its oil reserves than other oil companies because Aramco's primary concern had been a "sense of responsibility for future generations." Aramco had been less concerned about capital depreciation than IOCs and thus had treated its oil reservoirs with "velvet gloves."[92]

Simmons's dire predictions did not materialize. Aramco reached a capacity of 12.5 million barrels per day in 2016, while maintaining production from its older fields.[93] Aramco's 2016 annual review listed the company's crude oil and condensate reserves at 260.8 billion barrels. At a production rate of about 10 million barrels per day, Saudi Arabia would not deplete its reserves for about seventy years, but even this calculation ignores the likelihood of new reserve discoveries and technologies that improve the rate of recovery.[94] Saudi Arabia continued to discover new oil fields at least through 2016.[95]

Ambassador Smith, who served in Saudi Arabia shortly after the publication of Simmons's book, said the following: "In 2009, peak oil was the big thing. I haven't heard that term in years. When you ask the Saudis about running out, they go, 'Eh, it was Allah's blessing while it lasted.'"[96] Despite the nonchalance, Aramco continued to feel the weight of Simmons's allegations, and skeptics saw the company's continued secrecy as proof of the accuracy of Simmons's ominous predictions. Even Aramco's former leadership is divided on the topic. Ali al-Naimi, in 2017, described Saudi Arabia's reserves as "really phenomenal."[97] Former Aramco vice president Othman Alkhowaiter, on the other hand, was skeptical. Although he had not been privy to any data on the country's oil reserves since his retirement in the 1990s, he expressed concern that the company was overestimating the recovery rate of oil from its reserves.[98]

In a twist, warnings from Simmons and other skeptics in 2005 only served to raise the price of oil and increase revenue for Aramco and other oil producers. As the fear of peak oil remained, oil-consuming countries around the world worried about rising energy prices. They considered policies to improve energy efficiency and promote the development of renewable energy technologies, which also became popular because of the concurrent fear of global climate change. Meanwhile, oil-rich countries grew more prosperous. Some countries, like the UAE, used newfound revenues to transform cities into ultramodern hubs of finance and luxury consumerism. Forward-thinking oil-rich countries also used their now large sovereign wealth funds to make investments around the world. Saudi Arabia put away $800 billion in foreign reserves. Aramco continued its diversification and expansion plans. The company opened more joint-venture downstream projects in the 2000s, including major refineries and petrochemical plants within Saudi Arabia.

By 2008, however, the roller coaster was approaching its apex. The years of high prices had provided oil companies with profits to invest in developing new technologies. Known oil deposits that had long been considered too expensive to develop, such as

Canada's oil sands and Venezuela's Orinoco Belt, would soon flood the oil market. Just around the corner was the fracking revolution, in which North American oil companies used horizontal drilling techniques and high-pressure injections of water and chemical mixtures to flush crude out of shale deposits. These developments would soon take oil markets, and Saudi Arabia, on a roller coaster of volatility and uncertainty. Eventually, beginning in the second half of 2014, Saudi Arabia, at the head of OPEC, would be forced into tough decisions. Through the ride, Aramco continued to look toward the long-term future.

◆

In late 2008, Ali al-Naimi sat for an interview with Lesley Stahl of *60 Minutes*. In his traditional white Saudi *thobe* and with the folds of his starched white *ghutra* framing his face, the 73-year-old Saudi oil minister looked more like a kindly grandfather than one of the most powerful men of industry. Stahl found, behind the rimless glasses and carefully groomed mustache, an astute and intelligent leader who patiently answered her questions and gently corrected her misconceptions about Saudi Arabia and the oil market.

The two conversed in English, which Naimi spoke fluently, though with a slight accent. He learned the language as a boy in the 1940s, when he attended the Aramco-run school. Ali al-Naimi easily could have remained a shepherd like his grandfather, but instead he became the CEO of the most important energy company in the world and a close advisor to the Saudi king.

When Stahl brought up America's fossil fuel "addiction," which, in 2008, was fed largely by foreign sources of oil, she intimated that Saudi Arabia was to blame for America's reliance on fossil fuels.

Are the Saudis concerned, Stahl asked, that their society will suffer when renewable energies displace fossil fuels?

Naimi tried to explain that Saudi Arabia takes the long view. Someday, yes, the time will come when oil is no longer the fuel of choice.

"But listen," Naimi said slowly, "to what the professionals say and what do they advise. It's not going to happen today. It's not going to happen 10 years from now. It's probably not going to happen 20 years from now. It's not going to happen 30 years from now. Okay. Because you are still going to be using fossil fuels."

Even so, Naimi said, "we in Saudi Arabia are developing solar energy." He held up his hand and curved his fingers in an outline of the sun.

"Solar energy?" replied Stahl, her eyes wide and incredulous. "You're doing research in solar energy?"

"Yes," responded Naimi quickly. "Where else is the solar energy most intense?"

"The desert," Stahl replied, with a slight laugh, as if embarrassed she did not realize.

"The desert, of course," Naimi concurred softly, with a knowing smile.

"But won't that hurt your oil industry?" she pressed.

"No, no, not at all. It will . . . supplement it," Naimi explained. "Our vision is that we will be . . . exporters of gigawatts of electricity. We will be exporting both. Barrels of oil and gigawatts of power."

Against a tableau of a fiery sun dropping behind desert mountains and flaring natural gas in the foreground, Stahl concluded, "And so, he says, the kingdom will still be in the energy business, long after the sun sets on the age of oil."[99]

For those listening with open ears, Ali al-Naimi clearly laid out Saudi Arabia's long-term business strategy—a strategy the Saudis prioritized since the first oil wells were drilled in the desert kingdom, which was reaffirmed during the early years of economic struggles in the 1950s and the oil shocks of the 1970s and was echoed in the halls of OPEC and the words of Aramco executives. Saudi Arabia is in the energy business—now and for the future. Stability, expansion, profits, and diversification are the staples of its long-term policies, all with the aim of securing continued growth for future generations.

FOR THEIR SONS

n July 2008, the price of a barrel of West Texas Intermediate (WTI) oil peaked at $145.[1] Even though the price dipped dramatically that winter due to the global financial crisis, between the end of 2010 and the end of 2014, oil prices remained in a steady range of $80–$110 per barrel. Even adjusted for inflation, never before had oil been that expensive, and never before had it stayed at such high prices for such a long time. Though consumers complained, paying high prices for energy became a way of life, and OPEC appeared satisfied with these prices. "There wasn't much action," *S&P Global Platts* senior writer Herman Wang recalled. When he started covering the oil cartel in 2012, "OPEC was pretty much just rolling over" its allocation quotas, meaning member countries continued producing at the same rates. OPEC members were content with the large amounts of money they were making and not inclined to make any changes. Veteran reporters said OPEC's regular meetings every six months became "boring."[2]

Out in the field, however, oil production was anything but boring. Years of high prices enriched every oil producer, not just OPEC members. US producers were reviving the domestic oil industry in a phenomenon commonly referred to as the "shale revolution." Oil and natural gas that geologists had long believed were trapped within shale rock formations were unlocked through hydraulic fracturing. Fracking was expensive and complicated, but because the process did not require massive initial capital outlays, small companies could compete in the fracking industry. Seemingly overnight, tiny American towns like Williston, North Dakota, with large shale rock formations became hubs for oil production, and the media began to wonder if America could possibly produce more oil and gas than it consumed.

Throughout this fracking boom, Ali al-Naimi said he was not concerned. An energy journalist who covered OPEC recalled asking him several times about the growth of shale oil production. Naimi always said, "No, it's not a threat. I'm not worried about it."[3] By June 2014, however, Naimi and the rest of OPEC could no longer ignore the effect on the market of this new source of American oil production. Shale oil production in the United States and rising production from other global spots such as Canada and Brazil were rapidly increasing oil supplies.[4] Soon the high global oil supply would start to push prices lower. Growing supply from non-OPEC countries was not a new situation for OPEC. In fact, the cartel had faced a similar challenge in the early 1980s. At that time, OPEC had decided to cut production to support higher prices. Saudi oil minister Zaki Yamani had declared that Saudi Arabia would become the swing producer and reduce its production as necessary to keep prices up.

Yamani's strategy in the 1980s failed. Other OPEC oil producers had cheated and Saudi production had dipped so low that Aramco was forced to temporarily decommission key facilities—and the price of oil had continued to drop. Naimi, who was CEO of Aramco for some of that time in the 1980s, refused to let Saudi Arabia make the same mistake in 2014. Saudi Arabia was not willing to cut production alone, as it had in the 1980s, to prop up prices for other producers who continued to flood the market with oil supply. However, Naimi, as the same energy journalist explained, "liked to keep his cards to himself." When OPEC gathered in Vienna in June 2014 for the cartel's regular meeting, none of the reporters had any idea that Naimi was about to turn the entire cartel upside down.[5]

OPEC held its semi-annual meetings at its permanent headquarters in an unassuming building of gray stone in the heart of downtown Vienna. The building was nearly identical to the surrounding office buildings. It was distinguished only by a blue flag with the OPEC logo on the roof and a small sign attached to the corner of the building with the OPEC logo in blue lighting. As a safeguard against the type of attack perpetrated by Carlos the Jackal, a conspicuously armed Austrian policeman stood outside the glass doors.

Journalists waited outside for the building to open. They came from the United States, Gulf countries, Iran, the UK, Russia, South America, and Africa, and represented major publications, business news media, national papers, and even industry subscription services. Analysts from banks and other financial institutions attended the meeting as well to provide their clients and funds with the most updated information and to spread their brand through television appearances and quotes in the papers. The oil ministers and their entourages would not arrive until the reporters and analysts filed through security and set up in the basement pressroom. As the ministers appeared, chauffeured from nearby luxury hotels, they walked down a literal red carpet like movie stars at the Oscars, pausing to speak with reporters and the official OPEC hostess, whose commentary was broadcast for a live audience online. This was a typical start to an OPEC meeting.

"Everybody was writing the regular story of 'oh they are going to roll over [the same production numbers],'" the energy journalist recalled, indicating that the journalists and analysts expected OPEC to do nothing more than continue producing at its previous rate. Naimi, who was always the most anticipated arrival because of Saudi Arabia's outsized influence on OPEC, stopped to talk to reporters on the red carpet. "In typical Naimi fashion, [he] did not let the news leak of what his [desire] was."[6] Naimi's desire was indeed radical. He wanted OPEC to permit uninhibited production from its members. As always, after the red carpet walk and a brief appearance for the press and analysts, the oil ministers went behind closed doors for their meeting. As always, the deliberations were secret.

While the ministers met in private, most of the media waited in the basement pressroom, drinking coffee and snacking on cookies and small sandwiches provided by OPEC. Some stood outside smoking and chatting. A few reporters waited in the hallway and lobby, ready to catch the ministers for interviews on their way out. Almost everyone assumed nothing would happen for several hours, as even OPEC meetings with no important outcomes tended to drag on. "Everybody was relaxed . . . nobody expected people to come out." Suddenly, the reporters in the hallway saw movement and heard the rush of feet. "We saw the Saudi delegation come out." Naimi stormed out of the room. "It was a shock," the energy journalist said. Reporters scrambled after the Saudi oil minister.

Naimi told the press that this was "the worst OPEC meeting ever." He invited the press to an impromptu briefing in his suite at the Grand Hotel immediately. There, he explained that he had never been in a meeting "where no one was listening." He proceeded to shame the countries that had refused to consider his proposal. The "Libyans, Iranians, Algerians, and Venezuelans," the journalist recalled, all "preferred to keep the quota system." The quota system imposed production limits on each OPEC country, though the quotas at that time allowed healthy production. Naimi was unhappy with that quota system, because it kept the price high enough for non-OPEC producers to produce fully at their levels of capacity. The non-OPEC producers were benefitting from OPEC's restraint and non-OPEC production would soon flood the market and drive down the price of oil for all producers, including OPEC.

At the same time, Saudi Arabia was also unhappy that it had often accommodated for OPEC members that cheated on their production quotas and benefitted from Saudi Arabia's austerity. Naimi was "obviously angry" at the intransigence of the other oil ministers.[7]

That was "where things fell catastrophically apart." Some journalists wondered if OPEC could survive a rift of this scale or if the cartel would disband. "This was the biggest disagreement . . . since the Iraqis accused Kuwait of stealing their oil [before the 1990 invasion]. It was of that magnitude. Or bigger because everybody walked away and nobody knew if this group was going to be sitting in the same room again."[8] The price of oil rose slightly that day.[9] Then it began a steady decline through the summer and autumn. By November 27, 2014, the date of OPEC's next regular meeting, oil prices declined 40 percent. The price of a barrel of WTI oil dropped to $73.[10]

In the interim, Naimi tried to convince the Venezuelan oil minister, Rafael Ramirez, that OPEC could not cut production unless other oil producers from outside OPEC agreed to join the cartel in cutting production. According to Naimi, it was understood that there was "zero chance of a conversation, let alone agreement," with independent American oil producers, because US antitrust laws prohibited this.[11] However, Ramirez clearly thought there was a chance at convincing countries like Kazakhstan, Mexico, Norway, and Russia to cut their oil production along with OPEC.[12] The entire time, Naimi kept the failures of the 1980s in mind and remained convinced that Saudi Arabia could not sacrifice its own production for other countries to profit.

Two days before the November OPEC meeting, an anxious press gaggle in Vienna was "all set up in the lobby of the Grand Hotel waiting for [Ali al-Naimi] to come," according to Wang. When Naimi finally arrived, the oil minister stopped in front of the reporters. He read a short, prepared statement before continuing up to his suite. In a departure from his usual behavior, he did not answer questions, not even in his normally evasive manner.[13] The reporters and analysts could get nothing out of him.

Later that night, Naimi met with Ramirez of Venezuela; Russian oil minister Alexander Novak; Igor Sechin, the CEO of Russia's largest oil company, Rosneft; and Mexican energy minister Pedro Joaquin Coldwell at the Park Hyatt hotel in Vienna. Neither Russia nor Mexico was a member of OPEC, but they had come by invitation. When pressed about making production cuts, both Coldwell and Novak said it would be economically impossible for their countries. According to Naimi, everyone in the room turned and looked toward him, expectantly. He said that at the time he wondered if the Russians and the Mexicans "were hoping . . . that Saudi Arabia would once again have to swoop in and make a dramatic reduction in output" that would spare their economies. "Not this time," Naimi resolved.[14] Naimi was willing to let production flow freely, despite the inevitable negative impact on prices, because Saudi Arabia would not sacrifice and watch everyone else profit.

However, neither the media, nor the analysts, nor the oil traders following events from afar knew what happened at this private meeting. While Saudi Arabia, Russia, Mexico, and Venezuela met, the press was waiting, "for quite a long time," at the same hotel for a scheduled press briefing. Eventually, the oil ministers canceled the press briefing. As Wang described it, "Naimi went out a back exit [and] the Russians disappeared." Ramirez went down to speak to the press, and he tried "to put on a brave face [but] obviously it hadn't gone well."[15] Venezuela and other countries were hoping for some production cuts, which they must have believed would come primarily from Saudi Arabia.

Two days later, OPEC started its official, semi-annual meeting. Speculation was rampant among reporters, analysts, and oil traders. Everyone wondered about Saudi Arabia's intentions. Jamie Webster, an analyst who regularly attended OPEC meetings, recalled that the observers were exceptionally eager. After years of boring OPEC meetings that were largely ignored by reporters and oil traders alike, "suddenly . . . everybody was there."[16]

Most analysts believed Saudi Arabia would support a production cut as OPEC tried to keep oil prices high. Michael D. Cohen, the director of energy markets research at Barclays, the British bank, said that among all of the analysts, "there were a couple analysts that believed that a cut was not going to be the right way to go." He continued, "Irrespective of what the calls were and who got it right or wrong, I think there were a couple different pillars in the view on OPEC that deserved to have some questioning at that time."[17] However, at that time, not many questioned the generally held assumptions.

In Vienna, New York, London, and elsewhere thousands of investors and traders with significant bets on the line were waiting for a decision from Naimi and his colleagues. Webster said that waiting "was nerve wracking."[18]

When the meeting ended, several ministers arrived to brief the press. The cartel announced its stunning decision to withdraw any country-specific production limits. Each country could produce as much as it could and wanted to, though technically OPEC set a high limit for the organization as a whole of a "30 million [barrels per day] ceiling but with no mention of a commitment to comply with it."[19] The oil ministers, observers in Vienna, oil traders, and energy industry personnel around the world knew immediately that OPEC's decision would lead to more oil production. The price of oil would fall, forcing most oil producers to pump and sell still more oil to keep up revenue. Most of the OPEC countries along with Russia and Mexico had gone to Vienna seeking production cuts, but Naimi ruined their plans. Wang remembered that Naimi left the meeting "all smiles, saying it was a great decision and he pretty much got his way." The Venezuelan oil minister "left the meeting quite angry. He had a pinched expression on his face."[20]

That day, the price of WTI fell 7 percent.[21] In Wang's estimation, the outcome "demonstrated the power of Saudi Arabia in OPEC. Nothing [happened] in OPEC without Saudi Arabia."[22]

Webster explained Saudi Arabia's decision to, in effect, allow the price of oil to free-fall. "The Saudis and [other Persian Gulf oil-rich nations] had a fair amount of money in the bank . . . and could act more strategically as opposed [to] tactically." Other countries, such as Venezuela for instance, desperately needed to maintain high oil prices.[23]

Oil prices fell steeply throughout the rest of 2014 and 2015, with the WTI benchmark reaching a nadir of just below $27 per barrel in February 2016.[24] The Venezuelan economy unraveled with the low prices, because it had shifted in the previous decade to an overreliance on that single commodity. Other oil producers also suffered. In April 2016 alone, eleven fracking companies filed for bankruptcy in the United States. In September 2016, another 135 were so heavily indebted that they were on the edge of bankruptcy.[25] IOCs suffered as well. ExxonMobil reported a 58 percent drop in its fourth-quarter 2015 profits, and BP reported a loss of $3.3 billion dollars in the same period.[26] Texas, the unofficial capital of oil production in the United States, shed 250,000 jobs in 2015. Declining oil production also cost the state over $40 billion in investment.[27]

Ali al-Naimi defended Saudi Arabia's policy throughout. He was repeatedly questioned about when he would change his mind. The press and the industry seemed to assume that he would shortly agree to OPEC production cuts. However, he remained steadfast. With such low prices, observers began to speculate about how much Saudi Arabia was suffering under the economics of that time. As it had since the late 1940s, the majority of Saudi Arabia's government budget came from Aramco. Many wondered if the kingdom could withstand decreased oil revenue. However, Saudi Arabia had advantages that many geopolitical and industry analysts did not recognize. Most importantly, Saudi Arabia knew it had these advantages when Naimi implemented his strategy. First, Saudi Arabia benefitted from very low costs of oil production, reportedly the lowest in the world, and Aramco had diversified enough into downstream operations that would actually do well during periods of low crude prices.[28] As a result, Aramco could make a profit even if oil prices dropped into the teens, while its competitors could not. Second, the Saudi Arabian government could afford to take less cash from Aramco and operate, in part, off its foreign cash reserves, which were estimated at $800 billion in 2015. Third, there was no reason Saudi Arabia could not take on debt in the form of bank loans or government bonds, just as the governments of nearly every advanced economy did. When Saudi Arabia took a $10 billion line of credit in April 2016 at a time of very low interest rates, some observers openly questioned whether it marked the end of *al Saud*, but they did not realize that Saudi Arabia had taken on debt several times before to promote expansion.[29] Fourth, *al Saud* already had decided to embark on a large-scale strategic diversification of its economy. Economic reforms and diversification were, in part, the Saudi state's method of hedging against continued low prices. Moreover, lower oil prices would help, rather than hinder, the process of economic reform, because, with low oil revenue, the people were more likely to agree to the need for change. Saudi Arabia had had mixed results previously when the state had attempted economic reforms, though previous reforms had never been attempted with as high a proportion of educated young adults and prolonged periods of low oil prices.

However, neither King Abdullah nor Ali al-Naimi remained to see Naimi's strategy through. Abdullah died in January 2015, just two months after Naimi surprised the oil world in Vienna. The king was succeeded by his half brother Salman, a Sudairi and former governor of Riyadh. More significantly, for the first time, two members of the next generation would serve as Crown Prince and Deputy Crown Prince. Though several of Abdul Aziz's numerous sons still lived, King Salman would be the last king from that generation. The time had come for a new generation of leaders.

Ali al-Naimi, the ambitious geologist who had shaped Aramco's strategic vision and Saudi Arabia's oil policy for so many years, was retired at age eighty-one in a decree issued by King Salman in May 2016. Naimi had been Saudi Arabia's oil minister for twenty years. In his place, King Salman appointed former Aramco CEO Khalid al Falih, who was only fifty-six years old. According to the energy journalist, al Falih had a very different approach. Naimi was "the kind of guy that if people [did not] listen to him or give him time he [would] storm out of the room. Al Falih, on the other hand, [would] stay and argue with them until he brainwashed them into something. He [would not] give up."[30]

The time had come for a new generation of leaders.

◆

When Abdul Aziz set out to recapture his family's ancestral city, he had a plan for the future. He took Riyadh and planned a home for *al Saud*. Fifteen years later, he saw an opportunity to capture Mecca from the overextended Sharif Hussein and planned his expansion across the Arabian Peninsula. Just after establishing the Kingdom of Saudi Arabia in 1932, he saw opportunity in the American oilmen who wanted to search his land for petroleum so he planned a new approach to acquire funds for his depleted treasury. In Naimi's words, "the king—King Abdul Aziz—established a principle originally [and] listed what he wanted the company to do for Saudis, and the company honored that responsibility."[31] The story of Saudi Arabia, in many respects, is the story of leaders with plans, strategies, and visions for the future. Not all of those plans came to fruition or benefitted Saudi Arabia, but many did. Those that did succeed brought profit and power to *al Saud* and to future generations.

Like Abdul Aziz, the king's loyal finance minister Abdullah Sulaiman had plans. Sulaiman saw the Aramco oil business flourishing in Saudi Arabia and crafted a plan to increase Saudi Arabia's revenue. He continuously pushed the Americans for more and more money as a way to fund the kingdom's modernization and solidify the king's power as a successful provider for his people. Sulaiman was also the architect of what became a successful and oft-used Saudi strategy. He hired Westerners, learned from them, and eventually positioned Saudi Arabia to take over operations and build on its own. Saudi Arabia would do this in finance, construction, defense, oil refining, and, of course, oil extraction.

King Saud was a glaring exception. He lacked vision, plans, and strategy. He spent money without purpose, acted without thought for the future, and failed to listen to those who did. Ultimately, his brothers deposed him for these reasons. Saud's half brother Talal did have plans and vision for Saudi Arabia's future. However, his ideas were radical dreams of constitutional limits on the monarchy and political liberalization. They were, of course, rejected by his brothers in power. Similarly, the plans of oil minister Abdullah Tariki also were rejected by Feisal for the challenges they presented to *al Saud*'s profit and absolute authority. Tariki envisioned a nationalized Saudi Arabian oil industry and sought to create a body of oil-rich nations that would assert unified power against the oil-consuming nations. Tariki failed to achieve his first goal, but OPEC eventually achieved the power he sought, even if under a new leader.

Feisal, as Crown Prince and king, sought to make the Saudi government financially solvent. A healthy government with a surplus of money could have the flexibility to pursue greater modernization, invest in educating its children, and exert its power and influence regionally. His wife, Queen Iffat, had vision and plans to build schools for girls and promote the education of women to improve the lives of the Saudi people and their families in the future.

Feisal's oil minister Zaki Yamani had a similar goal to that of his predecessor, Abdullah Tariki, but a vastly different plan. Yamani also wanted Saudi Arabia to control its own commodity and its own industry, but not through nationalization. First, he planned to gain participation in the business to learn how it operated from the inside as a minority shareholder. Then he sought to exercise control over the oil market and the commodity itself, through unilateral pricing, production quotas, and export limitations. He used Tariki's OPEC to accomplish his goals. He continued working on his plan for the king to purchase Aramco, increasing Saudi Arabia's position in Aramco until the king owned it entirely. All the while, he remained committed to his plan to buy the company instead of nationalizing it so he could avoid costly disruptions. Not all of Yamani's plans succeeded for *al Saud*'s twin goals of profit and power. Though the purchase of Aramco paved the way for Saudi

Arabia to transform the company from an oil producer to a global energy conglomerate, Yamani failed when he attempted to use Saudi Arabia as a swing producer on the oil market in the 1980s. Saudi Arabia's profit and power suffered because of it.

King Khaled, who succeeded Feisal, reacted to the violent seizure of the Grand Mosque by increasing religious observance and religious strictures in Saudi society. His plan to make Saudi Arabia more devout, at least outwardly, was designed to satisfy elements in society and maintain power. The plan worked, but the unintended consequences altered the characteristics of the country and may have created a hurdle for future business development. The turn toward state-mandated religious observance and traditionalism in 1979 and earlier resulted in practices that made Saudi society and the economy less accessible to outside businesses. Travel to Saudi Arabia could be overwhelming, especially for foreign women. Businessmen, especially outside of Aramco facilities, had to adjust to a lack of certain amenities such as alcohol and movie theaters. Perhaps the feature that most restricted the accessibility of Saudi Arabia is a physical one—the stringent visa limitations. Saudi Arabia would not grant tourist visas, meaning foreigners essentially needed a sponsor to enter the kingdom. This limited casual business opportunities and familiarity by foreigners with the society.

Ali al-Naimi, first as CEO of Aramco and then as oil minister, pushed through a strategic plan for Aramco that would have been impossible under American ownership. He diversified and globalized Aramco, building businesses in shipping, refining, and petrochemical manufacturing. Aramco invested in energy opportunities with foreign companies in parts of the world that needed Saudi oil. Thus the company secured long-term relationships with key customers for the future and positioned itself to withstand fluctuations in the oil market. He and his successors authorized new research and development in alternative energies and introduced a venture capital unit to make investments in energy technology startups around the world. The plan was to become an energy conglomerate that could prosper with future changes in the industry.

Even after Naimi retired from government service, the company and the government continued to pursue his plans, which, in a sense, were designed to achieve the goals of King Abdul Aziz. As Yasser Mufti, an Aramco vice president, said in 2017, "I hope that we will be exporting great ideas, good people, good technologies that the world will find use for in energy and beyond. And I think that ultimately this will realize Naimi's vision."[32]

King Abdullah, like King Feisal and Queen Iffat before him, planned to educate the Saudi population. He supported the development of Saudi universities and centers of scientific excellence and provided scholarships to any Saudi with the ability and desire to study in a college or university abroad. Under Abdullah's programs, Saudi youth gained expertise and experience for a globalized economy. As a result, these young adults, men and women, planned careers and supported social changes with the possibility for a modernized and diversified economy. The financial health of the kingdom continued to rely, in large part, on the energy sector, but the goal was to harness the education and experience of the youth to eventually lead both the economy and the society.[33]

Like his father, King Salman's plans included preparing the next generation of kings to rule and opening Saudi Arabia and Aramco to the world economy on an unprecedented scale. Yet as always, Aramco and oil, God's gift to Saudi Arabia, remained the centerpiece of these plans and *al Saud*'s ambitions.

NOTE ON SOURCES

In researching this book I drew on a wide variety of sources, including government and private archival material; published memoirs; archived oral histories; newspaper articles; Aramco newsletters; the *Congressional Record*; interviews I conducted; archives of broadcast media; and published volumes of history, culture, and economics.

The lack of written records from the Saudi perspective for large periods of this history presented a particular challenge. In addition, there is very limited access for historians to the existing archives of the Saudi government, Saudi Aramco, and the former parent companies of Aramco. Fortunately, many vital conversations were preserved, often in State Department memoranda and documents. All quotes, conversations, and actions in this book were taken directly from sources. It is my hope that the number and range of sources—many of which were cross-referenced to ensure accuracy—make up for the lack of Saudi and Aramco records.

I am thankful for the work of historians who came before me, particularly those who enjoyed unique access to the Saudi royal family and Saudi government officials. These include Harry St. John Bridger Philby, Robert Lacey, David Howarth, D. Van Der

Meulen, David Holden, and Richard Johns. They provided some of the best accounts of the early days of the Saudi Arabian kingdom and intimate knowledge of the activities of *al Saud*. However, their narratives are not without biases, in large part because of the access they were granted. Furthermore, it should be noted that while the works of these men offer significant information, the authors rarely explained their own sources. As a result, the tales they told are largely uncorroborated. We rely on them, as they provide the most detailed accounts.

Some of the other published works that were particularly helpful in writing this book include the memoirs of Ali al-Naimi, the memoirs of Ambassador J. Rives Childs, the biography of Ambassador Raymond Hare (written by his son), the letters of Tom Barger (curated and edited by his son), and the oral history of Ambassador Parker T. Hart (compiled by the State Department). For a complete list of all primary and secondary sources, please consult the notes section.

NOTES

PROLOGUE: THE REFUGEE BECOMES KING

1. The tale of Abdul Aziz's conquest of Riyadh had been told and retold in the king's court so many times that it became almost mythical. The story here is based on retellings from a variety of sources, including the following: D. Van Der Meulen, *The Wells of Ibn Saud* (New York: Praeger, 1957), 44–53; David Howarth, *The Desert King: A Life of Ibn Saud* (London: Collins, 1964), 11–23; Robert Lacey, *The Kingdom: Arabia & The House of Sa'ud* (New York: Avon, 1981), 41–51; and David Holden and Richard Johns, *The House of Saud* (London: Pan Books, 1981), 3–7.

2. David Fromkin, *A Peace to End All Peace* (New York: Henry Holt & Company, 1989), 108.

3. "A Mystery War," *Boston Daily Globe*, September 24, 1924.

4. Shane Dixon Kavanaugh, "The mysterious Saudi prince leading the war in Yemen," *Week*, April 6, 2015, http://theweek.com/articles/548188/mysterious-saudi-prince-leading-war-yemen.

5. Fareed Zakaria, "Why Saudi Arabia can't get a nuclear weapon," *Washington Post*, June 11, 2015.

6. "Saudi Arabia is considering an IPO of Aramco, probably the world's most valuable company," *Economist*, January 7, 2016.

7. "Memorandum of Conversation with Saudi Finance Minister Regarding Aramco," General Records of the Department of State, Record Group 59, National Archives and Records Administration (NARA) (hereafter abbreviated as RG 59, NA), 886A.2553/7–653.

8. Abdullah Jumah, *60 Minutes: The Oil Kingdom*, produced by Richard Bonin and Kathy Lui (2008: CBS Broadcasting Inc.), DVD.

NOTES

PART I

ONE: "A DEVIL OF A TIME"

1. Holden and Johns, 106.
2. Holden and Johns, 107.
3. Thomas C. Barger, *Out in the Blue: Letters from Arabia 1930–1940* (Vista, California: Selwa Press, 2000), 104.
4. J. Rives Childs, *Foreign Service Farewell: My Years in the Near East* (Charlottesville: University Press of Virginia, 1969), 139.
5. Anthony Cave Brown, *Oil, God, and Gold* (New York: Houghton Mifflin Company, 1999), 48.
6. Tim Barger, interview with the author, June 1, 2017.
7. Lacey, *The Kingdom*, 239.
8. Tim Barger, interview with the author, June 1, 2017.
9. "Americans Get Oil Concession in Arabia; Transformation of Desert Life May Result," *New York Times*, July 15, 1933.
10. Standard Oil of California, *Desert Venture*, produced by Robert Yarnall Richie, 1948.
11. Fred A. Davies: An Inventory of His Papers at the Minnesota Historical Society, http://www2.mnhs.org/library/findaids/01049.xml?.
12. Chevron: history, http://www.chevron.com/about/history/1927/.
13. Wallace Stegner, "Discovery! The Story of Aramco Then," *Aramco World*, 19:1, 1998, http://archive.aramcoworld.com/issue/196801/discovery.the.story.of.aramco.then-chapter.1.contact.htm.
14. Aileen Keating, *Mirage* (New York: Prometheus Books, 2005).
15. Daniel Yergin, *The Prize* (New York: Free Press, 2009), 273.
16. Lacey, *The Kingdom*, 236, 237.
17. Anthony Sampson, *The Seven Sisters: The 100-Year Battle for the World's Oil Supply* (New York: Bantam Books, 1991), 111.
18. Holden and Johns, 67.
19. Tom Carver, "Diary," *London Review of Books* (34:19), October 11, 2002, 42–43.
20. Holden and Johns, 119.
21. Lacey, *The Kingdom*, 245.
22. Tim Brady, "Profile of Fred Davies," *Minnesota*, April/March 2006, http://www.minnesotaalumni.org/s/1118/content.aspx?sid=1118&gid=1&pgid=1500.
23. Lacey, *The Kingdom*, 246.
24. Barger, 15.
25. Yergin, 281.
26. Barger, 28.
27. Ibid., 26.
28. Ibid., 29.
29. Yergin, 281.
30. Barger, 14.
31. Yergin, 283.

32. Holden and Johns, 120. The numbers are different from different sources, but all tell the same story—that the well was increasing in productivity.
33. Lacey, *The Kingdom*, 256; and Holden and Johns, 121.
34. Yergin, 284.
35. William E. Mulligan, "Air Raid! A Sequel." *Aramco World*, 27:4 (1976), 2–3.
36. Yergin, 285; Thomas Lippman, "The Pioneers," *Aramco World*, 55:3 (2004), 14–21; and Wallace Stegner, "The Frontier closes," *Aramco World*, 21:4 (1970), 9–21.
37. Confidential Aramco Memorandum, undated, National Archives, ARC 2071559, Box 213 Folder 3; and "Ambassador Childs to the Secretary of State," December 4, 1947, RG 59, NA, 890F.00/12–447.
38. Memorandum by the Director of the Office of Near Eastern and African Affairs (Henderson) to the Secretary of State, Washington, January 26, 1948. FRUS 1948, V:I 217–218.
39. Childs, 149.

TWO: THE AMERICANS IN KING IBN SAUD'S COURT

1. Childs, 137.
2. Ibid., 137.
3. Ibid., 138.
4. Ibid., 20.
5. Ibid., 55.
6. Ambassador James B. Smith, interview with the author, Washington, D.C., January 11, 2016.
7. Childs, 142.
8. Ibid., 140.
9. Confidential Aramco Memorandum, undated, National Archives, ARC 2071559, Box 213 Folder 3.
10. "Duce, James Terry," William E. Mulligan Papers, Box 1 Folder 17, Georgetown University.
11. Ibid.
12. Laton McCartney, *Friends in High Places: The Bechtel Story* (New York: Ballantine Books, 1989), 88.
13. Ibid., 86.
14. America's Largest Private Companies." Forbes, Forbes Magazine, 2017, www.forbes.com/largest-private-companies/list/.
15. McCartney, 80.
16. "Letter from Tom Borman to Steve Bechtel," October 27, 1949, Box 4 Folder 4, Snodgrass Papers, 06571, American Heritage Center University of Wyoming (AHCUW).
17. McCartney, 89.
18. "Letter from John M. Rogers to Steve Bechtel," December 4, 1949, Box 4 Folder 4, Snodgrass Papers, 06571, AHCUW
19. "Letter from John M. Rogers to Steve Bechtel, 'Jeddah Situation,'" December 18, 1949, Box 4 Folder 5, Snodgrass Papers, 06571, AHCUW.

20. Lacey, *The Kingdom*, 285–286.

21. McCartney, 89–91.

22. "Letter from Van Rosendahl to Steve Bechtel," London, England, December 5, 1949, Box 4 Folder 4 Snodgrass Papers, 06571, AHCUW.

23. Inventory of the C. Stribling Snodgrass papers, 1918–1977, University of Wyoming, American Heritage Center, http://rmoa.unm.edu/docviewer.php?docId =wyu-ah06571.xml

24. McCartney, 121.

25. "Notes of Meeting with Mark—Tuesday evening September 5th, 1950," Box 4 Folder 7, Snodgrass Papers, 06571, AHCUW.

26. "Memorandum of Understanding between Cornelius S. Snodgrass and Representative of U.S. Government," December 20, 1951. Approved for Release by CIA, August 22, 2016.

27. "Agreement Between the Kingdom of Saudi Arabia and International Bechtel, Inc.," Box 4 Folder 7, Snodgrass Papers, 06571, AHCUW.

28. "Letter from C. Stribling Snodgrass to Steve Bechtel, 'SAG Government Program (1950),'" January 17, 1950, Box 4 Folder 4, Snodgrass Papers, 06571, AHCUW.

29. "Letter from Snodgrass to Steve Bechtel, 'SAG Program,'" January 21, 1950, Box 4 Folder 4, Snodgrass Papers, 06571, AHCUW.

30. Ibid.

31. "Paper Prepared in the Department of State, 'Middle East Oil,'" Washington, D.C., September 1950, FRUS 1950, V, 78.

32. The Export-Import Bank of the United States: About Us, https://www.exim.gov/ about/ and The Export-Import Bank of the United States: History, https://www .exim.gov/about/history-0.

33. "Letter from Snodgrass to Steve Bechtel, 'SAG Program,'" January 21, 1950, Box 4 Folder 4, Snodgrass Papers, 06571, AHCUW.

34. Ibid.

35. "Letter from Rogers to Rosendahl, 'Saudi Arab Government Project,'" March 19, 1950, Box 4 Folder 4, Snodgrass Papers, 06571, AHCUW.

36. "Cable to Aramco, Jeddah," February 1, 1951, Box 4 Folder 7, Snodgrass Papers, 06571, AHCUW.

37. Executive and Technical Staff: Petroleum Administration for Defense, January 2, 1952, Box 52 Folder 7, Snodgrass Papers, 06571, AHCUW, 1–2.

38. "Visit to Your office by Messrs. Bechtel and Snodgrass," January 16, 1951, Saudi Arabia, Bechtel Int'l Corp. 1951, General Records of the Department of State, Record Group 59, National Archives and Records Administration (NARA).

39. "Memorandum of Conversation," June 5, 1951, RG 59, NA 886.2553/6–551.

40. "American Embassy, Jidda to Department of State," Washington, July 2, 1951, RG 59, NA 886.2553/7–251.

41. "Letter from Earl F. English to Van Rosendahl," June 22, 1951 and "Enclosure 1," RG 59 NA 886A.2553/7–251.

42. "Boyhood Dream Come True in Big Way," *Pittsburgh Post-Gazette*, February 2, 1953.

43. "U.S. Embassy, Jidda to Department of State, Washington. Subject: Contract Negotiations between the Saudi Government and Michael Baker Jr. Inc. of Pittsburgh Pennsylvania," August 25, 1951 RG 59, NA 886A.2553/8–2551.
44. Robert Vitalis, *America's Kingdom* (New York: New Left Books, 2009), 169.
45. Saudi Binladin Group, http://www.sbg.com.sa

THREE: ACTUAL ACCRUED BENEFIT

1. Childs to Secretary of State, RG 59, NA, 886A.2553/1–3050.
2. Childs, 145.
3. Hill to Childs, RG 59, NA, 886A.2553/2–1050.
4. Childs to Department of State, RG 59, NA, 886A.2553/5–350.
5. James Terry Duce to Fraser Wilkins, May 25, 1950, RG 59, NA, 886A.2553/5–2550.
6. Lacey, *The Kingdom*, 291.
7. James Terry Duce to Fraser Wilkins, May 25, 1950, RG 59, NA, 886A.2553/5–2550.
8. Ibid.
9. Acheson to U.S. Embassy in Jeddah, RG 59, NA, 886A.2553/6–150.
10. Childs to Secretary of State, RG 59, NA, 886A.2553/6–1350.
11. Ibid.
12. Childs to Secretary of State, RG 59, NA, 886A.2553/6–2350.
13. Childs to Secretary of State, RG 59, NA, 886A.2553/6–2750.
14. "Memorandum of conversation with Najib Bey Salha, Assistant Deputy Minister of Finance," in Childs to Department of State, RG 59, NA 886A.2553/7–2550.
15. "Discussion with Aramco and Saudi Arabian Government Officials Regarding Saudi Arabian Government Requests for Increased Participation in Revenues of the Arabian American Oil Co.," July 25, 1950, NA, RG59, 886A.2553/7–2550.
16. Ibid.
17. Ibid.
18. "Conversation with Colonel Eddy, Regarding Conditions in Saudi Arabia," RG 59, NA, 886A.2553/8–1450.
19. "Memorandum of Conversation between Sheikh Yusuf Yassin, and Mohammed Effendi at Riyadh July 17, 1950," in Childs to Department of State, RG 59, NA, 886A.2553/7–2550.
20. Ibid.
21. "Statement of Aramco's position with regard to the Saudi Arabian Government's demands for increased participation in Aramco's earnings," in Childs to Department of State, RG 59, NA, 886A.2553/7–2550.
22. Childs, 158.
23. Ibid., 172.
24. Ibid., 177.
25. Paul J. Hare, *Diplomatic Chronicles of the Middle East: A Biography of Ambassador Raymond A. Hare* (Lanham, Maryland: University Press of America, Inc., 1993), 5.
26. Hare, 93.
27. Ibid., 87.

28. Raymond Hare, oral history interview, Georgetown University Library, 38, as quoted in Hare, 87.
29. Hare, 70.
30. "Memorandum of Conversation: Conversation with Aramco Officials," RG 59, NA 886A.2553/10–2650
31. Telegram from Department of State to Jeddah, RG 59, NA, 886A.2553/11–650.
32. Confidential Memorandum: Visit of Sheikh Asad al Raqih, RG 59, NA, 886A.2553/11–650.
33. "Memorandum of Conversation: SAG Demands for Renegotiation of Aramco Contract," RG 59, NA, 886A.2553/11–2250.
34. Childs to Secretary of State, RG 59, NA, 886A.2553/6–2350.
35. "Memorandum of Conversation: SAG Demands for Renegotiation of Aramco Contract," RG 59, NA, 886A.2553/11–2250.
36. Holden and Johns, 173.
37. Hare to Secretary of State, RG 59, NA, 886A.2553/12–150.
38. Hare, 89.
39. Hare to Secretary of State, RG 59, NA, 886A.2553/12–1250.
40. Hare to Secretary of State, RG 59, NA, 886A.2553/12–1350.
41. Hare to Secretary of State, RG 59, NA, 886A.2553/12–2950.
42. Ibid.
43. House Subcommittee of the Committee on Government Operations, *Foreign Tax Credits Claimed by U.S. Petroleum Companies: Hearings before a Subcommittee of the Committee on Government Operations.* 95th Cong. 1st sess. September 26, 27; October 4; and November 29, 1977, 497.
44. IRS Revenue Ruling on Saudi Arabian Tax Law, Rev. Rul. 55–296, 1955–1 C.B. 386.
45. Ellen R. Wald, "The United States, Great Britain and the Middle-Eastern Oil Industry, 1945–1960" (doctoral dissertation, Boston University, 2012), 74–76.
46. Memorandum of Conversation, RG 59, NA, 886A.2553/1–1051.
47. Ibid.
48. Hare to Secretary of State, RG 59, NA, 886A.2553/12–2950.

FOUR: AN ARABIAN DAWN

1. "Resume of audiences had by Aramco officials at Riyadh on June 2 & 3, 1951" July 2, 1951, RG 59, NA 886A.2553/7–251.
2. Ibid.
3. Letter from Garry Owen to Shaikh Abdulla Sulaiman, Minister of Finance, January 2, 1951, RG 59, NA 886A.2553/2–1051.
4. "Memorandum to Department of State, Subject: New Developments in Aramco Operations," May 24, 1951, RG 59, NA 886A.2553/5–2451.
5. Hare to Secretary of State, RG 59, NA 886A.2553/7–1451.
6. Hare to Secretary of State, RG 59, NA 886A.2553/7–1951.
7. Hare to Secretary of State, RG 59, NA 886A.2553/7–2451.
8. Ibid.

9. Ibid.
10. Ibid.
11. Hare to Secretary of State, RG 59, NA 886A.2553/8-1151.
12. Hare, 70–87
13. Hare to Secretary of State, RG 59, NA 886A.2553/8-1151.
14. "Discussion with Aramco on SAG Demands," RG 59, NA 886A.2553/8-2151.
15. Unsigned Telegram from Jiddah to Secretary of State, RG 59, NA 886A.2553/8-2451.
16. Memorandum of Conversation, RG 59, NA 886A.2553/10-3051.
17. "Status of Aramco-SAG Discussions of Concession Terms," RG 59, NA 886A.2553/4-2152.
18. William E. Mulligan, "A Kingdom and a Company," in *Aramco World Magazine* 35:3 (1984): 44.
19. "Memorandum of Conversation, Subject: Aramco Call on Mr. McGhee," RG 59, NA 886A.2553/10-3051.
20. Memorandum of Conversation, RG 59, NA 886A.2553/6-3052.
21. Memorandum of Conversation, RG 59, NA 886A.2553/11-652.
22. Hare to Secretary of State: "Exploratory Conversations: Aramco-SAG Petroleum Consultant," NA 886A.2553/12-652.
23. "Weekly Summary—Arabian Peninsula Affairs," RG 59, NA 886A.2553/12-1652.
24. Hare, 91, 95.
25. Ibid., 95.
26. "Memorandum of Conversation with Saudi Finance Minister Regarding Aramco," NA 886A.2553/7-653.
27. "Memoranda of Conversations with Saudi Officials Regarding Aramco," RG 59, NA 886.2553/7-653.
28. Ibid.
29. U.S. Embassy London to Department of State, Washington, RG 59, NA 886A.2553/9-2854.
30. "Memorandum of Conversation, Subject: ARAMCO Negotiating Plans," RG 59, NA 886A.2553/7-2853.

PART II

FIVE: HE MET HIS DUTY

1. Lacey, *The Kingdom*, 296.
2. Holden and Johns, 174.
3. Holden and Johns, 173.
4. J. Winston Porter, interview with the author, Savannah, GA, June 30, 2016.
5. "Faisal—a Perspective of 1945–1965," Parker T. Hart Papers Box 5 Folder 13, Georgetown University Archives.
6. Lacey, *The Kingdom*, 318.
7. Ibid., 296.

8. Holden and Johns, 173, 174.
9. Howarth, 230.
10. Holden and Johns, 174.
11. Holden and Johns, 174, Lacey, *The Kingdom*, 297, and Howarth, 230.
12. Lacey, *The Kingdom*, 297.
13. Holden and Johns, 174.
14. Brown, 203.
15. Howarth, 230.
16. Abdul Nabi Shaheen, "Sultan will have simple burial at Al Oud cemetery," *Gulf News* (Abu Dhabi, UAE), October 31, 2011.
17. Holden and Johns, 174.
18. Lacey, *The Kingdom*, 97.
19. Brown, 53.
20. "An 'Electronic Dialogue' with Ambassador Parker T. Hart," William Mulligan Papers, Box 1 Folder 20, Georgetown University Archives.
21. Howarth, 229.
22. Brown, 203.
23. Ihsan Bu-Hulaiga, interview with the author, Abu Dhabi (UAE), April 20, 2017.
24. Othman Alkhowaiter, interview with the author, Dhahran, Saudi Arabia, November 26, 2017.
25. Ali al-Naimi, *Out of the Desert* (Great Britain: Portfolio Penguin, 2016), 5.
26. Howarth, 231.
27. Holden and Johns, 177.
28. "Faisal—a Perspective of 1945–1965, Parker T. Hart Papers," Box 5 Folder 13, Georgetown University Archives.
29. Holden and Johns, 178.
30. Ibid., 199.
31. Ibid., 183.
32. Ibid., 183.
33. Alexei Vassiliev, *King Faisal: Personality, Faith and Times* (United Kingdom: Saqi Books, 2012); and "Wives of King Saud," King Saud Foundation, www.kingsaud.org.
34. "Faisal—a Perspective of 1945–1965," Parker T. Hart Papers, Box 5 Folder 13, Georgetown University Archives.
35. Lacey, *The Kingdom*, 250.
36. Ibid., 339.
37. Frank Jungers, *The Caravan Goes On: How Aramco and Saudi Arabia Grew Up Together* (Isle of Wight: Medina Publishing, 2013), 108.
38. Ibid., 108.
39. Lacey, *The Kingdom*, 359.
40. Ibid., 308.
41. Holden and Johns, 199.
42. Parker T. Hart (US Ambassador to Saudi Arabia), interviewed by William R. Crawford, January 27, 1989, transcript, The Association for Diplomatic Studies and Training Foreign Affairs Oral History Project.

43. Lacey, *The Kingdom*, 318–319.

44. Ibid., 320.

45. Memorandum of Conversation, Washington, March 26, 1958, FRUS 1958–1960, vol. XII, 721.

46. Lacey, *The Kingdom*, 320.

47. Ibid., 321–323.

48. Implications of Recent Governmental Changes in Saudi Arabia, Special Intelligence Estimate, April 8, 1958, FRUS, 1958–1960, vol. XII, 726.

49. Holden and Johns, 205.

50. Lacey, *The Kingdom*, 324.

51. Ibid., 325.

52. Telegram from the Embassy in Saudi Arabia to the Department of State, Jiddah, April 22, 1959, FRUS 1958–1960, vol. XII, 747.

SIX: PUTTING THE HOUSE IN ORDER

1. Vernon O. Egger, *A History of the Muslim World to 1405* (Upper Saddle River, New Jersey: Pearson Prentice Hall, 2004), 34.

2. Michael Cook, *Muhammad* (New York: Oxford University Press, 1996), 85.

3. Egger, 31.

4. Cook, 24.

5. Bernard Lewis, *The Arabs in History* (New York: Oxford University Press, 1993), 49.

6. Parker T. Hart (US Ambassador to Saudi Arabia), interviewed by William R. Crawford, January 27, 1989, transcript, The Association for Diplomatic Studies and Training Foreign Affairs Oral History Project.

7. Tim Niblock, "Social Structure and the Development of the Saudi Arabian Political System," in *State, Society and Economy in Saudi Arabia*, ed. Tim Niblock (London: Routledge, 1915), 100.

8. Lacey, *The Kingdom*, 336.

9. "Memorandum from the Director of Intelligence and Research (Cumming) to Secretary of State Herter," December 22, 1960, FRUS, 1958–1960, Vol. XII, 769.

10. "Memorandum From the Director of the Office of Near Eastern Affairs (Meyer) to the Assistant Secretary of State for Near Eastern and South Asian Affairs (Jones)," December 23, 1960, FRUS, 1958–1960, vol. XII, 771.

11. Parker T. Hart (US Ambassador to Saudi Arabia), interviewed by William R. Crawford, January 27, 1989, transcript, The Association for Diplomatic Studies and Training Foreign Affairs Oral History Project.

12. "Memorandum from the Director of the Office of Near Eastern Affairs (Meyer) to the Assistant Secretary of State for Near Eastern and South Asian Affairs (Jones)," December 23, 1960, FRUS, 1958–1960, vol. XII, 771.

13. Parker T. Hart (US Ambassador to Saudi Arabia), interviewed by William R. Crawford, January 27, 1989, transcript, The Association for Diplomatic Studies and Training Foreign Affairs Oral History Project.

14. Lacey, *The Kingdom*, 335–338.

15. Ibid., 338.

16. Parker T. Hart (US Ambassador to Saudi Arabia), interviewed by William R. Crawford, January 27, 1989, transcript, The Association for Diplomatic Studies and Training Foreign Affairs Oral History Project.

17. Ibid.

18. Lacey, *The Kingdom*, 342.

19. "Statements Made by Abdullah Tariki, Oil Advisor to Saudi Arabian Government," RG 59, NA, 886A.2553/9–1151.

20. "Memorandum of Conversation: General Discussion of Saudi Arabian Oil Problems," RG 59, NA, 886A.2553/10–2451.

21. Vitalis, 136–137.

22. Yergin, 254.

23. William L. Owen, interview with Carole Hicke, "American Perspectives of Aramco, the Saudi-Arabian Oil-Producing Company, 1930s to 1980s, University of California Berkeley Regional Oral History Office University of California Department Interview, 332–333.

24. Brown, 222.

25. Lacey, *The Kingdom*, 338–339.

26. Yergin, 488.

27. Owen, interview with Carole Hicke, 334–335.

28. Schwinn to Secretary of State, RG 59, NA, 886A.2553/9–2458.

29. "Saudi Members Participate in Aramco Board Meeting," RG 59, NA, 886A.2553/6–459.

30. Ibid.

31. "New Aramco President Pays Initial Call on Crown Prince," RG 59, NA, 886A.2553/6–459.

32. Ibid.

33. Ambassador Heath to Secretary of State, RG 59, NA, 886A.2553/8–2859.

34. "Memorandum of Conversation, Shaikh Abdullah Tariki, Director of Petroleum and Mineral Affairs and William D. Wolle, Embassy Economic Officer," November 28, 1959, RG 59, NA, 886A.2553/12–1559.

35. "Memorandum of Conversation, Shaikh Abdullah Tariki, Director of Petroleum and Mineral Affairs and William D. Wolle, Embassy Economic Officer," November 28, 1959, RG 59, NA, 886A.2553/12–1559.

36. Yergin, 505.

37. Ibid., 493–494.

38. Anna Rubino, *Queen of the Oil Club: The Intrepid Wanda Jablonski and the Power of Information* (Boston: Beacon Press, 2008), 185.

39. Rubino, 162.

40. Juan Carlos Boue, "The Forging of the Saudi-Venezuelan Petroleum Entente," Conference paper, *OPEC and the Global Energy Order*, NYU Abu Dhabi, April 18, 2017; and "Statements Made by Abdullah Tariki, Oil Advisor to Saudi Arabian Government," RG 59, NA, 886A.2553/9–1151.

41. Yergin, 504–505.
42. "Telegram from the Embassy in Saudi Arabia to Department of States," November 26, 1959, FRUS, Near East Region 1958–1960, 750.
43. Lacey, *The Kingdom*, 340.
44. Scott McMurray, *Energy to the World: The Story of Saudi Aramco*, vol. 2 (Houston: Aramco Services Company, 2011), 16.
45. Naimi, 212.
46. Lacey, *The Kingdom*, 348.
47. Ibid.
48. Ibid., 349.
49. Ibid.
50. Lacey, *The Kingdom*, 349, and Holden and Johns, 237.
51. Lacey, *The Kingdom*, 351.
52. Ibid., 351–352.
53. Ibid.
54. Holden and Johns, 235.
55. Ibid., 238.
56. Lacey, *The Kingdom*, 353.
57. Holden and Johns, 239.
58. Lacey, *The Kingdom*, 354.
59. Hamid Enayat, *Modern Islamic Political Thought* (Austin: University of Texas, 1982), 74; and Andrew F. March, "Islamic Political Thought," in Gerald F. Gaus and Fred D'Agostino, ed., *The Routledge Companion to Social and Political Philosophy* (New York: Routledge, 2013), 206.
60. Lacey, *The Kingdom*, 357.
61. Holden and Johns, 269–270.
62. Douglas E. Steusand, *Islamic Gunpowder Empires* (Boulder, Colorado: Westview Press, 2011), 71–73.
63. Holden and Johns, 240.
64. Lacey, *The Kingdom*, 360.
65. Michael Herb, *All in the Family: Absolutism, Revolution, and Democracy in the Middle Eastern Monarchies* (Albany: State University of New York Press, Albany, 1999), 102.
66. Lacey, *The Kingdom*, 360.
67. Holden and Johns, 241.
68. Ibid., 240.
69. Ibid., 266.
70. Lacey, *The Kingdom*, 361.
71. Ibid., 361.

SEVEN: WAHHABISM, WOMEN, WESTERNERS, AND RIYALS

1. Leslie McLoughlin, *Ibn Saud: Founder of a Kingdom* (New York: Palgrave Macmillan, 1993), 55.
2. Noel F. Busch, "The King of Arabia," *Life* magazine, May 31, 1943, 75.

3. Riyadh Population, http://population.city/saudi-arabia/riyadh/.

4. Steffen Hertog, *Princes, Brokers, and Bureaucrats: Oil and the State in Saudi Arabia* (Ithaca: Cornell University Press, 2010), 109.

5. John Duke Anthony, "Saudi Arabia: From Tribal Society to Nation-State," in *Saudi Arabia*, ed. Ragaei El Mallakh and Dorothea H. El Mallakh (Massachusetts: Lexington Books, 1982), 93–98.

6. Karen Elliot House, *On Saudi Arabia: Its People, Past, Religion, Fault Lines—and Future* (New York: Alfred A. Knopf, 2012), 66.

7. Natana J. Delong-Bas, *Wahhabi Islam: From Revival and Reform to Global Jihad* (New York: Oxford University Press, 2004), 8–25.

8. Ibid., 35.

9. William L. Cleveland and Martin Bunton, *A History of the Modern Middle East* (Boulder, Colorado: Westview Press, 2013), 402.

10. Ibid., 403.

11. Ambassador James B. Smith, interview with the author, January 11, 2016.

12. Lacey, *The Kingdom*, 435.

13. Robert Lacey, *Inside the Kingdom: Kings, Clerics, Modernists, Terrorists, and the Struggle for Saudi Arabia* (New York: Viking, 2009), 87.

14. Lacey, *The Kingdom*, 369.

15. Cleveland and Bunton, 403.

16. Holden and Johns, 261.

17. Associated Press, "Reported killer of Faisal knew drugs, radicals," *Record-Journal* (Meriden, CT), March 25, 1975, 18.

18. Holden and Johns, 262.

19. Yaroslav Trofimov, *The Siege of Mecca: The Forgotten Uprising in Islam's Holiest Shrine and the Birth of Al Qaeda* (New York: Doubleday, 2007), 30.

20. Ambassador James B. Smith, interview with the author, January 11, 2016.

21. Trofimov, 26–28.

22. Lacey, *Inside the Kingdom*, 87–90.

23. Trofimov, 28.

24. Ibid., 30–38.

25. Ibid., 38.

26. Ibid., 48–49.

27. Lacey, *Inside the Kingdom*, 22.

28. Ibid., 24–27.

29. Ibid., 28–30.

30. Trofimov, 150–152.

31. Lacey, *Inside the Kingdom*, 31–34.

32. Ibid., 35.

33. Ibid., 47.

34. Ibid., 48–52.

35. Ibid., 53.

36. House, 77; and Lacey, *Inside the Kingdom*, 85.

37. Lacey, *Inside the Kingdom*, 52.

38. Tim Barger, interview with the author, June 1, 2017.

39. Linda Porter, interview with the author, Savannah, GA, June 30, 2016.

40. Lacey, *Inside the Kingdom*, 46.

41. UNESCO, "Trends and Projections of Enrollment by Level of Education and by Age, 1960–2025," November, 1989, appendix A-61 http://unesdoc.unesco.org/images/0008/000852/085283EB.pdf.

42. Haya Saad Al Rawaf and Cyril Simmons, "The Education of Women in Saudi Arabia," *Comparative Education* 27:3 (1991), 287.

43. Hertog, 106; and UNESCO Institute for Statistics, Saudi Arabia, http://uis.unesco.org/country/SA.

44. Rawaf and Simmons, 292.

45. UNESCO Institute for Statistics, Saudi Arabia, http://uis.unesco.org/country/SA.

46. Nick Clark, "Higher Education in Saudi Arabia," *World Education News and Reviews*, November 3, 2014, http://wenr.wes.org/2014/11/higher-education-in-saudi-arabia.

47. UNESCO Institute for Statistics, Saudi Arabia, Education and Literacy, http://uis.unesco.org/country/SA.

48. Tim Niblock and Monica Malik, *The Political Economy of Saudi Arabia* (New York: Routledge, 2007), 194.

49. Ben Hubbard, "Young Saudis See Cushy Jobs Vanish Along with Nation's Oil Wealth," *New York Times*, February 16, 2016.

50. Dr. Janet Breslin-Smith, interview with the author, Washington, D.C., January 11, 2016.

51. Samir Madani, former Erikson employee in Saudi Arabia, conversation with the author, January 20, 2017.

52. Global Media Insight, "Saudi Arabia Social Media Statistics 2016," May 25, 2016, http://www.globalmediainsight.com/blog/saudi-arabia-social-media-statistics/; "Why Saudis are ardent social media fans," *Economist*, March 23, 2015; and "Social media in Saudi Arabia: A virtual revolution," *Economist*, September 13, 2014.

53. Mohammad al Sheikh, interview with Bret Baier, "Saudi minister of state talks arms deal, fighting terror," Fox News, May 22, 2017. https://www.youtube.com/watch?v=Bzj5KUHetg8.

54. Ambassador James B. Smith, interview with the author, Washington, D.C., January 11, 2016.

55. Jeffrey K. Walker, "The Rights of the Accused in Saudi Criminal Procedure," *Loyola of Los Angeles International and Comparative Law Review*, 15:4 (1993), 878.

56. Eleanor A. Doumato, "Gender, Monarchy, and National Identity in Saudi Arabia," *British Journal of Middle Eastern Studies*, 19:1 (1992), 34–35.

57. Fulya Dogruel, "A Long Road Ahead for Achieving Fully Fledged Equality: Saudi Women's Rights Activism," in *Authoritarianism in the Middle East: Before and After the Arab Uprisings*, eds. J. Karakoc Bakis and Julide Karakoc (London: Palgrave Macmillan, 2015), chapter 4.

58. Lacey, *The Kingdom*, 365–366.

59. Al Rawaf and Simmons, 289.

60. Ibid.,291–292.
61. Eleanor Abdella Doumato, "Women and Work in Saudi Arabia: How Flexible Are Islamic Margins?" *Middle East Journal*, 53:4 (1999), 569–570.
62. Doumato, 581.
63. Vivian Nereim and Matthew Martin, "Sarah Al Suhaimi to Become the First Woman to Head Saudi Arabia's Stock Exchange," *Bloomberg*, February 16, 2017, https://www.bloomberg.com/news/articles/2017-02-16/ sarah-al-suhaimi-said-to-become-first-woman-to-head-saudi-bourse.
64. Michael Pearson, "First women elected to office in Saudi Arabia," *CNN*, December 14, 2015, http://www.cnn.com/2015/12/13/world/first-women -elected-to-office-in-saudi-arabia/index.html.
65. Ben Hubbard, "Saudi Arabia Agrees to Let Women Drive," *New York Times*, September 26, 2017.
66. Lulwa Shalhoub, "Saudi women no longer need guardians' consent to receive services," *Arab News*, May 5, 2017.
67. Samah Damanhoori, interview with the author, June 5, 2017.
68. Maureen Dowd, "A Girls' Guide to Saudi Arabia," *Vanity Fair*, August 2010, http:// www.vanityfair.com/news/2010/08/maureen-dowd-201008.
69. Brid Beeler, interview with the author, May 5, 2017.
70. Laura, interview with the author, June 7, 2017.
71. Ibid.
72. Lee S. Wolosky, Maurice R. Greenberg, and William F. Wechsler, *Terrorist Financing: Report of an Independent Task Force Sponsored by the Council on Foreign Relations* (New York: Council on Foreign Relations, 2002), 8.
73. Gawdat Bahgat, "Saudi Arabia and the War on Terrorism," *Arab Studies Quarterly*, 26:1 (2004), 54.
74. Caroline Mortimer, "Jeremy Corbyn calls for 'difficult conversations' with Saudi Arabia and Gulf states over extremism funding," *Independent*, June 5, 2017. http://www.independent.co.uk/News/uk/politics/jeremy-corbyn -saudi-arabia-extremist-funding-terrorism-gulf-states-qatar-isis-al-qaeda -labour-a7773451.html.
75. David D. Kirkpatrick, "Saudi Arabia Said to Arrest Suspect in 1996 Khobar Towers Bombing, *New York Times*, August 26, 2015. https://www.nytimes.com/ 2015/08/27/world/middleeast/saudia-arabia-arrests-suspect-khobar-towers -bombing.html?_r=0 and "Perry: U.S. eyed Iran attack after bombing," *UPI*, June 6, 2007. http://www.upi.com/Business_News/Security-Industry/2007/06/06/ Perry-US-eyed-Iran-attack-after-bombing/UPI-70451181161509/.
76. United States Department of State, *Annual Briefing Saudi Arabia*, November 23, 2015.
77. Simon Henderson, "Al-Qaeda Attack on Abqaiq," *Washington Institute*, February 28, 2006.
78. Mohammad al Sheikh, interview with Bret Baier, "Saudi minister of state talks arms deal, fighting terror," Fox News, May 22, 2017. https://www.youtube.com/ watch?v=Bzj5KUHetg8.

79. Bruce Riedel, "The Prince of Counter-Terrorism," *Brookings*, September 29, 2015. http://csweb.brookings.edu/content/research/essays/2015/the-prince-of-counterterrorism.html.

80. "Declassified '28 pages' on 9/11—full text," *CNNpolitics*, http://www.cnn.com/2016/07/15/politics/28-pages-released-full-text/index.html.

81. Roba Dagustani, conversation with the author, Jacksonville, FL, November 10, 2016.

82. Lesley Stahl, "The Oil Kingdom: Part Two," *60 Minutes*, December 7, 2008.

83. Tim Barger, interview with the author, June 1, 2017.

84. Lee Ingham, interview with the author, May 8, 2017.

PART III

EIGHT: "MASTERS OF OUR OWN COMMODITY"

1. Jeffrey Robinson, *Yamani: The Inside Story* (New York: The Atlantic Monthly Press, 1988), 44.

2. Robinson, 45.

3. Ibid., 9.

4. "Biographical sketch of Ahmed Zaki Yamani," March 24, 1962, William Mulligan Papers, Box 1, Folder 6 Georgetown University.

5. Holden and Johns, 310.

6. Ibid.,313.

7. Ibid.

8. Holden and Johns, 309; and Yergin, 567.

9. Holden and Johns, 311.

10. Ibid.,318.

11. Ibid.,315.

12. Ibid.

13. Ibid.,316.

14. Ibid.,318.

15. *Multinational Corporations and United States Foreign Policy: Hearings Before the Subcommittee on Multinational Corporations of the Committee on Foreign Relations, United States Senate*, 93rd Congress, pt. 4 (1974), 56–57.

16. Yergin, 566; *Multinational Corporations and United States Foreign Policy: Hearings Before the Subcommittee on Multinational Corporations of the Committee on Foreign Relations, United States Senate*, 93rd Congress, pt. 4 (1974), 230; and *Multinational Corporations and United States Foreign Policy: Hearings Before the Subcommittee on Multinational Corporations of the Committee on Foreign Relations, United States Senate*, 93rd Congress, pt. 6 (1974), 52.

17. "Saudi Arabia And Aramco Reach Agreement On Takeover," *mees*, March 15, 1976.

18. Yergin, 496–503.

19. Ibid., 574.

20. Sampson, 292.

21. Ibid., 292.

22. Yergin, 581–583.

23. Lacey, *The Kingdom*, 404.

24. Yergin, 583, Sampson, 23, and Lacey, *The Kingdom*, 404.

25. Lacey, *The Kingdom*, 404.

26. Sampson, 294.

27. Ibid., 294.

28. Yergin, 574.

29. Lacey, *The Kingdom*, 414.

30. Ibid., 404.

31. Sampson, 23.

32. Yergin, 576; and Benny Morris, *Righteous Victims: A History of the Zionist-Arab Conflict, 1881–1999* (New York: Alfred A. Knopf, 1999), 434.

33. Sampson, 287.

34. Yergin, 576.

35. Ambassador Childs to the Secretary of State, December 4, 1947, RG 59, NA, 890F.00/12-447.

36. Noel F. Busch, "The King of Arabia," *Life* magazine, May 31, 1943, 77.

37. Sampson, 289.

38. Yergin, 576, but the calculations have been corrected from the original.

39. Ibid., 576.

40. *Multinational Corporations and United States Foreign Policy: Hearings Before the Subcommittee on Multinational Corporations of the Committee on Foreign Relations, United States Senate*, 93rd Congress, pt. 7 (1974), 441.

41. Yergin, 587.

42. Ibid., 588.

43. "Memorandum of Discussion at the 303d Meeting of the National Security Council," Washington, November 8, 1956, *FRUS 1955–1957, X*, 628–30.

44. Holden and Johns, 341.

45. Ibid.

46. Frank Jungers, interview with Carole Hicke, "American Perspectives of Aramco, The Saudi-Arabian Oil-Producing Company, 1930s to 1980s, University of California Berkeley Regional Oral History Office University of California Department Interview, 133.

47. Sampson, 296; and *Multinational Corporations and United States Foreign Policy: Hearings Before the Subcommittee on Multinational Corporations of the Committee on Foreign Relations, United States Senate*, 93rd Congress, pt. 7 (1974), 515.

48. Jungers, *The Caravan Goes On*,156.

49. Holden and Johns, 350.

50. Ibid.

51. Ibid.

52. Sampson, 302–303.

53. Lacey, *The Kingdom*, 420.

54. Yergin, 612–613.

55. Lacey, *The Kingdom*, 420.

56. Yergin, 597.

57. Henry Kissinger, *Years of Upheaval* (Boston: Little Brown & Co., 1982), 854.

58. Sampson, 294.

59. Yergin, 576.

60. Ambassador Childs to Secretary of State, December 4, 1947, RG 59, NA, 890F.00/124–47.

61. Sampson, 299.

62. Telegram, US Embassy in Tehran to Secretary of State, "Iran's Version of the Quito Meeting," July 5, 1974.

63. *Multinational Corporations and United States Foreign Policy: Hearings Before the Subcommittee on Multinational Corporations of the Committee on Foreign Relations, United States Senate*, 93rd Congress, pt. 7 (1974), 516.

64. Frank Jungers, interview with Carole Hicke, "American Perspectives of Aramco, The Saudi-Arabian Oil-Producing Company, 1930s to 1980s, University of California Berkeley Regional Oral History Office University of California Department Interview, 89.

65. *Multinational Corporations and United States Foreign Policy: Hearings Before the Subcommittee on Multinational Corporations of the Committee on Foreign Relations, United States Senate*, 93rd Congress, pt. 7 (1974), 408.

66. *Multinational Corporations and United States Foreign Policy: Hearings Before the Subcommittee on Multinational Corporations of the Committee on Foreign Relations, United States Senate*, 93rd Congress, pt. 7 (1974), 416.

67. Ibid.

68. Frank Jungers, interview with the author, May 8, 2017.

69. Jungers, *The Caravan Goes On*, 157.

70. Tim Barger, interview with the author, May 8, 2017.

71. Holden and Johns, 369.

72. Telegram, Akins to Secretary of State, "New Saudi-Oil Company Relationship, Yamani's Views and Plans," May 27, 1974.

73. Ibid.

74. *Multinational Corporations and United States Foreign Policy: Hearings Before the Subcommittee on Multinational Corporations of the Committee on Foreign Relations, United States Senate*, 93rd Congress, pt. 7 (1974), 433.

75. Telegram, Secretary of State to Jeddah Embassy, "Saudi Arabia-Aramco Interim Agreement on Participation," June 12, 1974.

76. William D. Smith, "Saudis to Increase Their Share in Aramco from 25% to 60%," *The New York Times*, June 11, 1974.

77. Telegram, Akins to Secretary of State, "Yamani's Views on the Future of Aramco," August 22, 1974.

78. Telegram, US Embassy in Jidda to Secretary of State, "Aramco Plans (Or Lack of Plans For The Future," July 10, 1974.

79. Telegram, Akins to Secretary Kissinger, "Yamani Plans on Price and Aramco," November 9, 1974.

80. Telegram, Akins to Secretary Kissinger, "Yamani Plans on Price and Aramco," November 9, 1974.

81. Telegram, Akins to Secretary of State, November 29, 1974.

82. Terry Robards, "Talks Are Halted In Aramco Bid," *New York Times*, December 11, 1974.

NINE: "NATIONALIZATION WAS NOT THE THING AT ALL"

1. Lacey, *The Kingdom*, 425.
2. Ibid., 425.
3. Jungers, *The Caravan Goes On*, 169.
4. Lacey, *The Kingdom*, 429.
5. Juan De Onis, "Faisal's Killer Is Put to Death," *New York Times*, June 19, 1975.
6. Lacey, *The Kingdom*, 425.
7. Ibid., 425.
8. Jungers, *The Caravan Goes On*, 176.
9. AP Archive, "Sheikh Ahmed Zaki Yamani Speaks About Carlos the Jackal," October 12, 1997. http://www.aparchive.com/metadata/UK-SHEIKH-AHMED-ZAKI-YAMANI-SPEAKS-ABOUT-CARLOS-THE-JACKAL/44a3f3c2cadcccbacbd54043b9 216a3b?query=aaliyah.
10. Edward Hudson, "Yamani Reported in Florida Talks," *New York Times*, March 7, 1976.
11. United Press International, "Security Blacks Out Oil Meeting," *New York Times*, March 8, 1976.
12. Nassir Ajmi, interview with the author, Dhahran, Saudi Arabia, November 27, 2017.
13. *Saudi Arabia v. Arabian American Oil Company* (Aramco), ARAMCO-Award, ILR 1963, at 117 et seq.
14. "New Saudi-Oil Company Relationship: Yamani's Views and Plans," Telegram from US Embassy in Jeddah to Secretary of State, May 27, 1974.
15. "Effect on US-Saudi Relations of Suspension of US Peace Efforts," Telegram from U.S. Embassy in Jeddah to Secretary of State, February 20, 1974 and "Future of Aramco," Telegram from U.S. Embassy in Jeddah to Secretary of State, March 25, 1974.
16. H.E. Ali al-Naimi, interview with the author, Dhahran, Saudi Arabia, November 27, 2017.
17. Frank Jungers, interview with the author, May 8, 2017.
18. United Press International, "Security Blacks Out Oil Meeting," *New York Times*, March 8, 1976.
19. "Saudi Arabia and Aramco Reach Agreement on Takeover," *mees*, March 15, 1976.
20. H.E. Ali al-Naimi, interview with the author, Dhahran, Saudi Arabia, November 27, 2017.
21. Nassir Ajmi, interview with the author, Dhahran, Saudi Arabia, November 27, 2017.
22. Naimi, 119.
23. Ibid., 118–119.
24. Frank Jungers, interview with the author, May 8, 2017.
25. Dr. Majid al Moneef, interview with the author, Abu Dhabi (UAE), April 19, 2017.
26. H.E. Ali al-Naimi, interview with the author, Dhahran, Saudi Arabia, November 27, 2017.
27. Naimi, 118–119.

28. H.E. Ali al-Naimi, interview with the author, Dhahran, Saudi Arabia, November 27, 2017.
29. Frank Jungers, interview with the author, May 8, 2017.
30. Lee and Jackie Ingham, interview with the author, May 8, 2017.
31. Yasser Mufti, interview with the author, Dhahran, Saudi Arabia, November 27, 2017.
32. Naimi, 187.
33. Yasser Mufti, interview with the author, Dhahran, Saudi Arabia, November 27, 2017.
34. "Saudi Aramco gets new supreme council headed by deputy crown prince—statement," *Reuters*, May 1, 2015, https://www.reuters.com/article/saudi-oil-aramco/saudi-aramco-gets-new-supreme-council-headed-by-deputy-crown-prince-statement-idUSL5N0XS0LR20150501.
35. Yasser Mufti, interview with the author, Dhahran, Saudi Arabia, November 27, 2017.
36. Anthony J. Parisi, "Final Saudi Payment for Aramco Is Made," *New York Times*, September 5, 1980.
37. "No Production Cut Envisaged in Saudi Arabia," *mees*, June 29, 1981. https://mees.com/opec-history/1981/06/29/no-production-cut-envisaged-in-saudi-arabia/.
38. Naimi, 117; and Lacey, *Inside the Kingdom*, 90.
39. Robinson, 258.
40. Lacey, *Inside the Kingdom*, 88.
41. "The Latest Oil Price Crisis: A Saudi View," *mees*, December 3, 1984. https://mees.com/opec-history/1984/12/03/the-latest-oil-price-crisis-a-saudi-view/.
42. Naimi, 136.
43. Ibid., 135.
44. H.E. Ali al-Naimi, interview with the author, Dhahran, Saudi Arabia, November 27, 2017; Othman Alkhowaiter, interview with the author, Dhahran, Saudi Arabia, November 26, 2017; and Nassir Ajmi, interview with the author, Dhahran, Saudi Arabia, November 27, 2017.
45. Naimi, 110.
46. Valerie Marcel, *Oil Titans National Oil Companies in the Middle East* (Washington, D.C.: Brookings Inst. Press/Chatham House, 2006), 87.
47. Zaki Safar, interview with the author, February 9, 2016.
48. Naimi, 173.
49. Glenn Labhart, interview with the author, December 15, 2015.
50. Naimi, 141.
51. "Motiva Enterprises' co-owners to split U.S. refineries on May 1," *Reuters*, March 6, 2017. http://www.reuters.com/article/us-refineries-motiva-split-idUSKBN16E05B.
52. Yergin, 728.
53. Robinson, 264.
54. Ibid., 269–270.
55. Leonardo Maugeri, *The Age of Oil: The Mythology, History, and Future of the World's Most Controversial Resource* (Westport: Praeger, 2006), 138–139.
56. Yergin, 731.
57. Ibid., 743–744.

58. Robinson, 268.

59. Ibid., 272.

60. Rubino, 276.

61. "Biographical Sketch—Hisham Nazer," William Mulligan Files, Box 1 Folder 69, Georgetown University.

62. John Tagliabue, "New Saudi Minister Begins Test of Skill," *New York Times*, December 14, 1986.

63. Naimi, 114.

64. Lee and Jackie Ingham, interview with the author, May 8, 2017.

65. H.E. Ali al-Naimi, interview with the author, Dhahran, Saudi Arabia, November 27, 2017

66. Ibid.

67. Scott McMurray, *Energy to the World: The Story of Saudi Aramco*, vol. 1 (Houston: Aramco Services Company, 2011), 212.

68. Yousef al-Naimi, conversation with the author, April 12, 2017.

69. Naimi, 182–183.

70. Richard Eason, interview with the author, Jacksonville, FL, December 10, 2015.

71. Ibid.

72. Herman Wang, interview with the author, July 28, 2017.

TEN: "BARRELS OF OIL AND GIGAWATTS OF POWER"

1. Lacey, *Inside the Kingdom*, 128.

2. Ibid., 130.

3. Dick Cheney, *In My Time: A Personal and Political Memoir* (New York: Simon and Schuster, 2011), 186.

4. Cheney, 187–189.

5. Ibid., 189.

6. Ibid., 190.

7. Ibid., 187.

8. Lacey, *Inside the Kingdom*, 130.

9. Ibid., 131.

10. Ibid., 132.

11. Cheney, 191.

12. Lacey, *Inside the Kingdom*, 133, and Cheney, 191.

13. Cheney, 192.

14. Robert S. "Bo" Smith, Captain U.S. Navy (Ret.), interview with the author, Jacksonville, FL, March 15, 2017.

15. Lacey, *Inside the Kingdom*, 131.

16. Ibid., 134.

17. Neil MacFarquhar, "After the Attacks: The Saudis; Battle Against Terrorism Test Fragile Relationship Between U.S. and Saudis," *New York Times* (New York: NY), September 15, 2001.

18. Lacey, *Inside the Kingdom*, 148.

19. Ibid., 150.

20. Michael Scott Doran, "Somebody Else's Civil War," *Foreign Affairs*, 81:1 (2002), 26.

21. Doran, 33.

22. Neil MacFarquhar, "After the Attacks: The Saudis; Battle Against Terrorism Test Fragile Relationship Between U.S. and Saudis," *New York Times*, September 15, 2001.

23. Lacey, *Inside the Kingdom*, 291.

24. Oliver Burkeman, "America signals withdrawal of troops from Saudi Arabia," *Guardian* (London, U.K.), April 30, 2003; and "Why the U.S. Is Pulling Out of Saudi Arabia," *Time*, April 29, 2003.

25. Anthony H. Cordesman, "Saudi Arabia Enters the 21st Century: The Military and Internal Security Dimension," *Center for Strategic and International Studies*, October 30, 2002, 1, https://csis-prod.s3.amazonaws.com/s3fs-public/legacy_files /files/media/csis/pubs/saudimilbook_04.pdf.

26. Lacey, *Inside the Kingdom*, 295.

27. Adam Bouyamourn, "Saudi Arabia becomes biggest defence equipment importer with $9.8bn set to be spent this year," *National*, March 8, 2015.

28. Naimi, 155.

29. Thomas C. Hayes, "The Iraqi Invasion; Invading Iraqis Seize Kuwait and Its Oil; U.S. Condemns Attack, Urges United Action," *The New York Times*, August 3, 1990.

30. Robert S. "Bo" Smith, Captain U.S. Navy (Ret.), interview with the author, Jacksonville, FL, March 15, 2017.

31. Nassir Ajmi, interview with the author, Dhahran, Saudi Arabia, November 27, 2017.

32. Ian Seymour, "OPEC's Vienna Agreement Should Go Far to Defuse Oil Supply Crisis," *mees*, September 3, 1990.

33. Ibid., September 3, 1990.

34. Naimi, 158.

35. R. W. Apple Jr., "War in the Gulf: Scud Attack; Scud Missile Hits a U.S. Barracks, Killing 27," *New York Times*, February 26, 1991.

36. "What Chances for Oil Exports from Iraq?" *mees*, April 8, 1991.

37. Matthew L. Wald, "After the War; Gulf Oil Spill Vexing Cleanup Efforts," *New York Times*, April 7, 1991.

38. Naimi, 160–163.

39. Tom Pledge, "War Within a War," *Aramco World*, 42:3 (1991), 35–39.

40. Eric Schmitt, "War In The Gulf: The Fouled Sea; The Gulf Oil Spill Cleanup Flounders in Bureaucracy," *New York Times*, February 21, 1991; and Naimi, 163.

41. Pledge, 39, and Naimi, 163.

42. Naimi, 164.

43. U.S. Energy Information Administration, "Table 11.1b World Crude Oil Production: Persian Gulf Nations, Non-OPEC, and World," https://www.eia.gov/ totalenergy/data/monthly/pdf/sec11.pdf.

44. H.E. Ali al-Naimi, interview with the author, Dhahran, Saudi Arabia, November 27, 2017; and Naimi, 165–169.

45. H.E. Ali al-Naimi, interview with the author, Dhahran, Saudi Arabia, November 27, 2017.

46. H.E. Ali al-Naimi, interview with the author, Dhahran, Saudi Arabia, November 27, 2017; and Saudi Aramco 2011 Annual Review, 30–33 http://www.saudiaramco .com/content/dam/Publications/annual-review/2011/AR2011En-1.pdf and Naimi, 173–184.

47. Naimi, 177; and "Aramco sells Petron stake to Ashmore for $550M," *Reuters*, March 19, 2008.

48. H.E. Ali al-Naimi, interview with the author, Dhahran, Saudi Arabia, November 27, 2017.

49. "Showa Shell," Aramco Japan, http://japan.aramco.com/en/home/services/ projects/showa-shell.html and Naimi, 175.

50. Lacey, *Inside the Kingdom*, 293.

51. "Saudi Aramco Signs Agreement on Okinawa Storage," *Gulf Oil & Gas*, June 15, 2010, http://www.gulfoilandgas.com/webpro1/main/mainnews.asp?id=11561.

52. "Saudi Aramco, PETRONAS sign SPA," Aramco Singapore, February 28, 2017, http://singapore.aramco.com/en/home/news-and-media/news/saudi-aramco-- petronas-sign-spa-for-equity-participation-in-mala.html.

53. Saudi Aramco 2016 Annual Review, http://www.saudiaramco.com/content /dam/Publications/annual-review/2016/English-PDFs/2016-AnnualReview -full-EN.pdf.

54. Ambassador James B. Smith, interview with the author, January 11, 2016.

55. WSJ News Graphics, "Barrel Breakdown: Source: Rystad Energy UCube," *Wall Street Journal*, April 15, 2016, http://graphics.wsj.com/oil-barrel-breakdown/.

56. Salam Salamy, interview with the author, Dhahran, Saudi Arabia, November 27, 2017.

57. Dan Arthur, interview with the author, August 11, 2016.

58. Marcel, 82.

59. Ibid., 84–85.

60. Ibid., 134.

61. Frank Jungers, interview with the author, May 8, 2017.

62. Naimi, 139.

63. Ibid., 187.

64. "Saudi Arabia studies fuel subsidy reform," *Economist*, October 29, 2015.

65. Rania El Gamal, "Burning less oil at home will help Saudi exports and Aramco IPO," *Reuters*, March 7, 2017.

66. Lacey, *Inside the Kingdom*, 180.

67. Ibid., 185.

68. Ibid., 182.

69. Ibid., 185.

70. Ibid., 183.

71. Naimi, 190.

72. Ibid., 187.

73. H.E. Ali al-Naimi, interview with the author, Dhahran, Saudi Arabia, November 27, 2017.

74. Naimi, 150.

75. Harry St. John Bridger Philby, *The Empty Quarter: Being a Description of the Great South Desert of Arabia Known as Rub' Al Khali* (New York: Henry Holt and Company, 1933).

76. Barger, 47.

77. Richard Eason, interview with the author, Jacksonville, FL, December 10, 2015.

78. Saudi Aramco, "Shaybah Project," http://www.saudiaramco.com/en/home/inaugurations/Shaybah-Project.html.

79. Naimi, 212–214.

80. Ibid., 215.

81. Ibid., 218.

82. Saudi Aramco, "Shaybah Project," http://www.saudiaramco.com/en/home/inaugurations/Shaybah-Project.html.

83. Richard Eason, interview with the author, Jacksonville, FL, December 10, 2015.

84. Ibid.

85. "Declassified '28 pages' on 9/11—full text," CNNpolitics, http://www.cnn.com/2016/07/15/politics/28-pages-released-full-text/index.html.

86. Peter Maass, "The Breaking Point," *New York Times Magazine*, August 21, 2005.

87. Russell Gold, "Why Peak-Oil Predictions Haven't Come True," *Wall Street Journal*, September 29, 2014.

88. Peter Maass, "The Breaking Point," *New York Times Magazine*, August 21, 2005.

89. Matthew L. Simmons, *Twilight in the Desert* (Hoboken, New Jersey: Wiley, 2005), 315.

90. Simmons, 344–350; and Peter Maass, "The Breaking Point," *New York Times Magazine*, August 21, 2005.

91. Naimi, 245.

92. Marcel, 72.

93. "Saudi oil output capacity 12.5 million b/d, but investment needed: Falih," *S&P Global Platts*, June 2, 2016.

94. "Oil production: investing in capacity," *Saudi Aramco 2016 Annual Review*, 19.

95. "Exploration: adding to our resource base," *Saudi Aramco 2016 Annual Review*, 18.

96. Ambassador James B. Smith, interview with the author, Washington D.C., January 11, 2016.

97. H.E. Ali al-Naimi, interview with the author, Dhahran, Saudi Arabia, November 27, 2017.

98. Othaman Alkhowaiter, interview with the author, Dhahran, Saudi Arabia, November 26, 2017.

99. *60 Minutes: The Oil Kingdom*, produced by Richard Bonin and Kathy Lui (2008: CBS Broadcasting Inc.), DVD.

EPILOGUE: FOR THEIR SONS

1. "Cushing, OK WTI Spot Price FOB" U.S. Energy Information Administration.

2. Herman Wang, interview with the author, July 28, 2017.

3. Energy journalist, interview with the author, July 25, 2017.

4. Jamie Webster, interview with the author, August 4, 2017.

5. Energy journalist, interview with the author, July 25, 2017.

6. Ibid.

7. Ibid.

8. Ibid.

9. Summer Said, Benoît Faucon, and Sarah Kent, "OPEC Ministers Agree to Maintain Output Quota" *Wall Street Journal*, June 11, 2014.

10. Herman Wang, "Petrodollars: Looking back at the latest OPEC meeting" *S&P Global Platts Oilgram News*, December 8, 2014.

11. Naimi, 283.

12. Ibid., 283.

13. Herman Wang, interview with the author, July 28, 2017.

14. Naimi, 286.

15. Herman Wang, interview with the author, July 28, 2017.

16. Jamie Webster, interview with the author, August 4, 2017.

17. Michael D. Cohen, interview with the author, August 22, 2017.

18. Jamie Webster, interview with the author, August 4, 2017.

19. Herman Wang, "Petrodollars: Looking back at the latest OPEC meeting," *S&P Global Platts Oilgram News*, December 8, 2014.

20. Herman Wang, interview with the author, July 28, 2017.

21. Alanna Petroff, "Oil prices crash below $70," *CNNMoney*, November 28, 2014.

22. Herman Wang, interview with the author, July 28, 2017.

23. Jamie Webster, interview with the author, August 4, 2017.

24. Charles Riley, "Oil crash taking stocks down . . . again," *CNNMoney*, February 11, 2016.

25. Christopher Helman, "The 15 Biggest Oil Bankruptcies (So Far)," *Forbes*, May 9, 2016; and David Hunn, "135 oil companies are on edge of bankruptcy. So why is that good news?" *Fuelfix*, September 12, 2016.

26. Clifford Krauss and Stanley Reed, "Exxon Mobil's Profits Fall and BP Cites Low Oil Prices in $3.3 Billion Loss," *New York Times*, February 2, 2016.

27. Robert T. Garrett, "Report: Oil price slump costs Texas 65,000 energy jobs—and 250,000 overall," *Dallas News*, March, 2016.

28. WSJ News Graphics, "Barrel Breakdown: Source: Rystad Energy UCube," *Wall Street Journal*, April 15, 2016, http://graphics.wsj.com/oil-barrel-breakdown/.

29. Andy Chrichlow, "$10 Billion Loan to Saudi Arabia Carries Risks," *New York Times*, April 21, 2016.

30. Energy journalist, interview with the author, July 25, 2017.

31. H.E. Ali al-Naimi, interview with the author, Dhahran, Saudi Arabia, November 27, 2017.

32. Yasser Mufti, interview with the author, Dhahran, Saudi Arabia, November 27, 2017.

33. House, 119; and Zaki Safar, interview with the author, February 9, 2016.

ACKNOWLEDGMENTS

This project has spanned many years and several continents. It has also benefitted from the time and contributions of many individuals. First, to my excellent agent, William Clark: Thank you for taking a chance on a new author and for finding *Saudi, Inc.* the perfect home at Pegasus Books. Thank you to my incredible publisher, Claiborne Hancock, and amazing editor, Jessica Case. Your enthusiasm for this project, careful attention, and astute comments during revisions made working with you both a pleasure. Thank you for making this book a reality. Thank you also to Marc Melzer, Esq., of Hoguet Neman Regal & Kenney.

The initial research for this project took place during my graduate studies at Boston University. Thank you to the Boston University History Department for the Engelbourg Travel Fellowship and to the Boston University Graduate School of Arts and Sciences for the Graduate Research Abroad Fellowship. Thank you as well to the American Heritage Center at the University of Wyoming, where I was able to do significant research for this project as the Bernard L. Majewski Fellow in Economic Geology. Thank you also to the Cambridge University Faculty in History for hosting me as a visiting scholar and giving me the opportunity to conduct additional research in the United Kingdom. Thank you to *Aramco*

World magazine and editor Arthur Clark for providing many of the photographs in this book. Thank you to the archivists at the U.S. National Archives and Records Administration, the British National Archives at Kew, the British Petroleum Archives at the University of Warwick, the Georgetown University Archives, and the American Heritage Center at the University of Wyoming for preserving, organizing, and providing access to important historical records.

I'd like to thank those who took the time to share with me their personal and professional stories, and, in some cases, their parents' stories. These include: Ambassador James B. Smith, Dr. Janet Breslin-Smith, Frank Jungers, Lee and Jackie Ingham, Samah Damanhoori, Laura, Roba Dagustani, Yousef al-Naimi, Ann-Louise Hittle, Robert "Bo" Smith Capt. USN Ret., Richard Eason, Dr. J. Winston and Linda Porter, Brid Beeler, Glenn Labhart, Dan Arthur, Herman Wang, Amena Bakr, Jamie Webster, Michael Cohen, Samir Madani, Dr. Ihsan Buhulaiga, Dr. Majid al Moneef, Yasser Mufti, and most expressly, Tim Barger. Thank you to Karen Alexander for connecting me with some of the Aramcons and "Aramco brats" from her childhood in Dhahran and to Anas Alhajji for introducing me to several Saudis who contributed their thoughts and personal experiences to this book. Thank you to Dr. Taleb Jawab for facilitating my conversations with Saudi women who were eager to share their perspectives.

I am particularly grateful to H.E. Ali al-Naimi for taking the time to have lunch with me and for offering his thoughts and candid opinions. I so appreciated the hospitality of two former Aramco vice presidents, Othman Alkhowaiter and Nassir Ajmi, in Dhahran. Both welcomed me into their homes and to meet their families and openly discussed the history of Aramco.

To Stephen Power and Jade Mamarbachi—thank you for your patience and persistence in arranging my visit with Aramco. Thank you to Saudi Aramco for facilitating my visa for visits to Saudi Arabia and to the media relations department for arranging tours and interviews during my visit to the company. I want to especially thank Rawan Nasser and Abdulaziz Shalfan who accompanied me on my tour of the company and recognize their efforts in arranging certain invaluable

ACKNOWLEDGMENTS

meetings. It is impossible to name everyone I met at Aramco, but I wish to thank all of them for taking the time to speak with me and answer my questions at various sites including the Research and Development Center, the Upstream Professional Development Center, the Heritage Gallery, the King Abdulazziz Center for World Culture, Sadara Chemical Company, the Young Leadership Council, and the Oil Supply Planning and Scheduling (OSPAS) center.

I greatly appreciate all of the Aramco-affiliated people and Saudis I have spoken with over the years who shared background information, general thoughts, and anecdotes.

Zaki Safar deserves special thanks here, not only for sharing his story and his candid thoughts on everything Saudi but also for his friendship. It has been a pleasure and an honor getting to know you, and by extension, the generation of young Saudis who are working toward a better life and toward a new future for their country.

Thank you to New York University Abu Dhabi and the organizers and funders of the OPEC and the Global Energy Order conference for enabling me to travel to Abu Dhabi, where I met several people who were influential to this book. My work has particularly benefitted from conversations with and the personal insights of industry journalists including Summer Said, Anjli Raval, Reem Shamseddine, Nader Itayim, Amena Bakr, Herman Wang, Michael Amon, and Reza Zandi.

Thank you to my beta readers, Dr. Kate Jewell, Judy Lewis, and Dr. Benjamin Plotinsky for taking the time to read and comment on my manuscript. Ben's thoughtful comments, in particular, helped me reorganize several chapters.

I'd like to thank my family and particularly my aunt, Susan Radlauer. Sue, you have opened so many doors and helped me in more ways, professionally and personally, than I can say. Thank you.

Finally, I offer my most heartfelt thank you and a great deal of gratitude to my husband, Sam. Your faith in me and in this story is the reason this book exists. This book is better for every draft you read, every error you caught, and the countless insights you offered. Thank you for everything.

INDEX